Advance praise for *Kremlin Capitalism*

"Joseph Blasi and his colleagues have written a valuable and timely account of the vital and often turbulent process of privatizing the old Soviet economy in Russia. For the specialist, this book is larded with useful facts, figures, and details, and makes the case that privatization has been a greater success than most Americans think."

—Hedrick L. Smith, author of *The New Russians*

"*Kremlin Capitalism* is required reading for business and government officials with economic interests in Russia."

—The Honorable Robert S. Strauss, former
U.S. Ambassador to Russia

"The stress of Western media on crime and corruption in contemporary Russia has diverted public attention from what the authors of *Kremlin Capitalism* rightly call an unprecedented event in world history: in the space of five years, the industrial economy of Russia, once 100 percent state-run, has passed 80 percent into private hands. Based on thorough study of the published sources and direct inspection of the privatized firms across the vast country, this authoritative book helps explain why in the recent elections Russians have rejected a return to the communist past."

—Richard Pipes, Harvard University

"This perceptive, wonderfully well-informed investigation into the doings and undoings of privatization is an illuminating voyage through the Russian economy, whose epic transformation is shaping Russia's entire future, and thus some part of our own."

—Edward N. Luttwak,
Center for Strategic and International Studies

"*Kremlin Capitalism* is about much more than privatizing the Russian economy. It is a highly significant in-depth look at the prospects for successful transition from communism to democratic capitalism. Offering a rare glimpse of the process at work, this book is must

reading for those who wish to get beyond political rhetoric and superficial headlines."
—Jeffrey B. Garten, Dean, Yale School of Management, and former Under Secretary of Commerce, Clinton Administration

"An innovative and informative study of the Russian privatization program. The authors make a major contribution in showing how Russian society really works. And no one can responsibly conduct relations with Moscow without appreciating the true nature of Russian capitalism."
—Dimitri K. Simes, Nixon Center for Peace and Freedom

"This account of Russia's privatization efforts during the last half decade is comprehensive, lucid, and insightful. The revolutionary transformation of Russia's economy is one of the great stories of the twentieth century, and Joseph Blasi—as the expert insider—tells it magnificently. A must read for business men and women and scholars alike."
—Eugene K. Lawson, President, U.S.–Russia Business Council

"This book provides significant new material for scholars, analysts, and anyone who wants to understand the political and economic foundations of post-communist Russia. An absorbing and well-written work."
—Stephen Handelman, author of
Comrade Criminal: Russia's New Mafiya

KREMLIN
CAPITALISM

KREMLIN
CAPITALISM

ILR Press AN IMPRINT OF

Cornell University Press ITHACA AND LONDON

The Privatization of the Russian Economy

Joseph R. Blasi,

Maya Kroumova,

and Douglas Kruse

Foreword by **Andrei Shleifer**

with the research assistance of
Daria Panina, Ekaterina Grachova,
Elena Zakrevskaya, Tatyana Voronina,
Aleksei Krivolapov, Joanne Mangels, Iuliia Cole,
and **Ekaterina Dementieva**

135234

First published 1997 by Cornell University Press.

Printed in the United States of America

This book is printed on Lyons Falls Turin Book, a paper
that is totally chlorine-free and acid-free.

Library of Congress Cataloging-in-Publication Data

Blasi, Joseph R.
    Kremlin capitalism : the privatization of the Russian economy / by Joseph Blasi, Maya Kroumova, and Douglas Kruse ; with the research assistance of Daria Panina . . . [et al.].
        p.   cm.
    Includes bibliographical references and index.
    ISBN 0-8014-3351-7 (alk. paper). —ISBN 0-8014-8396-4 (pbk. : alk. paper)
    1. Privatization—Russia (Federation)   2. Russia (Federation)—Economic policy—1991–   I. Kroumova, Maya.   II. Kruse, Douglas.   III. Title.
HD4215.15.B58   1997
338.947—dc20   96-33557

Contents

Foreword

Andrei Shleifer

Since 1991 the Russian economy and society have gone through a major transformation, almost a revolution. Russia started the last decade of the twentieth century as part of a declining Communist dictatorship called the USSR, unable to provide its people with even basic consumer goods, facing a political crisis, and accumulating foreign debts at a breathtaking pace in a vain attempt to prop up its moribund industry. By the middle of the decade, Russia was an independent country, a transformed market economy, no longer a threat to its neighbors, and holding a free democratic election for president. The changes Russia went through during this period were momentous, with many setbacks but many triumphs as well.

An essential part of transforming Russia was the radical economic reform envisioned by President Boris Yeltsin. The four legs of this reform were liberalization of prices, demilitarization of the economy, reduction of inflation, and privatization. Price liberalization made sure that markets rather than bureaucrats set prices; it had the effect of ridding the Russian economy of its infamous queues. Demilitarization ensured that Russia no longer spent its vast wealth on building arms; it made Russia a safer place for both its citizens and the rest of the world. The difficult fight against inflation forced the Russian government to control its budget, and prevented it from wasting the national wealth on subsidies to declining industries and agriculture.

Last but not least, in a few short years, Russia managed to privatize more than 15,000 industrial firms—to turn over their ownership from the state to private investors. Together with more than a million new businesses and tens of thousands of newly privatized shops, over half the output of the Russian economy is now produced by the private sector—a higher fraction than in much of Western Europe. But privatization did a lot more than just reshuffle assets. It gave the declining state firms real owners, with real desires to assert their rights as investors, and hence gave Russian firms a hope of surviving in a market economy. Privatization also, and perhaps even more important, put an end to central planning as a way to organize economic life and hence became the decisive step into capitalism. As it destroyed central planning, it also destroyed the very roots of the Soviet state as the all-powerful Soviet ministries lost their power and were reduced to renting space in their offices to new private firms. Perhaps most important, privatization created a new class of Russians, those with a keen economic interest in seeing a market economy take root and succeed in Russia, willing to let their voices be heard in the voting booth and in the parliament. Politically and economically, privatization truly transformed Russia.

This book by Joseph R. Blasi and his colleagues tells the remarkable story of the Russian privatization process in vivid detail. Blasi was in Moscow as an adviser to the State Committee for the Management of State Property (the privatization agency). More than that, he and his colleagues traveled through Russia to witness privatization turn from a set of government documents into reality, and to watch as Russian firms evolved into private companies. Blasi and his colleagues spent time with the managers of privatized firms; they heard their concerns, their ambitions, and on occasion their lies. All over Russia they saw the battles for corporate control as investors tried to protect their claims against ever more rapacious managers, while managers did their utmost to deter investors, in part by taking away workers' voting rights in their companies. The story of the struggles and maneuverings of Russian managers after their enterprises were privatized is perhaps the most exciting part of the book. Here we can see corporate governance being born.

This book documents the Russian privatization process with passion but also with a keen analytical eye. The interviews that Blasi and his colleagues have conducted have been put together and converted into the first systematic data set on privatization and corporate governance in Russia. The analysis of how the privatized firms are managed brings many surprises and is certain to provoke debate among scholars concerned with Russia, with transition more generally, and with corporate governance. Some of the conclusions paint an optimistic picture of the future of Russian firms, but many raise serious concerns about how the economy is working. Some of these conclusions will surely be challenged. But as the first systematic account of what happened to Russian firms during this momentous transformation, this book is certain to remain of great value to both current observers and future historians of Russia.

Chronology of Major Events

1985
March 11   Mikhail Gorbachev becomes general secretary of Communist Party of Soviet Union.

April 23   Communist Party Central Committee approves resolution to reform economic management.

December 24   Boris Yeltsin is elected first secretary of Moscow City Communist Party.

1986
January 15   Gorbachev proposes total elimination of nuclear weapons by the year 2000.

February 18   Yeltsin becomes candidate member of Politburo of Communist Party.

June   Gorbachev attacks State Planning Commission of USSR.

November 19   USSR Law on Individual Labor Activity allows some private enterprise.

1987
January 27   Plenary session of Communist Party Central Committee focuses on democratization.

June 30   Supreme Soviet (parliament) of USSR adopts Law on State Enterprises, effective January 1988.

October 21   Yeltsin criticizes Gorbachev's approach to reforms and falls from favor.

November 11   Yeltsin is removed as first secretary of Moscow Communist Party.

1988
February 18   Yeltsin is removed from candidate membership in Politburo.

May   USSR Law on Cooperatives allows private enterprises to be formed.

June 28	Gorbachev proposes elections for a new legislature, the Congress of People's Deputies.
October 1	Gorbachev is selected chairman of Presidium of Supreme Soviet, or head of state.
December	USSR decree permits sale of state-owned apartments to individuals.
December 1	USSR Supreme Soviet approves law providing for contested elections.

1989

March 26	Elections for Congress of People's Deputies. Yeltsin wins seat as deputy from Moscow.
May 25	USSR Congress of People's Deputies convenes. Gorbachev is selected as chairman of Supreme Soviet.
April	USSR decree allows leasing of state enterprises by their workers.
May 29	Yeltsin achieves membership in USSR Supreme Soviet when another deputy yields his seat.
July 5	Gorbachev creates Commission on Economic Reform under Deputy Prime Minister Leonid Abalkin.
July 6	Gorbachev tells Council of Europe that USSR will not block reforms in Eastern Europe.
October	Abalkin Commission presents a program emphasizing a market economy, freeing of prices, competition, a convertible currency, and stock exchanges.
End of year	10,000 apartments have been privatized.

1990

January	Gorbachev tacitly allows leasing of family farms.
February	Grigory Yavlinsky and others discuss a 500-day program for transition to a market economy.
March	Supreme Soviet of USSR passes law on property, with no mention of private ownership of land. Yeltsin is elected to Russia's Congress of People's Deputies from Ekaterinburg.
March 13	USSR Congress of People's Deputies amends Constitution to eliminate Communist Party's monopoly on power and create post of president.
March 14	USSR Congress of People's Deputies selects Gorbachev as president.
May 24	Prime Minister Nikolai Ryzhkov announces price increases but rescinds them when wave of panic buying sweeps country.
May 29	Yeltsin is elected chairman of Russia's Supreme Soviet.
June	Russia's Supreme Soviet declares its sovereignty and precedence of its laws over those of USSR.
June 4	Supreme Soviet of USSR passes Law on Enterprises, emphasizing a market economy.
June 12	Supreme Soviet of USSR passes law guaranteeing freedom of press.
Summer	Grigory Yavlinsky enters Russian government as deputy prime minister; Boris Fedorov becomes minister of finance.

July	Gorbachev is reelected general secretary of Communist Party with much opposition. Yeltsin quits Communist Party.
August	Group of economists under Stanislav Shatalin, convened jointly by Gorbachev and Yeltsin, develops 500-day plan for economic reform.
August 9	USSR Council of Ministers (cabinet) legalizes private ownership of business.
August 31	Gorbachev orders reform plans of Ryzhkov government and Shatalin group to be combined.
September 11	Russian Supreme Soviet approves Shatalin's 500-day plan by vote of 213 to 1.
September 24	USSR Supreme Soviet grants Gorbachev decree powers for 18 months to implement economic reforms.
October	Gorbachev rejects 500-day economic reform plan. USSR Supreme Soviet approves another transition plan and passes law authorizing multiparty system.
October 1	USSR Supreme Soviet legislates freedom of worship.
November	Russian Congress of People's Deputies adopts law authorizing family farms.
November 7	Gorbachev escapes assassination attempt.
November 13	Yeltsin says Russia cannot implement Shatalin reform plan without cooperation of USSR.
December	Russian Congress of People's Deputies adopts Law on Land Reform.
December 25	Russian Law on Enterprises and Entrepreneurial Activity allows sole proprietorships, partnerships, and closed and open joint-stock corporations, and eliminates restrictions on their activities.
End of year	53,000 apartments and 4,432 family farms have been privatized.

1991

January	Wholesale prices are freed but retail prices remain unchanged and subsidies to consumers rise.
February	In television address Yeltsin calls for Gorbachev's resignation.
March	USSR referendum shows support for voluntary union of Soviet republics and popular election of Russian president.
March 31	Warsaw Pact is dissolved.
April	Nine leaders of Soviet republics agree to negotiations to replace Soviet Union.
April 1	USSR increases consumer prices but also expands subsidies.
April 4	Russian Supreme Soviet gives Yeltsin extensive powers.
April 24–25	Gorbachev threatens to resign.
June	Soviet Union considers but does not adopt Draft Law on Fundamental Principles of Destatization and Privatization of Enterprises.
June 12	Yeltsin is elected president of Russia with 57.3% of vote.
Summer	Gorbachev rejects plan presented by Grigory Yavlinsky, Graham Allison and Jeffrey Sachs of Harvard University, and others for rapid economic and political reform in return for massive Western aid.

July	Russian Housing Privatization Act is adopted.
July 3	Russian Supreme Soviet adopts Law on Privatization of State and Municipal Enterprises and Law on Personal Privatization Accounts.
July 17	Gorbachev meets with Group of 7 in London and receives little economic aid.
August 4	Gorbachev leaves Moscow to vacation near Sochi, on Black Sea.
August 10	Gorbachev signs decree authorizing privatization in USSR.
August 18	Delegation of antireform Communists tries unsuccessfully to persuade Gorbachev to declare a state of emergency.
August 19	Emergency committee announces it has assumed power.
August 21	Takeover attempt fails; Gorbachev returns to Moscow.
August 24	Gorbachev suspends Communist Party and resigns as general secretary.
August–September	Most Soviet republics declare independence.
October 28	Before Russia's Congress of People's Deputies Yeltsin announces radical economic reforms, including price liberalization, privatization, and tight monetary and fiscal policies.
November	Yeltsin appoints Anatoly Chubais minister of privatization and chairman of State Committee for Management of State Property.
November 1	Russian Congress of People's Deputies grants Yeltsin decree powers to implement economic reforms.
November 4	Soviet republic leaders agree to abolish all USSR ministries other than Defense, Foreign Affairs, Railways, and Nuclear Power.
November 6	Yeltsin bans Communist Party of Soviet Union and of Russia.
November 6–8	Yeltsin becomes prime minister of Russia in addition to president; delegates economic reform to deputy prime ministers Gennady Burbulis, Yegor Gaidor, and Aleksandr Shokhin.
November 15	Russian decree on social partnership envisions tripartite agreements between trade unions, government, and employers. Additional decrees empower enterprises to determine their own wage levels and engage in import and export activities, and give Yeltsin control of all financial and economic activity on Russian territory.
December 7–8	Yeltsin and heads of Ukraine and Belorus decide to end Soviet Union.
December 22	Eleven former Soviet republics form Commonwealth of Independent States.
December 25	Gorbachev resigns. Russian flag replaces Soviet flag over Kremlin.
December 27	Presidium of Russian Supreme Soviet unanimously adopts provisional privatization program.
December 29	Yeltsin issues decree on basic provisions of Program of Privatization of State and Municipal Enterprises in Russian Federation; decree on land reform, mandating transfer of property of collective and state farms; and decree on freedom of trade.
End of year	175,000 apartments and 49,013 family farms have been privatized; 250,000 new small businesses have been started.

1992

January 2	Prices are freed on most products and economic reform begins.
January 29	Yeltsin issues decree to accelerate privatization of state and municipal enterprises.
February 27	Russia signs memorandum on economic policy with International Monetary Fund (IMF).
March	Most food prices still under state control are freed.
March 25	Yeltsin issues decree authorizing sale of land under privatized enterprises.
April	Yeltsin announces that privatization vouchers will be distributed at end of 1992. Congress of People's Deputies defeats measure to permit privatization of land.
April 1	Western governments announce support in principle for $25 billion in aid to Russia linked to a future IMF agreement.
April 2	Ruslan Khasbulatov, chairman of Supreme Soviet, calls for reintroduction of price controls.
April 3	Burbulis is sacked as first deputy prime minister.
April 11	Congress of People's Deputies criticizes economic policy of Russian government.
May 30	Viktor Chernomyrdin becomes minister of energy and deputy prime minister.
May 31	Anatoly Chubais, minister of privatization, is appointed deputy prime minister.
June 1	Russia becomes member of International Monetary Fund.
June 11	Supreme Soviet adopts privatization program for 1992.
June 15	Yeltsin appoints Gaidar acting prime minister.
July 1	Yeltsin issues decree mandating corporatization of state-owned enterprises by November 1, 1992.
July 17	Supreme Soviet names Viktor Gerashchenko as acting chair of Central Bank.
July 24	Chubais chairs government commission to accelerate pace of reform.
August 5	Russia and IMF sign agreement for $1.04 billion loan.
August 19	Yeltsin delivers speech on voucher privatization.
December	Voucher privatization program for mid-sized and large enterprises begins.
December 12	Yeltsin dismisses Gaidar as prime minister.
December 14	Yeltsin appoints Viktor Chernomyrdin prime minister.
End of year	18 mid-sized and large companies, 46,797 small shops, 2,788,000 apartments, and 182,787 family farms have been privatized; 3,485 industrial enterprises have been leased; and 503,203 new small businesses have been started.

1993

March	Constitutional Court rules Yeltsin's decree on emergency rule unconstitutional.
March 28	Vote to impeach Yeltsin in Supreme Soviet is narrowly defeated.
April 25	Economic reform and Yeltsin receive narrow vote of confidence in national referendum.

May 1	Nationalists and communists organize violent May Day demonstration in Moscow.
June 30	Russia and IMF sign agreement for $1.5 billion loan.
September 18	Gaidar rejoins government as first deputy prime minister and minister of economy.
September 21	Yeltsin dissolves Congress of People's Deputies and Supreme Soviet.
October 3–4	Armed uprising in Moscow; military units storm White House.
October 27	Yeltsin issues decree on land relations and agrarian reform.
December 12	Elections for Duma (new parliament) and referendum on new constitution.
December 24	Yeltsin issues decree initiating State Program of Privatization of State and Municipal Enterprises.
End of year	8,509 mid-sized and large companies, 80,491 small shops, 8,592,000 apartments, and 270,000 family farms have been privatized; 784,509 new small businesses have been started.

1994

January	Gaidar resigns as first deputy prime minister and minister of economy; Fedorov resigns as deputy prime minister and minister of finance.
April 7	Government adopts post-voucher privatization policies to sell state-owned enterprises and unsold shares of privatized enterprises for cash.
April 20	Russia and IMF sign agreement for $1.5 billion loan.
July 1	Formal end of voucher privatization program for mid-sized and large enterprises.
July 22	Yeltsin's decree overrides Duma's veto of cash privatization program.
October 11	Ruble collapses on currency markets.
October 14	Gerashchenko is sacked as chairman of Central Bank.
November 5	Chubais is named first deputy prime minister in charge of economic affairs.
November 15	Vladimir Polevanov is appointed deputy prime minister and chairman of State Committee for Management of State Property (GKI).
December 12	Russia moves troops into break-away republic of Chechnya.
December 14	Polevanov says privatization in strategic sectors may be detrimental to national security, and privatized companies in such sectors may be renationalized.
End of year	16,462 mid-sized and large companies, 95,538 small shops, 10,975,000 apartments, and 279,000 family farms have been privatized; 779,462 new small businesses have been started.

1995

January 24	Yeltsin fires Polevanov as deputy prime minister and chairman of GKI.
February	Yeltsin appoints Sergei Belyaev as chairman of GKI.
March 1	Commission on Securities and Capital Market acquires status of cabinet ministry.
April 11	Russia and IMF sign agreement for $6.8 billion loan.

April 22	Chubais is appointed Russia's representative to World Bank and IMF.
June 20	Belyaev announces 2,809 enterprises in which the government will not sell remaining state-owned shares until 1996 at the earliest.
June 23	Bank of New York announces National Registry Company to provide share registration services and access to American depositary receipts.
July 14	Duma passes land reform bill permitting lease of agricultural land but prohibiting its sale.
July 26	Presidential decree calls for establishment of mutual funds.
December	Elections for Duma.
December 26	Russian Corporate Law is passed by Duma and signed by Yeltsin.
End of year	17,937 mid-sized and large companies, 105,111 small shops, and 12,118,000 apartments have been privatized; 794,889 new small businesses have been started.*

1996

January	Yeltsin removes Chubais from all his positions in government.
March	Dmitry Vasiliev is appointed chairman of Commission on Securities and Capital Market. Chubais joins Yeltsin's presidential campaign team as senior aide.
March 7	Presidential decree entitles any agricultural worker to claim a share of land controlled by his or her collective farm, with power to sell, mortgage, and bequeath it.
March 26	Russia and IMF sign agreement for $10.087 billion loan.
April 22	Yeltsin signs Law on Securities Market.
June 16	Yeltsin narrowly beats Gennady Zyuganov, Communist candidate, in presidential election but fails to win a majority of votes.
June 19	Yeltsin fires First Deputy Prime Minister Oleg Soskovets and other opponents of reform.
July 3	Yeltsin wins presidential runoff election by a substantial margin; Chubais is appointed presidential chief of staff; Viktor Chernomyrdin is confirmed by Duma as new prime minister; Aleksandr Lebed is named national security adviser.
August 15	Aleksei Bolshakov, Viktor Ilyushin, and Vladimir Potanin are named first deputy prime ministers; Aleksandr Livshits is named deputy prime minister and minister of finance; Yevgeny Yasin is renamed minister of economy.

* The figure for privatized apartments is for the end of the third quarter of 1995. The number of private family farms in 1995 is not available.
Sources: The Cambridge Encyclopedia of Russia and the Former Soviet Union, ed. Archie Brown, Michael Kaser, and Gerald Smith (Cambridge: Cambridge University Press, 1994); Jack Matlock, *Autopsy on an Empire: The American Ambassador's Account of the Collapse of the Soviet Union* (New York: Random House, 1995); Anders Åslund, *How Russia Became a Market Economy* (Washington, D.C.: Brookings Institution, 1995); Boris Yeltsin, *The Struggle for Russia* (New York: Random House/Times Books, 1994); Goskomstat, 1995; Reuters, Lexis/Nexis; International Monetary Fund; *Russian Economic Trends,* 1992–96.

KREMLIN
CAPITALISM

INTRODUCTION

The Bolshevik Biscuit
Company Goes Private

In December 1992 the Bolshevik Biscuit Company in Moscow became one of the first large Russian factories to be sold at auction as part of the Russian government's program to transfer state-owned enterprises to private ownership. The reformers hoped that in four years the privatization program would convert Russia from a command economy in which all means of production were owned by the state to a mostly private economy. Thousands of small shops and stores had been sold to citizens during 1992 and the sale of state-owned apartments to citizens was under way; now the sale of the Bolshevik Biscuit Company kicked off the program to privatize the large factories that represented the core of the Russian economy. It could be the beginning of the end of the state's domination of ownership of the large industries of Russia.

The auctioning of the Bolshevik Biscuit Company was a risky beginning. Under communism, no one had ever sold a whole factory. Who would own the first chunk of communism to go on the auction block? Workers and managers of the cookie company, government officials, representatives of mutual funds, private citizens, and owners of small companies milled about the large auction room. Before the auction, workers and managers had bought more than half of the giant factory's stock, so they knew—or at least they thought they knew—they could protect the firm against "bad" investors. But until the deal was done, everything was in question. The general director of the plant was on pins and needles. Maybe some government offi-

1

cial would announce that the Moscow city government would buy the plant. After all, under communism, whatever the government wanted it simply announced as a fact. Maybe someone had bribed the petty bureaucrats acting as auctioneers.

Workers suspected that perhaps a few top managers would buy up all the stock, or that a Keebler, an RJR Nabisco, or a Pepperidge Farm would waltz in and buy its way into the Russian sweets market for a song. Maybe someone had already bought huge chunks of stock from the workers, and these unknown owners would corner the auction and take control of the company. Grandmothers stood by ready to lay down their bids. Agents of various corporations in Moscow who came to place their bids cast wary glances at one another. The country's reformers waited to see if the first sale would go off without a hitch or a scandal.

Who would win this struggle for property? As it transpired, employees of the Bolshevik Biscuit Company, Russian investors, and foreign investors would all win, and Moscow would have a restructured biscuit factory. The workers purchased most of Bolshevik's stock. Then just a year later, France's yogurt-making Danone group stepped in and bought out almost all of the stock from its original purchasers. The workers made money. Management made money. Citizen stockholders made money. Now the tables were turned. Workers and citizens owned about a fifth of the company and Danone owned most of it. The French promised to invest $10 million to modernize the factory to bake their tasty Danone chocolate-covered and -filled cookies for the local market. The Bolshevik-Danone story was the first of thousands of such stories. Together they provide a detailed picture of the way the communist economic system tried to change itself into something else.

By December 1992, eighteen large companies had been sold to citizens; by July 1994, the number of large and mid-sized companies transferred to private ownership had reached 15,052. These companies accounted for about 17 million employees in 1992. By the beginning of 1996, 17,937 industrial enterprises were privatized, producing 88.3 percent of industrial production, employing 79.4 percent of industrial workers, and accounting for 77.2 percent of large and mid-sized industrial enterprises.

The news media provide shifting, sometimes contradictory impressions of Russian privatization and economic reform, and it has been difficult to see beyond the current headlines. One month Russia is all Mafia, the next month all emerging stock market, then all communism, then all entrepreneurial savvy. In 1992, images of the Bolshevik Biscuit Company auction were flashed around the world, and privatization was heralded as the promise of great things to come. In October 1993, the violent struggle between President Boris Yeltsin and the Duma, or parliament, created uncertainty about the country's move toward democracy. In 1994, some Russian politicians were jubilant as the infant Russian stock market seemed to take off. But then it crashed. In 1995, members of the Communist opposition scored a significant victory in the parliamentary elections and began their race for the Russian presidency with strong charges that reform had failed. In early 1996, an article in *New York* magazine declared that most Russian banks were controlled by the Mafia, and other sources had the Mafia in control of a large proportion of Russian industry. In July 1996, Boris Yeltsin was reelected president of Russia and monthly inflation was 0.7 percent, the lowest rate since the start of free-market reforms.

This book is based on the only available continuous nationwide study of the privatization process in Russia, a remarkable opportunity to gauge this vast economic transformation. The Russian National Survey covered the significant companies—those that averaged about 2,000 employees—in most regions of the sprawling nation from 1992 to 1996. Joseph Blasi and Andrei Shleifer served as advisers to the Russian government and codirected this research effort. Shleifer, as senior foreign adviser, organized and directed the strategic advisory team of Harvard University's Institute for International Development (HIID) for the U.S. Agency for International Development. The Russian government asked this team of advisers to work with Deputy Prime Minister Anatoly Chubais and his deputy, Dmitry Vasiliev. Chubais was then the cabinet minister responsible for privatization. In July 1996 he was appointed chief of staff for the Russian president. Blasi served as an ongoing member of the advisory team and coordinated the work of the research unit on a day-to-day basis. Both Shleifer and Blasi have worked closely with and advised the Russian Federation's State Committee on the Management of State Property (the cabinet ministry in charge of privatization, or GKI, as it was called), which planned and implemented the program; the Russian Privatization Center, a government-sponsored agency that manages Western technical assistance to Russia; the Russian Federation's Commission on Securities and the Capital Market (the Russian version of the U.S. Securities and Exchange Commission), which oversees the emerging Russian stock market and shareholder rights; and the Institute for a Law-Based Economy, which collaborates with the parliament, the Legal Office of the President, and other government legislative agencies. These associations made it possible to observe policy being made and implemented and the activities, complicated achievements, and noted failures of the transition process. Maya Kroumova and Douglas Kruse have helped with analysis of the evidence.

The research group, which has been funded by the Eurasia Foundation of Washington, D.C., was intended to operate independently of the Russian government in order to serve the Western advisers, the Russian government, its reform-minded officials, and relevant aid institutions as a source of objective information on the transformation of the Russian economy as it was played out in thousands of companies across Russia.

We tell the story revealed by evidence collected in the old-fashioned way. To take the Russian National Survey, our team of Russian research assistants left Moscow weekly for cities throughout the sprawling Russian Federation and traveled the side roads to interview regional government officials responsible for privatization and top managers at the larger factories. In the summer and fall of 1992, before the privatization of the large factories actually began, we had extensive conversations at many factories in an effort to understand the problems and the prospects of privatization. During 1993 and 1994, our researchers conducted long interviews and surveys of management leaders to examine an additional 142 companies that had just begun to implement privatization in 32 regions. From May 1994 to August 1995, they visited 322 corporations with 612,000 employees in 44 of the 89 regions (we call this "the 1995 study"). Finally, from September 1995 to June 1996, just before the presidential elections, they made visits to 357 companies with 628,737 employees in 46 regions (we call this "the 1996 study"). The maps give an indication of the distances covered by the research team.

Each Sunday evening or Monday morning for four years, research teams left Moscow on trains and planes and traveled hundreds, often thousands of miles. The teams covered every major area of the Russian Federation, from Murmansk, north of the Arctic Circle, where some liberals are determined to create capitalism, to Novorossisk, on the Black Sea in the province of Krasnodar, which was once a Cossack settlement; from the western province of Pskov, a twelfth-century export center that now has thriving industries, to Krasnoyarsk and Irkutsk in central Siberia, previously forced-labor regions, where we were told that the main growth industry used to be "exile." The only areas our research did not cover were some Far Eastern provinces, such as Yakutsk, Sakhalin, Kamchatka, and some areas of the North Caucasus sector that were subject to hostilities, such as the Chechen and Ingush regions, Dagestan, and North Ossetia.

Visits to the diverse production facilities across the many regions offered glimpses of important sites in Russian history. There is a heavy equipment plant in Ulyanovsk (Simbirsk), the birthplace of Lenin, where until recently the regional government still enforced price controls. The Chuvash Republic, which has consistently struggled to maintain its cultural uniqueness, has a large textile factory. The many mills in Ivanovo, where Peter the Great established the textile industry, are now suffering from the competition of cheap Asian imports and the rising costs of raw materials. At the electronics plant in Kursk, scene of the decisive tank battle of World War II, the local administration once tried to push a xenophobic form of privatization. Arkhangelsk, where U.S. troops landed in 1918, supposedly to guard supplies stockpiled before the Revolution, still has its ship repair station. Military-related industries have fallen on hard times in Volgograd (earlier Stalingrad). The city has a margarine plant, which the researchers visited. Novgorod, which was already a fast-growing commercial center by the thirteenth century and whose university now sports its own World Wide Web page, has a mixed fodder plant, where we interviewed the top managers. Ekaterinburg (formerly Sverdlovsk), where the last tsar and his family were murdered, has an engine plant, where we had long talks with the general director.

Arriving in an administrative region, the researchers were hosted by the local government and often worked out of the state capitol or a nearby office. For two or three days they visited large enterprises; then they returned to Moscow to write up their experiences. The fieldwork involved long visits; extensive conversations with the top managers of the enterprises, which often went on for hours and overflowed into lunches, dinners, and the occasional vodka; and lengthy surveys of every aspect of their businesses. Several members of the senior management team frequently worked together in one big group or in a series of separate meetings with the research team until all the questions were answered. Often local government privatization officials who were familiar with the enterprise sat in and offered comments afterward. In general, although Russian managers made occasional attempts to conceal information (after four years of talking to the same people, these efforts became all too obvious), their statements were remarkably blunt and determinedly irreverent. The collection of information on Russian companies is extremely difficult.

RUSSIAN FEDERATION

The boundaries, colors, denominations and any other information shown on this map do not imply, on the part of The World Bank Group, any judgment on the legal status of any territory, or any endorsement or acceptance of such boundaries.

"M" ROADS
OTHER FEDERAL ROADS
SELECTED SECONDARY ROADS
SIGNIFICANT PORTS:
LOCAL
REGIONAL

RAILROADS
SELECTED TOWNS AND CITIES
NATIONAL CAPITAL
RIVERS

UNITED KINGDOM

Norwegian Sea

North Sea

NORWAY

SWEDEN

Gulf of Bothnia

FINLAND

Barents Sea

Kara Se

NETHERLANDS
DENMARK
GERMANY

Baltic Sea

RUSSIAN FED.
Kaliningrad

POLAND

CZECH REP.
SLOVAK REP.
HUNGARY

ESTONIA
LATVIA
LITHUANIA

BELORUS

Vyborg
St. Petersburg
Novgorod

Murmansk
Kandalaksha

Onega
Petrozavodsk

Arkhangelsk
Mezen

Naryan Mar

Dicks

Amderma

Vorkuta

ROMANIA
MOLDOVA

UKRAINE

Cherepovets
Vologda
Kostroma

MOSCOW

Bryansk
Tula
Vladimir
Lipetsk
Voronezh

Nizhny Novgorod

Kazan

Syktyvkar

Ob R.

Khanty-
Mansiysk

Ob R.

Nizhny
Jagil

Black Sea

Novorossisk
Tuapse
Sochi

Taganrog
Rostov na Donu
Volgograd

Saratov

Volga R.

Samara
Magnitogorsk

Ufa

Ekaterinburg
Tyumen

Chelyabinsk

Tobol

Omsk

Tor

Novosibirsk

Astrakhan

TURKEY

GEORGIA
ARMENIA
ISLAMIC REP. OF IRAN
AZERBAIJAN
SYRIAN ARAB REP.
IRAQ

Makhachkala

Caspian Sea

Aral Sea

KAZAKHSTAN

UZBEKISTAN

Gorno-A

UNITED STATES OF AMERICA

Chukchi Sea

Bering Strait

Bering Sea

○ Providenya

Egvekinot ○

Beringovsky ○

Anadyr ○

Pevek ○

East Siberian Sea

Laptev Sea

Kolyma R.

Indigirka R.

Ossora ○

Ust Kamchatsk ○

Tiksi ○

Khatanga ○

Lena R.

Magadan ○

Petropavlovsk Kamchatsky ○

Norilsk ○

Sea of Okhotsk

Arctic Circle

Yakutsk ○

Nikolayevsk ○

Boshnyakovo ○ Poronaysk ○
Shakhtersk ○
Uglegorsk ○
Vanino ● Yuzhno Sakhalinsk ○
Korsakov ○

Amur R.

Tynda ○

Khabarovsk ○

JAPAN

Enisei R.

Angara R.

Lake Baikal

Blagoveshchensk ○

Sea of Japan

Bratsk ○

Chita ○

Amur R.

Krasnoyarsk ○

Ulan-Ude ○

Vladivostok ○ Vostochnyy ●
Nakhodka ●

Abakan ○

Irkutsk ○

Posyet ●

Novokuznetsk ○

Kyzyl ○

CHINA

0 100 200 300 400 500 MILES

0 200 400 600 800 KILOMETERS

D.P.R. OF KOREA

MONGOLIA

MAY 1996

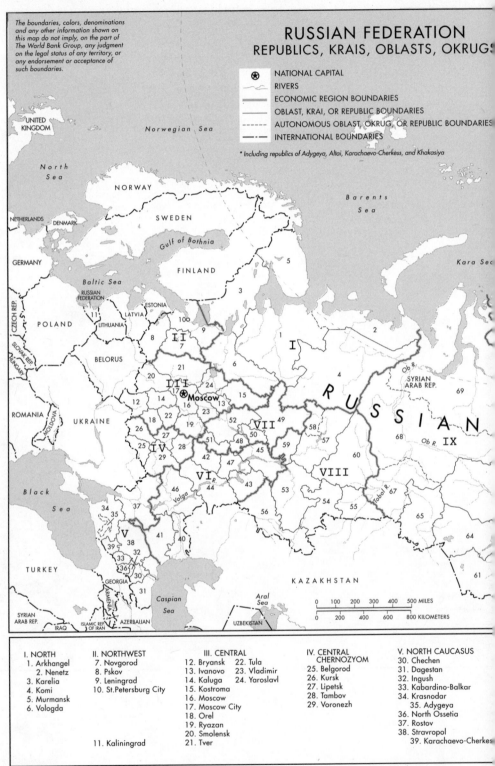

RUSSIAN FEDERATION
REPUBLICS, KRAIS, OBLASTS, OKRUGS

The boundaries, colors, denominations and any other information shown on this map do not imply, on the part of The World Bank Group, any judgment on the legal status of any territory, or any endorsement or acceptance of such boundaries.

⊛ NATIONAL CAPITAL
RIVERS
ECONOMIC REGION BOUNDARIES
OBLAST, KRAI, OR REPUBLIC BOUNDARIES
AUTONOMOUS OBLAST, OKRUG, OR REPUBLIC BOUNDARIES
INTERNATIONAL BOUNDARIES

* Including republics of Adygeya, Altai, Karachaevo-Cherkess, and Khakasiya

I. NORTH
1. Arkhangel
2. Nenetz
3. Karelia
4. Komi
5. Murmansk
6. Vologda

11. Kaliningrad

II. NORTHWEST
7. Novgorod
8. Pskov
9. Leningrad
10. St.Petersburg City

III. CENTRAL
12. Bryansk   22. Tula
13. Ivanovo   23. Vladimir
14. Kaluga   24. Yaroslavl
15. Kostroma
16. Moscow
17. Moscow City
18. Orel
19. Ryazan
20. Smolensk
21. Tver

IV. CENTRAL CHERNOZYOM
25. Belgorod
26. Kursk
27. Lipetsk
28. Tambov
29. Voronezh

V. NORTH CAUCASUS
30. Chechen
31. Dagestan
32. Ingush
33. Kabardino-Balkar
34. Krasnodar
35. Adygeya
36. North Ossetia
37. Rostov
38. Stravropol
39. Karachaevo-Cherkess

Courtesy of the Map Unit of The World Bank

UNITED STATES OF AMERICA
Bering Strait

Chukchi Sea

Bering Sea

East Siberian Sea

86

Laptev Sea

82

Indigirka R.

Kolyma R.

85

81

78

Lena R.

89   XI

Sea of Okhotsk

Arctic Circle

X 76

83

88

E D E R A T I O N

Amur R.

Enisei R.

Angara R.

80

JAPAN

75

73

84

Lake Baikal

70   71

87

Amur R.

Sea of Japan

74

72

77

CHINA

79

D.P.R. OF KOREA

M O N G O L I A

VOLGA	VII. VOLGO-VYATKA	VIII. URAL	IX. WESTERN SIBERIA	X. EASTERN SIBERIA	XI. FAR EAST
Astrakhan	48. Chuvash	53. Bashkir Republic	61. Altai	70. Buryat	80. Amur
Kalmykia-Khalmg Tangch	49. Kirov	54. Chelyabinsk	62. Gorny Altai	71. Chita	81. Kamchatka
Penza	50. Mariy El	55. Kurgan	63. Kemerovo	72. Agin Buryat	82. Koryak
Samara	51. Mordovia	56. Orenburg	64. Novosibirsk	73. Irkutsk	83. Khabarovsk
Saratov	52. Nizhny Novgorod	57. Perm	65. Omsk	74. Ust-Ordyn Buryat	84. Jewish AO
Tatar Republic		58. Komi-Permiak	66. Tomsk	75. Krasnoyarsk	85. Magadan
Volgograd		59. Udmurt	67. Tymen	76. Evenk	86. Chukot
Ulyanovsk		60. Sverdlovsk	68. Khanty-Mansi	77. Khakas	87. Primorsky
			69. Yamalo-Nenets	78. Taimir	88. Sakhalin
				79. Tuva	89. Yakutsk

Many questions remain unanswered, but some trends are clear. The names of all the people interviewed have been changed to protect their confidentiality.

This book is intended to help general readers understand some of the key facts, ideas, and interpretations necessary to evaluate the privatization process in Russia. Each chapter looks at what the privatization effort was trying to achieve and then discusses the available evidence about what happened and why it happened. We focus squarely on the privatization of the largest enterprises of Russia; we discuss the privatization of small shops and apartments only very briefly.

The attempt to dismantle the Communist economic and political system in the Soviet Union and later in the Russian Federation is one of history's major efforts to transform a society. The success or failure of the Russian Federation's transition from communism to some form of market economy will have a profound impact on the welfare of millions of Russian citizens and on the peace and security of citizens of countries throughout the world. In view of the importance of these events, it is unfortunate that what really took place in the privatization process has been obscure to most readers. Many books have been written about Mikhail Gorbachev and the breakup of the Soviet Union, but little has been available on the important events that occurred from 1991 to 1996 as the Russian Federation actually began its economic and political reforms. *Privatizing Russia,* by Maxim Boycko, Andrei Shleifer, and Robert Vishny, discusses the design of privatization. This book examines the results.

We pull back the curtain and offer an initial argument on how to interpret this encounter between the old Kremlin and capitalism. This book is not meant to be a point-by-point examination of every relevant aspect of privatization; we want to give an overview of its major themes and issues. The tables at the end of the book summarize evidence on several important questions. For the reader who wants to go further, the notes recommend additional reading. We will offer a more detailed analysis in a series of articles in scholarly journals. Certainly, historians and scholars will be looking at these events more closely as their ultimate implications become clearer. We plan to update this book in coming years as new information becomes available. The Chronology of Major Events will help readers find their way through the many important historical events that form the stage for this story.

Chapter 1 offers a perspective on some key events in Russian history and some introductory facts about Russia. It provides an overview of the political and economic situation in Russia before privatization was implemented and discusses the privatization program and the debate it aroused. We argue that the need to act quickly to reduce the power of the Communist Party over Russia's political and economic life, the economic crisis in which the country found itself, and the importance of beginning with a reform that Russian citizens wanted made a program of rapid privatization inevitable. And certainly the possibility of privatization was strengthened by the breakup of the Soviet Union and Boris Yeltsin's rise to power. But rapid privatization also planted the seeds of later conflicts, as we shall see as the story unfolds.

Chapter 2 answers the question: Who owns Russian industry after privatization? We examine who initially secured ownership of the factories in 1993–94 and how the ownership situation had changed by 1996. The ownership of Russian industry is put in some international perspective. It matters whether the majority of the owners of a privatized company are the employees of the firm, only its managers, or outsiders, or whether the company has no controlling block of owners. Since privatization was supposed to distribute property among citizens, it is important to know how much property ordinary citizens actually got. Chapter 2 makes it clear that privatization actually began rather than ended the struggle for property. Apportioning ownership of a firm among its employees got privatization off to a fast start, but unfortunately, this strategy has encouraged resistance to the outside investors that the newly privatized enterprises desperately need.

In Chapter 3 we consider who has the power in these new private corporations and how they are run. Here we see the problems that shareholders encounter in their efforts to supervise managers and make sure they can profit from their investment. We discuss how the struggle for control of these companies developed from 1993 to 1996. With so much stock in Russian companies held by workers, we investigate how much influence workers and their trade unions have and the impact economic reform has had on them. We also consider the extent of the influence of the Mafia and organized crime. We argue that the governance of the new private corporations is an extremely serious problem that threatens the future of reform.

Chapter 4 tells the story of the restructuring of privatized companies. The critical elements of real restructuring of a formerly state-owned company are managerial leadership and new capital investment. We look closely at what newly privatized companies did to restructure themselves in 1993 and 1994, immediately after privatization, and more recently, in 1995 and 1996. We examine in detail the adjustments these companies have made in their efforts to survive in a market economy. Have they fired managers? Have they changed what they produce and how they produce it? Have they reduced the many social services—apartments, day-care centers, kindergartens, cafeterias, vacation resorts, sports complexes—that large Soviet firms typically provided for their employees? Do the companies have access to capital to modernize their operations? Chapter 4 presents evidence on the many barriers to restructuring that are impeding the progress of companies across Russia. We present evidence of the role that strategic investors, takeovers, financial-industrial groups, banks, mutual funds, and the emerging Russian stock market are playing in the restructuring of the Russian economy. We conclude that many Russian companies are not restructuring enough in meaningful ways, and that managers and investors confront a daunting task when they attempt to persuade these corporations to change their ways.

Chapter 5 discusses the future of reform in light of the successes and failures of privatization and the challenges Russia faces after the parliamentary elections of December 1995 and the presidential elections of 1996. Was there an alternative to rapid privatization? What are the next steps in reform? Privatization went forward as overall economic reform in Russia faltered in significant ways; signs of progress appeared only in 1995 and 1996. The next stage of the reform process is as important as the initial privatization, and the challenges still facing the country are no less daunting. A program for further reforms is urgently needed, but the effort will be complicated by the distress of a large segment of the Russian population and the substantial opposition that reformers face. Still, Yeltsin's victory over the Communists in the presidential election offers the possibility of continued reform.

1

Privatization

The privatization of industries in Russia is only one part of a larger process of economic and political reforms. This process, difficult in the best of circumstances, is complicated by the country's enormous size and complexity and by its seventy-four years under a system that was hostile to private property. Stalin went so far as to reenserf the peasants in the 1930s. The breakup of the Soviet Union influenced the prospects for reform. To understand what has happened, we have to understand the road the country traveled from Mikhail Gorbachev as head of the Soviet Union in the late 1980s to Boris Yeltsin as leader of Russian reform in 1991. This is where the story of privatization really begins.

Russia's Past: The Context for Economic Reforms

Present-day reforms cannot be understood without an understanding of some of the forces exerted by Russia's past. Strict control of the economic activities of individuals has been a staple of Russian policy since a legal code enshrined serfdom in 1649. Peter the Great tried to force Russia to change when he sponsored the Westernization of the country in 1689. He established state-owned factories, took control of commerce, and brought foreign specialists to develop industries and exports. As Western nations moved headlong toward capitalism, Russia veered back and forth between encouraging private property and controlling it. This pattern has continued right up to the present day. In 1721, Peter the Great permitted merchants to purchase serfs, entire villages of them, for industrial labor. These serfs then became the property of industrial enterprises. For the next 270 years, Russia was never able to offer coherent support for private property; both the emancipation of the serfs and the Bolshevik Revolution complicated the move toward a market economy. On February 19, 1861, Tsar Alexander II emancipated 22 million serfs—40 percent of the population. The serfs had to buy back their land through annual payments over forty-nine years, and the total cost has been estimated to be well in excess of the market price at the time. In the end, the peasants had 13 percent less land than they had cultivated for their own use when they were serfs. The tsar ensured that their village societies remained segregated by restricting peasants' property rights and their freedom of movement. This reform can be seen as a kind of failed privatization. The peasants, by 1897 a majority of the population, bitterly resented the fact that the emancipation land settlement left a bulk of the land in the hands of the nobles, and millions of them left their villages for wage labor in city factories.

By 1900 capitalism had only weakly taken root in Russia; almost half of the capital invested in Russian industry came from other countries. Foreign capital was heavily invested in metallurgy and mining, engineering and machinery, chemicals, leather processing, paper, textiles, cement, ceramics, glass, and lumber. Foreign managers helped build, equip, and manage these enterprises. Modern business institutions were clustered in major cities. One student of the period says that corporations at this time "wore a foreign face" and demonstrated the weakness of an entrepreneurial tradition in Russia. The government tried to keep corporate development under strict control. A revolution erupted in 1905. It failed, but Nicholas II was persuaded to establish a parliament (the Duma) and to grant some civil liberties. Both the First and Second Dumas were dissolved by the government. To get the sort of duma he wanted, the tsar then changed the electoral law to permit the landed gentry to be assured of 50 percent of the seats. In an effort to build a class of free prosperous farmers, Prime Minister Peter Stolypin pushed legislation that permitted peasants to travel freely and encouraged them to farm independently, but by 1914 fewer than 25 percent of all peasant households had established independent farms.

The tide was to turn again. After Lenin and his Bolsheviks seized power in October 1917, the economy veered back to state control. The Soviet state was hard pressed to provide food for the urban population. Land was nationalized and the government began compulsory requisitions of food from the uncooperative peasantry. Lenin instituted a mixed economy and even toyed with the idea of private cooperatives. At first, industry was decentralized, each factory under the control of a workers' committee, or soviet. But the factory soviets came to be viewed as a threat to the state's power, and were abandoned in favor of strong centralized control by the state. By 1921, gross output had fallen to less than a third of its prerevolutionary level. Private banks were abolished. As all enterprises were now financed by the state, they were relieved of the need to pay and be paid by one another.

Under the New Economic Policy (NEP), introduced in 1921 after peasant uprisings, forced requisitions of agricultural products were replaced by a tax in kind related to level of income and number of household members. Peasants were now allowed to sell their production and trade freely. Private enterprise was expanded to allow sale of goods produced by small-scale private manufacturers in both kiosks and permanent facilities. Private real estate, hospitals, savings and loan associations, publishing, and manufacture were allowed. Nevertheless, most of the industrial labor force remained in a small number of nationalized enterprises. Seventy-six percent of retail sales were in private hands by 1923 and state companies were largely restricted to wholesale trade. The economy had recovered to its 1913 level when Lenin died in 1924.

The NEP did not long survive him. In 1928 his successor, Josef Stalin, deliberately magnified a temporary curtailment of grain marketed by independent peasants into a "grain crisis" and launched a campaign against the better-off peasants, the so-called kulaks. All agriculture was to be collectivized and the entire kulak class eliminated. At the same time Stalin inaugurated an industrialization drive with unprecedented investment in capital goods industries. State ownership had returned. By 1937, almost all cultivated land was in collective farms (*kolkhozy*) or state farms (*sovkhozy*). Private garden plots were allowed after the collectivization of the peasantry in 1929–32. After 1932, workers on the collective farms were allowed to sell produce to citizens directly from their private plots. By 1940, such sales accounted for 50 percent of total farm sales. Private plot production accounted for 24 percent of total farm output by 1989. Even under the Soviet system, common people were expressing their interest in private entrepreneurship. It took until 1953 for food production per person to regain its 1928 level. Throughout the 1930s Stalin continued a massive program of industrial investment through a series of five-year plans. Production was rapidly increased, but little attention was paid to costs and efficiency. Wages and living standards were low; the trade unions were arms of the Communist Party.

After World War II, Russia reconstructed its battered economy, but the Stalin regime put little emphasis on the production of consumer goods. After Stalin died in 1953, Nikita Khrushchev began to experiment with economic reforms. In 1957 he abolished all the central economic ministries that controlled factories throughout the Soviet Union and turned their control over to regional economic organs and hence to the first secretary of the Communist party of the given geographic region. When their economic performance did not improve, control over factories was centralized again.

The situation did not improve under Leonid Brezhnev, who presided from 1964 to 1982. In September 1965 he tried to reform industry again by putting into practice ideas advanced by an economist in the city of Kharkov, Evsei Libermann. Libermann proposed to link managers' bonuses to sales and profits rather than to the sheer volume of production. In January 1966, forty-three enterprises in seventeen industries with a total of 300,000 workers began working under the new system. In the end, there was very little difference between the old system and the new, and these reforms were reversed after the Soviet invasion of Czechoslovakia in 1968. From 1970 to 1990, the report card for Soviet agriculture was even more disappointing. According to one estimate, investment in agriculture rose an average 7 percent a year per farmworker in this period, but farm output declined by 1 percent a year. This uneven record of attempts to create private enterprise and reform the economic system over the centuries is the background against which the reforms of the 1990s must be seen.

It would be morally obtuse to see the imposition of the Communist system as merely a struggle of ideas or a question of the inefficiency of an economic system. The Stalin regime killed millions of people. Communism was not merely an alternative economic system. Millions were murdered and died in forced labor camps. When Stalin collectivized agriculture from 1928 to the mid-1930s, according to a Soviet estimate of the 1980s, the Communist state murdered one million peasants. Some scholars say that the true figure may be as high as 6.5 million. Ten million peasants went to labor camps. Soviet sources admitted that 5 million people died in the forced famine as part of this program; some Western estimates place the number as high as 8 million. From 1934 to 1939, Stalin's Great Terror executed

800,000 people and arrested 8 million more, or about 5 percent of the population. Historians estimate that 10 percent of the prisoners in the forced labor camps died each year. With a ten-year sentence the standard, as many as a million prisoners died each year during this period. It has been estimated that throughout the world, 100 million people fell victim to the communist system. The industrial and military might that Stalin and his successors achieved was bought at the cost of this international disaster.

From Gorbachev to Yeltsin

The system simply did not work well, and efforts to reform it made little difference. Up into the 1980s, most retail and wholesale prices were determined by the state, and they remained the same for years. Soviet prices simply bore no relation to prices on the world market. Crude oil fetched a penny inside the Soviet Union for every dollar of its value outside the country. Though the Soviet economic machine could claim enormous industrial and agricultural output, it was very inefficient. The annual growth rates of both the entire Soviet economy and its standard of living declined into the 1980s. The key failure of the Brezhnev period was the grain harvest and the inability to reform Soviet agriculture. Agricultural productivity grew at only 1.7 percent a year from 1964 to 1982.

After the brief tenures of Konstantin Chernenko and Yury Andropov, Mikhail Gorbachev became general secretary of the Communist Party of the Soviet Union in 1985. Gorbachev's solution was familiar: massive investment in industry with the goal of doubling the national income by the year 2000 and increasing the living standard of the average Russian. He wanted to use technology to restructure Soviet industry. When it became clear that economic performance could not be improved by these measures, Gorbachev tried to adjust the way the state controlled the economy. He announced that he was going to reform the Communist system by introducing glasnost (free discussion in speech and print) and perestroika (restructuring), and he rejected the notion that nuclear war had a role to play in human affairs. Boris Yeltsin was elected first secretary of the Moscow Communist Party in 1985 and became a nonvoting member of the Politburo of the Communist Party of the Soviet Union in 1986. On October 21, 1987, Yeltsin harshly criticized the substance and the speed of Gorbachev's reforms, and he was subsequently removed from both positions. The future president of the Russian Federation remained only deputy chairman of the State Committee on Construction of the USSR.

Gorbachev faced a daunting task. The government budget deficit was soaring because the prices of consumer goods were controlled and supported by government subsidies. Massive amounts were being spent to subsidize Soviet industry. Gorbachev had to reform the economy as a whole and at the same time he had to change the way enterprises worked. The two were linked. Gorbachev tinkered with the command economy but he never succeeded in changing it significantly. He encouraged different wage systems and the development of a system of quality control. In his 1987 book *Perestroika,* despite many uplifting remarks, Gorbachev avowed his opposition to privatization and political pluralism and his unwavering support for Lenin and the Communist Party. On January 1, 1988, the Law on State Enterprises gave more independence to enterprise directors, reorganized enterprises into bigger associations, and allowed workers to elect the managers of their enterprises. These changes did not improve performance. On the contrary, wages rose quickly, managers started raising prices, and in general they made no effort to cut costs or respond to consumer demand.

Support was growing for a market economy, for private property, for less control over prices, and for less control by the Communist Party. Earlier, in November 1986, new legislation permitted some limited private labor activity, but it did not envision privatization. After May 1988, when the government promulgated a law permitting cooperatives, hundreds of cooperatives—in essence private businesses with a more acceptable label—were founded, including some banks. In December 1988 the government issued a decree permitting the sale of apartments to individuals. A decree in November 1989 allowed the leasing of state enterprises by their workers. In 1990 Gorbachev said he would allow the leasing of family farms. On balance, the Gorbachev reforms added up to half-measures and a *discussion* of reform concepts without much radical action and without any serious attempt to change the giant sector of state-owned industry.

Gorbachev's political reforms were more extensive. Both his political reforms and the open discussions about the system's failures encouraged some further questioning and change. Many Russians and foreigners remember the shock of seeing the congresses openly discuss the failures of the Communist system in this period. In 1988 the 19th Conference of the Communist Party approved the creation of a legislature, the Congress of People's Deputies. After elections were held in 1989, 85 percent of the deputies were members of the Communist Party. A third of the deputies are actually selected from public organizations dominated by the Party. (Domination of the legislature by conservatives has hobbled the transition to a market economy right up to the present day.) Gorbachev was then elected head of state by the Congress, and Boris Yeltsin received a seat in the new legislature when another deputy withdrew in his favor. Gorbachev then created a state commission under the economist and deputy prime minister Leonid Abalkin to draft an economic reform program. The plan he received emphasized the creation of a market economy, the freeing of prices, competition, a convertible currency, and the creation of stock markets.

The year 1989 will be remembered as the year when events simply ran away from Gorbachev and the Soviet leadership. The last Soviet troops left Afghanistan. Estonia, Latvia, and Lithuania took steps toward declaring their sovereignty. Soviet troops started to leave Hungary. Candidates backed by Solidarity won elections and Poland formed a noncommunist government. Gorbachev declared that the USSR would not block reforms in Eastern Europe and that he would use no force against any member of the Warsaw Pact that withdrew from that Communist alliance. East Germany's leader, Erich Honeker, resigned, the Berlin Wall came down, and Germany announced plans for its reunification. A noncommunist government came to power in Czechoslovakia. There was a revolution in Romania, the Bulgarian Communist bosses were removed, and various Soviet republics started to articulate their desire for independence.

In 1990, Russia was still part of the Soviet Union and Yeltsin began his rise to power. The stage was set for the later conflict between Yeltsin and Gorbachev on the extent of economic reform, the autonomy of Russia, and the fate of the Soviet Union itself. Russia, as one of the republics of the USSR, had its own legislature, the Russian Congress of People's Deputies. Yeltsin was elected as a deputy in the smaller standing legislative body, the Supreme Soviet, in March 1990 and was elected its chairman, or speaker, in May. He pushed for a declaration of the sovereignty of Russia as a separate nation in June. He quit the Communist Party in July. In September 1990 the Russian Supreme Soviet approved a radical plan to transform the Soviet economy (the Shatalin plan) by 213 to 1. In December 1990, the Russian Republic of the USSR moved in the direction of a private sector economy by adopting a Law on Enterprises and Entrepreneurial Activity, which allowed for all kinds of enterprises —sole proprietorships, partnerships, and private and state-owned corporations. Russia was already pursuing its own economic reform course before the Soviet Union fell apart.

Gorbachev, too, continued to push for reform in 1990. The young Russian economist Grigory Yavlinsky and others put together a 500-day plan for transition to a market economy which was inspired by Poland's "shock therapy." The plan included rapid freeing of prices, stabilizing the economy, increasing state revenues, and privatizing state-owned enterprises by offering them for sale. The USSR's Congress of People's Deputies eliminated the Communist Party's monopoly on power, and Gorbachev was selected president of the USSR by a vote of only 59 percent of the deputies, an indication that hardliners were now turning against him. The USSR Supreme Soviet passed a Law on Enterprises which opened the way for a market economy, but this law actually had little effect. Gorbachev and Yeltsin finally agreed to appoint another commission chaired by Stanislav Shatalin to draft a 500-day plan for the transformation of the Soviet economy.

Then events took a different direction. Several Soviet republics, in addition to the Russian Republic, declared their sovereignty in 1990 and elected leaders who were independent of Moscow. It was becoming clear to everyone that the Soviet Union itself would have to undergo a restructuring. The USSR Supreme Soviet passed a law to become a multiparty political system. Gorbachev finally rejected the 500-day plan in October 1990 after recommending that it be merged with a less radical plan drawn up by his government. In November he escaped an assassination attempt.

There is no question that Yeltsin lost patience when Gorbachev rejected the radical 500-day plan. The former U.S. ambassador Jack F. Matlock writes:

> During a meeting on September 4, Yeltsin told a group of American senators and me that no merger between the two plans was possible and that he would not accept the result of an attempt to reconcile them. He thought the USSR Council of Ministers (Gorbachev's government and cabinet) had outlived its usefulness and should be replaced by a smaller Presidential Council. He added that he was not seeking a confrontation with the USSR government but that [Russia] and other republics would insist on assuming many of its current functions because they wished to move ahead more rapidly with economic reform and did not want to be held back by a standpat central bureaucracy. He was willing, however, to leave functions such as defense, communications, energy distribution, and rail and air transportation to the central government.

Matlock adds that Yeltsin later denounced Gorbachev's idea of combining the radical reform plan with a more watered-down plan on which his government was working. Gorbachev's economic reform plan, Yeltsin said, left Russia "with three choices: to reject it outright, to go its own way with its own program, or to wait six months until the inevitable economic collapse would force another approach." The former American ambassador considers Gorbachev's rejection of the Shatalin plan one of his "fateful errors." There was increasing evidence that Gorbachev would not support a truly radical privatization plan. In December 1990 he said, "When owners have appeared, private property may emerge; in any case, I imagine it will be small-scale property. It will be decisive only in certain spheres, where the cooperative and state sectors don't work as they should"; and "I am in favor of the market . . . but I don't accept private ownership of land, for instance, whatever you do with me."

The final report card on Gorbachev's reforms was mixed at best. On political reform, he unleashed forces that led to the demise of communism in many countries. On reforming the Soviet economy as a whole, he failed miserably. At the end of 1990 his prime minister, Nikolai Ryzhkov, tried to raise prices in order to reduce state subsidies, but opposition was so fierce that he had to reverse this plan. Later the Soviet Union freed most wholesale prices, but because retail prices stayed the same, subsidies for consumers actually rose. Then Gorbachev significantly increased wages and social expenditures despite the fact that the overall performance of the economy was declining. These moves put more pressure on the Soviet budget. As a result of Gorbachev's enterprise reforms, some economic experimentation was going on at the beginning of the 1990s. Almost 3 million workers, or 4 percent of the Russian Federation's workforce, were in cooperatives, and workers had leased almost 10,000 state-owned enterprises. Yet Gorbachev's chance to change the Soviet Union was drawing to a close. In 1991 he came increasingly under the influence of hard-line conservatives in the Communist Party and the KGB, despite the fact that he remained a progressive force in international foreign policy by supporting Operation Desert Storm against Iraq and going along with the dissolution of the Warsaw Pact. He allowed an attempt to repress the independence movement in Lithuania. Yeltsin called for Gorbachev's resignation in February. Gorbachev ordered a national referendum throughout the Soviet Union on whether citizens favored a voluntary Soviet Union. The referendum was not even implemented in some republics, it was changed in others, and it did not pass in yet others. Yet the overall result was a clear majority in favor of preserving the USSR in some form. Yeltsin was against holding the referendum in Russia, but then he added a question of his own: Did Russians favor creation of the post of president, to be filled by democratic election by individual citizens? His own legislature, the Russian Supreme Soviet, refused to amend the Russian constitution to establish the presidency. Matlock points out that Gorbachev had set a trap for himself, because if Yeltsin won a direct presidential election, his authority would rise dramatically in comparison with that of Gorbachev, "the unelected president of a faltering state machine." Yeltsin had set the stage for a power play, and Russia was poised to gain in importance in relation to the union of which it was a part.

Events, both political and economic, then moved very quickly. Gorbachev started to negotiate a voluntary treaty with the various republics that were formally part of the Soviet Union in order to create a voluntary union with himself as president. Yeltsin and the heads of eight other republics agreed to negotiate. In June 1991, Yeltsin was elected president of Russia with 57.3 percent of the vote. The USSR Supreme Soviet discussed a draft law on privatization in a marathon session filled with conflict. Communist opponents attacked Gorbachev bitterly and charged that the law would lead to a new middle class and to an influx of foreign investors, who would buy up the entire economy; the law was intended not to reform the Soviet system, they said, but actually to replace it. In July the Russian Supreme Soviet adopted laws that envisioned the privatization of state-owned enterprises, the establishment of individual privatization accounts in the state savings banks, and the privatization of the apartments in which citizens lived. Russia was moving to institute its own radical economic reforms. On August 10, at his vacation house on the Black Sea, Gorbachev departed from his usual passivity on the issue of privatization by signing a decree setting up a USSR Property Fund to design and organize a plan of privatization. It is unclear what kind of privatization he actually envisaged, but this decree went far beyond his previous initiatives on the question. It is possible that this action played some role in the conservatives' decision to oust him. His prime minister, Valentin Pavlov, one of the organizers of the committee that later declared a state of emergency, had spoken about the danger of Russia's enslavement by foreign bankers, and he strongly opposed any talk of the Shatalin and Yavlinsky plans.

A struggle between the conservatives and the reformers then took place. On August 18, 1991, representatives of the emergency committee went to the president's retreat in the Crimea and tried to persuade Gorbachev to agree to a state of emergency. Gorbachev refused.

On August 19, the emergency committee announced that it was taking power because Gorbachev was incapacitated. Their effort failed after Yeltsin declared the action a coup and led resistance from the Russian White House. After a halfhearted attempt to take over control of the country, the emergency committee collapsed. Gorbachev returned to Moscow. He suspended the Communist Party, and one Soviet republic after another declared its independence. Just after these events, Gorbachev's decree on privatization was published and a major Moscow newspaper wrote, "It is impossible to overestimate the significance of this decree in the internecine struggle between the President and the Prime Minister." Some observers believed that Gorbachev was the innocent victim of a coup; others suggest that he may have encouraged the hard-liners in his own government in order to challenge Yeltsin's growing power. Whatever the case, there is no doubt that Yeltsin used these events to buttress his political power and maneuver both Gorbachev and the USSR off center stage.

After the coup against Gorbachev, in October 1991, Yeltsin assumed the role of prime minister of a new Russian government and delegated economic reform to Yegor Gaidar and Gennady Burbulis as deputy prime ministers. Anatoly Chubais became minister of privatization and chairman of the State Committee for the Management of State Property, as the ministry of privatization was called. Yeltsin made a major speech on radical economic reform on October 28, 1991. The Russian Supreme Soviet allowed him to rule by decree. In November Yeltsin banned the Communist Party. In December, in a shocking move that some historians consider a power play against Gorbachev, Yeltsin and the leaders of Belorus and Ukraine refused to sign the treaty creating a voluntary union of republics and met in secret at a hunting lodge in Belorus and abolished the Soviet Union as a state. They created a very loose Commonwealth of Independent States. On December 25, Gorbachev had to resign as president of the USSR and the Soviet flag was replaced by the Russian flag over the Kremlin. The Soviet Union was dead, and a period of reform was about to begin in the Russian Federation. Given the interest in privatization and the tension it aroused, few observers were surprised when Yeltsin's government moved quickly in this direction.

Some Facts on Russia

The Soviet Union is no more, but the Russian Federation is still the world's largest country, extending over 11 million square miles from Europe to the Pacific. It is the largest and most influential part of the former Soviet Union, accounting for 51 percent of its population, 76 percent of its territory, and a substantial proportion of its industrial and economic might. Its population is about 149 million, about 109 million urban and 40 million rural. About 110 million people are voters; the rest are under the age of 17. Around 30 million people are on pensions. The total number of workers in 1995 was about 67 million. About 17 million were working in industry and about 9.9 million in agriculture. The others were involved in the construction trades, catering, education, health, social security, sports, culture, public administration, transportation and communications, and the military.

The death rate is 15.6 per thousand people, up by over a fifth since 1992. The birth rate has dropped significantly, from 12.1 per thousand people in 1991 to 9.4 in 1994. Russia's infant mortality rate, 18.6 per thousand, is three times that of the European Community. The number of children aged 3 to 6 was projected to drop by more than a quarter in 1997, and the number of children 7 to 9 to fall by just over a tenth. From 1991 to 1994, average life expectancy dropped by almost 5 years. The average life expectancy of Russian men is just 58 years, but it is 71 years for women. In 1994 the average Russian produced $4,031 worth of goods and services; the figure for the average agricultural worker was $1,777.

Since Stalin's time, Russian industry has been oriented toward military production, with huge investments in metals, machinery, and technology related to the military. Light industry and consumer goods producers always came second. In 1989, all machine building accounted for about a third of everything that was produced in the Soviet Union, compared with 20 to 25 percent in most industrialized countries, and only about 4 percent of this output was exported. Until the fall of the Soviet Union, the country made up for its distorted industrial structure by exploiting an abundance of raw materials from its major reserves of oil, gas, coal, diamonds, and other minerals. These exports earned the money the Soviet government used to subsidize the inefficient manufacturing economy. With more than 15 billion tons of proven and probable oil reserves and vast deposits of gas, Russia could be one of the world's biggest sources of fuel in the next century. Many of these deposits, as well as coal, diamonds, gold, platinum, nickel, and timber, are found in remote parts of Siberia, north of the Arctic Circle and in the Far East.

Russia's rich natural resources had another impact on economic reform. Much of the corruption and skimming off of supplies from heavy industries occurred between 1989 and 1994. Because the prices of these goods were strictly controlled, a person could buy or skim off refined oil, which was 146 times cheaper in Russia than on the world market, smuggle it across a border that had become permeable as the Soviet Union collapsed, and become rich overnight. Many other products sold in Russia for only a fraction of world prices: crude oil (100 times cheaper), machines (27 times cheaper), gas (12 times cheaper), coal (61 times cheaper), and some products of light industry such as food and textiles (13 times cheaper). After 1992, price controls were lifted, and these prices began to rise to world levels.

The Starting and Ending Points for This Story

As the discussion of economic reform began in Russia in the late 1980s and early 1990s, it was clear that large and mid-sized industrial enterprises—those with more than 200 employees—dominated the economy. At the beginning of 1988, such enterprises accounted for about 95 percent of both employees and production; 75 percent of employees and production were in enterprises with more than 1,000 employees. It was far easier for the Soviet government to control a few enormous enterprises than a multitude of small ones. Our investigations focus on Russia's program to turn over most of these large enterprises to private ownership. Producing oil, gas, and petroleum products, basic materials such as steel, aluminum, and other metals, industrial machinery, high technology, consumer products, and utility services, they constituted the jewels of the economy.

Our story begins in 1991 and ends in 1996. At the beginning of 1991 the Russian Federation had approximately 23,766 mid-sized and large industrial enterprises and 170,000 smaller ones, mostly retail shops. By the end of that year, Russian entrepreneurs had established about 250,000 new small private enterprises. Some of them were cooperatives that had gotten their start from Gorbachev-era legislation. Many owed their existence to the more favorable environment for private enterprise created by the 1990 Russian Law on Enterprises and Entrepreneurial Activity. These firms accounted for a modest amount of employment. Some managers and workers had already begun to experiment with freedom by leasing their enterprises from the state. By February 1992, 9,451 state enterprises, accounting for 8 percent of total employment, were leased by their workers and managers.

By 1996 most enterprises slated for privatization had been privatized, including those that earlier had been leased. (The year-by-year progress of the privatization of both small and large enterprises is shown in Table 1, which also shows how the development of new small businesses paralleled the privatization of state-owned businesses.) Here is the final report card: By the beginning of 1996, 77.2 percent of mid-sized and large enterprises were privatized. They account for 88.3 percent of the total industrial output of the Russian Federation. They have downsized considerably by pensioning employees and laying them off. About 82 percent of small shops and retail stores, accounting for 9 million employees, are now privatized. They include 900,000 new small businesses established by Russian entrepreneurs.

Privatization has been meaningful, but Russia has much farther to go in its economic reforms. And the level of privatization that has taken place should not be exaggerated. While most Russian industrial employment is indeed privatized, most employment is not in the private sector. We estimate that of the 67 million members of the employed Russian population, no more than 27 million are in the private sector. A rough estimate is that a quarter of the larger enterprises, a fifth of the smaller enterprises, and an agricultural sector of 10.5 million people remain to be completely turned over to private owners. If earlier figures are still valid, there are approximately 25,600 collective and state farms. Some of the remaining 40 million people who are employed in the state sector are likely to remain there. Russia has far to go before it is a normal market society. Millions of people are still working in state-related enterprises that in other societies are in the for-profit sector, such as coal, transport, communications, and the military-industrial sectors. And millions are working in organizations that make up vibrant nonprofit and nongovernmental sectors in market economies, such as education, culture, art, health, and science. Because of the country's severe budget deficits, some of these organizations may be viable only as private corporations. Russia's small-business sector is still tiny in comparison with that of the typical Western country, where small businesses usually account for well over half of the workforce.

Why Was Privatization Necessary?

Privatization was necessary for two reasons. Decades of state control had created a mentality that prevented improvements in economic performance because private property rights were neither accepted nor clear-cut. Whatever laws and decrees were passed and whatever reforms were implemented, the results made little difference. And the Soviet Union's economy was collapsing. The story of how reform zigzagged back and forth throughout Russian history and the Communist period fails to capture the deep-seated mentality among Russian bureaucrats and managers that was a major barrier to the privatization of enterprises.

The Soviet Union operated as one giant corporation, with none of the formal markets and competition through which companies in the free market economies gain their labor, capital, managerial talent, information about consumer preferences, raw materials, and energy. In a free market economy, the managers of a factory depend on the market to tell them what to produce, and the profits of shareholders, the compensation of workers, and their own bonuses depend on the success of the business. A business in an open economy has real owners who put their capital into it and take responsibility for its profits and losses. These owners are shareholders who have the right to oversee the management of the company through the board of directors and to share in the profits. Other countries may have tax breaks and subsidies for various industries and agriculture, but no government in a market economy has managed to exert as much control and pump as many subsidies into enterprises as the Soviet Union did.

The Soviet factory had no individual owners. The state was the owner. The employees received modest wages with significant perks, such as enterprise-provided apartments, utilities, cafeterias, a day-care center and a kindergarten, health care, a vacation retreat, and a cultural center. They could look forward to modest but stable pensions, and they did not worry about inflation. Since the stores offered them little to buy, they could save part of their modest wages in the state savings bank. Instead of commercial banks that lent money to businesses to expand, the government supplied enterprises with money. Managers may have been chosen for technical competence but they were not required to have training in financial management. Quite bluntly, the manager needed to worry only about getting supplies and producing his quota. He often was not aware what individual products actually cost or whether the plant made a profit on them. For this reason, he had no real incentive to improve his employees' productivity. The firm did little advertising and placed scant emphasis on product development or style. It had no sales or marketing department. Many imported products were not available to consumers, and because the country was generally cut off from world markets, Soviet firms had no need to compete with foreign products on the basis of quality, price, function, availability, or style. Many managers were not even aware of world performance standards for products, management, or labor. Managers did not downsize and restructure; they expanded. Some industrial managers actually sold finished goods for less than it cost to produce them.

The support services common in free market economies were virtually nonexistent. There were no checking accounts and no checks, so that after the fall of communism one factory could not easily transfer payment to another factory. Some people hired a truck to carry a big payment across the country so it could be made on time. The country had no extensive business law or lawyers, no private bankers, few insurance companies, no consulting firms, no accounting firms or public disclosure of financial information, no stock market or bond market, no securities laws, and no boards of directors to oversee the managers of corporations.

In 1991, the Soviet Union's economy was collapsing (see Table 2). Domestic production shrank 12.8 percent, and the budget deficit jumped to 30 percent of all domestic production from only 2 percent at the beginning of Gorbachev's administration. The USSR's member republics started to withhold tax revenues from the central government. The government was sending money through the Soviet pipeline to enterprises and regions but getting less and less back. Gorbachev was playing a dangerous game with socialism. He could not make the economy more efficient, yet he wanted to improve the lot of the population. So he simply increased their benefits by using deficit spending on a gargantuan scale. From 1989 to 1991, wages were allowed to grow at two to three times the normal rate, and social benefits were increased by 25 percent in 1990 alone.

Prices were still controlled, so that pumping all this money into the economy ignited the first serious inflation in the Soviet Union for decades. Consumer prices shot up 93 percent while wholesale prices for industry rose 138 percent. The manufacture of consumer goods started to drop; production of such basic foodstuffs as meat, milk, eggs, and grains plummeted. The only good news was that there was still no recorded unemployment.

In the waning days of the Cold War, Russia propped up its economy by exports of oil, gas, gold, and other commodities. But now many of Russia's raw materials were used up. Perhaps the USSR could have dealt with a drop in production and efficiency if it had secured new capital and equipment to build up its production. But such steps were not being taken, and in the period from 1989 to 1991, capital investment began to sink. Without significant capital investments in technologies to extract natural resources more efficiently, the already plundered source of cash for investment was blocked. Gorbachev had used much of the Soviet Union's gold reserves, built up massive international loans that required billions a year simply to keep current, and drawn down its hard currency reserves to the danger point of about $100 million. In 1991, trade with the Warsaw Bloc countries fell by over half; the entire COMECON—the Communist economic market, consisting of the USSR, the Communist countries of Eastern Europe, Vietnam, and Cuba—fell apart; military expenditures were out of control; and the USSR defaulted on its international loans. The crisis was felt very starkly when productivity of factories and farms fell. Long lines formed at most shops as stocks dwindled.

As 1991 drew toward its close, Yeltsin said that he was determined to move forward quickly with privatization. His speech on October 21, 1991, could not have been clearer: "For impermissibly long, we have discussed whether private property is necessary. In the meantime, the party-state elite have actively engaged in their personal privatization. The scale, the enterprise, and the hypocrisy are staggering. The privatization of Russia has gone on [for a long time], but wildly, spontaneously, and often on a criminal basis. Today it is necessary to grasp the initiative, and we are intent on doing so."

Privatization was only part of a larger program of economic reform. Anders Åslund, an expert on the Russian economy, has written in detail about the design of Yeltsin's overall economic reform program. He and the Harvard economist Jeffrey Sachs were among a group of foreign advisers on larger economic questions from November 1991 to the end of 1993, when Yeltsin's principal reformers, First Deputy Prime Minister Yegor Gaidar and Minister of Finance Boris Fedorov, left the government. Åslund's explanation of economic reform hinges on two propositions: first, in a market economy individuals have the right to create, manage, profit from, and liquidate companies, and within these companies they have the right to decide what to produce, what to buy, what to sell, and with whom to do business; and second, in a market economy companies must be hungry for profits and recognize that money is scarce if they are going to have any incentive to compete and respond to consumers' demands by making products consumers want and will buy. If the state has a soft attitude toward providing money to enterprises—economists often call it a soft budget constraint—companies will not care about what buyers want. Firms will then have little incentive to cut their costs and increase their sales and profits. One principle underlines freedom for any form of private property, and the other underscores a small role for the state in the economy. The Soviet state controlled the economy. The government subsidized the enterprises, set their prices, and preserved them from competition. A state planning committee, Gosplan, and a state supplies committee, Gossnab, controlled the allocation of goods and the trade between enterprises. A few big enterprises had monopolies on oil, gas, grain, and timber. The right to engage in foreign trade was dominated by government organizations. And the government purchased foreign imports at high world market prices and then resold them to Soviet companies at a fraction of their cost. The Soviet Union was defined by its point-by-point opposition to basic free market principles.

These principles prescribed that the Russian state had to (1) both free prices and stop controlling domestic and foreign trade so that all companies could compete; (2) give citizens the freedom to start any kind of company they wanted to start and give companies the right to produce anything they wanted; (3) reduce its large budget deficit and make it perfectly clear that enterprises were no longer going to be subsidized; (4) establish a stable convertible currency and control inflation; (5) simplify its legal and tax systems in order to promote small business; and (6) divest itself of all commercial and industrial enterprises and move toward privatization. Because so much of Soviet industry was tied to the military-industrial complex and the manufacture of products that no one wanted to buy, significant drops in production were expected under such a scenario.

In 1992 Yeltsin's chief economic strategist, Yegor Gaidar, took some steps to implement these plans. The task was complicated by a lack of coordination among many parts of the central government and between the central government and the many local governments spread across Russia's far-flung regions. Contrary to popular belief, it was also complicated by the slow pace of key international financial institutions' involvement in support of Russia's reforms. As 1992 began, Russia was not yet a member of the International Monetary Fund.

On January 2, 1992, the Russian government stopped controlling 80 percent of wholesale prices and 90 percent of retail prices. It set some ceilings on other prices but continued to set the prices of some food, energy, and some services, such as air fares. Russia signed a shadow program with the International Monetary Fund on February 27, 1992, and in March submitted to the IMF a Memorandum of Economic Policies that set out the framework for its reform. In March and again in May 1992, the prices of many basic foods were freed.

Shortages stopped and products began to appear on store shelves. The government already allowed any kind of enterprise to be established, and small businesses appeared rapidly. The government had said that citizens could engage in any kind of trade and purchasing activities without permission. Controls over foreign trade were somewhat relaxed. Reform was not complete. The country had no import controls or tariffs in the first half of 1992, but certain imports continued to be controlled by the government and subsidized well into 1993. And state-controlled farms continued to dominate agriculture and the government continued to control the distribution of food.

After liberalizing prices and trade, the Russian government faltered on the larger economic reforms in 1992. One important cause of the large budget deficit was extensive subsidies and subsidized loans to enterprises and the government's desire to continue financing the investments of some enterprises. In addition, the Central Bank was financing the huge government budget deficit and issuing credits to other former Soviet republics. All of these activities fueled inflation. At this time, Russia really implemented only half of the economic reform program. A quick rise in prices had been expected when prices were freed, but Russia was experiencing continuing inflation as a result of confused government policies.

Jeffrey Sachs blames the international community for its lack of financial support and profound failures in policy advice at this critical moment. The International Monetary Fund, he says, was unwilling to provide Russia with financing to stabilize the exchange rate of the ruble until it was no longer needed. Russia became a member of the IMF only on June 1, 1992, when another plan to reform its economy was approved. The IMF approved the Russian Federation's request for support on August 5, 1992, after Gaidar had implemented most of his initial macroeconomic reforms. The IMF made about $1 billion available to support economic reform and said the goals of its support were to reduce inflationary pressures during the remainder of the year and to reduce the country's budget deficit by about 12 percent. The IMF asked Russia to limit the growth of Central Bank credit, develop a flexible interest rate policy, and push reforms in the area of privatization, agriculture, and its financial sector.

To casual observers of this stage of Russian "shock therapy," it might seem as though economic reform had been designed to hurt the average person. In fact, proponents such as Sachs argued that rapid implementation of these reforms would concentrate the pain in one short period and minimize suffering over the long term. Military expenditures and enterprise supports could be cut and social support could be substantially increased. In 1992 the Russian government did not follow this approach. It continued to subsidize powerful industries, factories, and political lobbies, and ignored the plight of the common people. By continuing to avoid a plan to make farmers independent property owners, it maintained the need for huge subsidies to an inefficient agricultural system. The government specifically promised the IMF that it would protect the most vulnerable groups in the population during the economic transformation process and that it would ensure that what it spent on maintaining a social safety net was consistent with the pain that efforts to stabilize its economy would cause. That promise was not kept. As the presses of the Central Bank worked overtime printing money to subsidize the economy, consumer prices soared at an annual rate of 1,354 percent and industrial prices 1,949 percent.

In 1992, as all domestic production fell again by 14.5 percent, capital investment in production fell again by over a third, and even the production of electricity sank by 6 percent nationwide. The Central Bank of Russia, which was under the control of the Supreme Soviet, the parliament that Yeltsin had inherited from the Gorbachev era, printed rubles and pushed loans at negative interest rates through its regional branches to big and medium-sized enterprises. Most enterprises used the funds to pay for raw materials, labor, and energy. The budget deficit equaled over a fifth of all domestic production.

As inflation changed the value of everything weekly, the managers of the big enterprises tried to juggle prices, subsidies, loans, and payments to suppliers so that none of them crashed. Wages went up only a bit more than half the rate of consumer prices during 1992. Pensions never kept pace with inflation, and the living standards of pensioners plummeted. Before 1991, Russians had a low but stable standard of living because the state kept unemployment, wages, and pensions under control. By 1992 it could not afford to do so. Official unemployment was 4.9 percent at the end of 1992. People's lives were getting worse.

Despite its inability to move ahead forthrightly with all elements of radical economic reform, the Russian government continued to plan for widespread privatization in 1992. The notion that the state must not own and operate companies had been gaining increasing support since the 500-day program was discussed under Gorbachev and the conservative Russian Supreme Soviet had adopted several preliminary laws calling for privatization in late 1991. In 1992–93, the Russian federal government accounted for 70 percent of the capital investment in enterprises through seven industrial funds created by government ministries. This expenditure alone constituted 10 percent of the gross domestic product of the country. A respected public opinion poll had indicated that Russian citizens favored the Shatalin plan—which included privatization—by 5 to 1. In fact, some observers report that both the left and the right agreed that privatization should precede the other elements of economic reform. The actual plan of privatization was unclear in the summer and fall of 1991, but by the summer of 1992 less than a quarter of the workers polled thought it was not necessary. Privatization was one element of the economic reform program that had not yet been implemented and that had some popular support—despite the polls that showed that Russians were suffering as a result of initial attempts at economic reforms and were turning against those reforms in significant numbers.

The most cynical view of the privatization process was that the Communist elite, the *nomenklatura*—the enterprise managers and top government and Party bureaucrats—were planning to appropriate all the property of Russia and that privatization was really a convenient cover for this hijacking. In 1991, Gorbachev inadvertently opened the door to one form of hijacking when, in his efforts to reform the lumbering Soviet economic system, he experimented with removing the power of the big Soviet cabinet ministries over the individual general directors of thousands of enterprises. The Russian general director is similar in authority to the chief executive officer (CEO) of a capitalist company, but the terms are not completely interchangeable because a Russian factory director was never answerable to a board of directors. The idea was to keep state ownership of the means of production and let individual enterprises have a bit more autonomy. Let's consider a general director, Mr. Smirnov. In the past, a Soviet ministry could hire and fire him. Once Gorbachev removed cabinet supervision from the top managers of Smirnov's plant, the only formal authority over his enterprise was a distant state bureaucracy that was spinning out of control, and the now independent, authoritarian Smirnov could do what he pleased. Smirnov was probably tempted to treat the company as his personal property. This process has been called spontaneous privatization. Certainly the gap between prices charged for goods in Russia and the prices they could fetch if they were shipped across a border gave the Smirnovs in the system many opportunities to privatize wealth informally.

One journalist reports that a worker might get an order for 120 kilograms of sausage for some shop but ship only 100 kilograms and store the other 20 in the manager's private stock so that he could sell them for a profit. Workers would have to cover up the loss. Before a factory was privatized, the top managers would also start smaller related corporations and joint ventures with foreign or domestic producers. Before they had a board of directors looking over their shoulders, they began the simple physical transfer of equipment to these daughter companies. They sold them goods or services at low rates and used their financial accounts to transfer funds to them. Managers and their families now own significant parts of these new corporations. The trade unions were largely puppet organizations, and they did not stand in Smirnov's way. Though the workers elected the general directors at their factories, most authoritarian general directors were able to exert great influence once they were elected.

The only constraints on Smirnov were his moral scruples and how much he dared do blatantly in front of the rest of the senior management team and the employees, who were so dependent on the enterprise and his leadership. We may never know the extent to which the factory managers really took advantage of their positions. It is hard to quantify the property that was stolen and appropriated. But managers did sell equipment and products at ridiculously low controlled prices to friends, associates, and family, who resold them at higher prices or exported them. Managers were known to set up joint ventures with foreigners or other companies, transfer assets and machinery to those entities without paying for them, and take excessive personal profit from the businesses. Managers abused their personal expense accounts. They paid friends, relatives, and cronies for services to the enterprise and received kickbacks. Many oil and mineral products and types of machinery and equipment could be "honestly" sold for far less than the world market price. The temptation was enormous and the line between legal and illegal dealings very fuzzy. Can all the people who participated in this racket be called "Mafia"? Perhaps not. It is clear, however, that some people took advantage of their opportunities and some broke laws.

Some political leaders may not have objected to these trends, but others recognized that it would be possible for a few thousand managers to take the country's wealth if privatization were not rapidly concluded. Within the Russian government's reform team there was concern that the property of the state had to be divided up quickly, before this skimming operation went any further. Without at least some formal program of privatization, the pilfering of assets by factory directors and the *nomenklatura* could only be expected to expand. In a speech in December 1992 Yeltsin himself publicly recognized this problem: "Bribery, privatization for the sake of and by the *nomenklatura,* the plunder of natural resources, and *nomenklatura* separatism threaten the disintegration of Russia." Though rapid formal privatization would limit the plundering, one could also argue that privatization could help the official and managerial elite accelerate their plan to get as much property as they could. Doing nothing would surely be the worst course.

There was a brief window of opportunity for sweeping change. No one really knew how long it would remain open. The 1991 coup against Gorbachev had not succeeded, and the military and the Communist intelligentsia were certainly not committed to reform, as the top officials of the Russian Federation were former Communist officials who had changed hats a few months or years earlier. Opponents of communism believed that the economy had to be wrenched from state control before the traditional forces could mount another coup or attempt to reassert the importance of state control over enterprises by pressuring the weak reform regime. (In view of the Communists' resurgence in 1995 and calls for the renationalization and state ownership of important industries in their political platform, this assessment may have been correct.)

Privatization of shops and industry was the one radical change that might be politically possible, because, on the face of it, it amounted to giving something to the people rather than taking something from them.

The Fight over Privatization

The job of designing and implementing the Russian privatization program was given to Anatoly B. Chubais, a 36-year-old economist and former professor with a doctorate from the Leningrad Institute of Economics and Engineering in 1977. He was appointed minister of privatization in November 1991. In 1990 and 1991, as an official in the city government of St. Petersburg, he had overseen the privatization of shops and smaller businesses. His top aides were Dmitry Vasiliev and Maxim Boycko. Vasiliev served as deputy chairman of the privatization ministry, with responsibility for implementation of the program. Boycko served as the Russian economist working on policy with Chubais's American advisory team, directed by Andrei Shleifer. Vasiliev later became a cabinet minister when his Federal Commission on Securities and the Capital Market became a full-fledged cabinet ministry in the Russian government; and Boycko moved on to become the director of the Russian Privatization Center, which coordinates Western technical assistance after privatization; deputy chairman of the government's committee on economic reform; and deputy chief of staff of the president in 1996. A small Western advisory team supported by the U.S. Agency for International Development, the World Bank, the European Bank for Reconstruction and Development, and the European Community, with a technical staff of accountants, lawyers, public relations experts, and investment bankers, helped implement specific programs.

There was extensive public disagreement over how to sell off more than 170,000 small shops and retail outlets. Larisa Pyasheva, the head of privatization for the city of Moscow, argued for turning over all the shops to their workers. In the end, it was decided that they would be sold at simple auctions. Ultimately, workers and managers were able to win a large number of these auctions. The fate of large and mid-sized enterprises, however, was a matter of more serious and complicated contention. Workers and managers wanted these enterprises to be given or sold cheaply to them and to no one else. Workers opposed any significant initial role for domestic or foreign investors because they feared that outsiders would drastically cut employees, and managers feared outsider owners would fire them or curtail their power. Both were also concerned that outsiders who had criminal connections might get control of their enterprise. These fears were not groundless. Most observers assumed that at least half of the workers in Soviet plants were unnecessary. But employees had always been told that they were the legitimate owners of the means of production, and Gorbachev strengthened this perception by allowing the workers to vote out general directors at their factories. Why shouldn't Kremlin capitalism be true to its Marxist roots? they reasoned.

Though the top managers publicly proclaimed their support for employee ownership, in interviews held out of public view in 1992 and 1993 they repeatedly voiced the opinion that they should control the enterprises and own a large amount of the stock. For many managers, employee ownership was a cover for pursuit of their own interests, a kind of Trojan horse. The present and former bureaucrats in the ministries traditionally responsible for certain industries also entered the property battle. They wanted the enterprises in their former areas of responsibility to be organized into production associations, holding companies, or financial-industrial groups. In combination with the top managers and perhaps the workers in a passive ownership role, the former officials would have large ownership stakes and a good deal of control over these huge conglomerates of companies. Sometimes they envisioned the state as retaining ownership of the enterprises while they ran them.

Advocating yet another approach, liberal Russian economists, such as Boris Fedorov, former minister of finance and deputy prime minister, and the 1996 presidential candidate Grigory Yavlinsky, wanted to sell the enterprises to the highest bidders who would bring capital to restructure them. Yavlinsky and some Western economists predicted that any significant role for employee ownership would doom privatization because workers would take over the board of directors, vote themselves huge wage increases, and never invest profits in the future of the enterprise. Other economists hoped that foreign investors would be the ones to supply the necessary capital, and still others looked to the privatization program of what is now the Czech Republic, in which vouchers were distributed to every citizen. An individual could use the vouchers to purchase a few shares in enterprises or groups of citizens could deposit their vouchers in mutual funds, which could then buy bigger blocks of shares in companies. Still other economists wanted a mixed economy, in which the state retained a significant portion of the ownership in the companies.

Meanwhile, the managers and the former and present government bureaucrats were not waiting for the government to take action. During 1991 and 1992, they tried to get their hands on whatever assets they could or to position themselves for a form of privatization that would favor them. Our evidence indicates that about 8 percent of the companies had negotiated some kind of special deal under Gorbachev or Yeltsin. In most of these cases, the employees were allowed to lease the enterprise with an option to buy it if privatization ever went forward. The general director of a large high-technology firm in southern Russia proudly told visitors that before the official privatization program went into effect he got a decree signed by a high government official allowing him to privatize his company the way he wanted.

The reform team spent 1992 weighing these alternatives. They finally settled on three key principles to guide the assignment of property rights to the Russian people. They were spelled out in an early book on the ideas behind Russian privatization by Maxim Boycko, Andrei Shleifer, and Robert Vishny, *Privatizing Russia*: First, Russians would respond rationally to economic incentives. Second, the state's influence over the economic life of Russia was the fundamental cause of inefficiency, and the principal objective of reform was to end it. Third, the Russian government did not really own the assets that needed to be privatized. If Russians were simply allowed to do so, they would take advantage of the opportunity to become owners. These analysts rejected the widely held view that Russians were lacking in entrepreneurial ability. They saw a strong link between the freeing of prices and privatization, because once prices are freed, goods are no longer allocated by politicians. Privatization then finishes the task of price liberalization by robbing politicians of their control over firms. The goal of privatization was to sever the dependency between enterprise managers and politicians, but the tie proved more durable than many observers had believed or hoped. The reality was that the government did not have firm control over the companies to be privatized. By now, managers, employees, and other stakeholders had considerable leverage over the enterprises, and these groups could stop privatization if they were not given a strong incentive to participate.

These central principles suggested the working rules of the privatization program. First, privatization had to proceed quickly, before the window of political opportunity closed, the possibility of rapidly separating the economy from state power disappeared, and the stealing of assets developed from an art into a science.

Second, each interest group would be offered enough potential ownership of the economy to persuade the Supreme Soviet (most of whose members had not been democratically elected) to pass the privatization law. The reform team felt that one interest group, the *nomenklatura,* had to be opposed as strongly as possible. The reformers feared that if the *nomenklatura* were given any significant favors, they would run away with all the country's property. Opposition to them, however, had to be carefully handled, since without question the enterprise managers were the most knowledgeable individuals in each enterprise, and some of them were quite necessary to the future restructuring of the enterprises.

Third, the privatization process had to be simple, because the state bureaucracy was incapable of managing anything efficiently and there were initially 15,000 enterprises to put on the auction block. "Simple" meant giving incentives to all the participants to implement privatization on their own, without government approval.

Fourth, privatization would occur only if Russian citizens wanted it to. No one could force them to take part in it. Russia had no legal regime, no corporate or related law to speak of, no real independent judiciary, no culture of the rule of law, and no way for the courts or the police to enforce government orders.

Last, most of the shares in the enterprises would have to be given away or sold at very low prices because ordinary citizens would not have enough money to participate otherwise. Citizens would have to be given some type of "currency" that they could use to "buy" their shares.

The decision to sell Russia's large industrial enterprises, its crown jewels, at low prices to the population became one of the most politically controversial aspects of the program. To the reform team, the speed at which ownership was transferred was of primary importance. The managerial elite and criminals would increase their advantage with each month that passed, and the methods traditionally used to sell a company in a market economy were viewed as too time-consuming. The traditional way to sell an enterprise in the West involved bringing in an accounting firm to value each building, each machine, each account, and other experts to advertise its sale and handle negotiations with buyers. In a free market economy, it takes six months to a year to sell most large firms, and it is not uncommon for ten professionals to spend most of their time throughout this period on a single deal. One calculation indicated that it would take decades to privatize Russia this way, and the professional fees alone would be greater than the book value of all the firms. Another calculation predicted it would take 15,000 person-years at 10 people per firm. With a staff of 1,000 lawyers, accountants, and consultants with all the luck running high, the whole process could be accomplished in 150 years!

The Privatization Program

On June 11, 1992, the Russian parliament passed the new privatization program and Yeltsin signed it into law. The plan put forward by the reform team was a political compromise to cut short a year of debates. The central plan was to distribute property rights to most of the big firms in about eighteen months, from January 1993 to June 1994. The privatization program sold a majority of the shares to workers and managers at low prices and a small number of shares to individuals not in the firm, and it reserved the opportunity for any outside investor to buy the rest of the shares at auction. Every citizen received a 10,000-ruble voucher that could be exchanged for shares in a diverse array of enterprises.

The program included most industrial enterprises but excluded those that were in any way controversial, such as military industries, oil companies, and medical facilities. Many companies with more than 1,000 employees were left out, and most companies with more than 10,000 employees did not have to privatize until they got special permission to do so. The idea was to cut short political battles and get the program rolling. Many people knew they could profit once the scramble for ownership started. This plan involved a serious compromise by Chubais on the question of employee ownership. He originally wanted a design that would result primarily in outside ownership, with no more than 25 percent of shares reserved for workers.

The program called for an interim step called corporatization: when a state-owned enterprise, which earlier had no separate legal identity as a business unit, was incorporated, an economic value was assigned to its assets and it acquired stock, a senior management, and a board of directors. At this stage, all of the enterprise's shares were still owned by the state, but now the enterprise was structured so that it could be sold off quickly. The managers and employees of each state-owned enterprise were required quickly to submit papers to turn their enterprise into a corporation with shares of stock owned by the state. They calculated the value of all assets aside from the land at book value and divided the sum by 1,000 rubles to arrive at the number of shares in their enterprise. The shares of stock were considered property of the state and were handed over to the Russian Property Fund, at that time an arm of the parliament, until they could be sold. The workers and managers then selected a board of four members: the general director with two votes, a representative of rank-and-file employees, and one representative each of the local and federal governments. The corporatization step was designed to bar well-placed members of the Communist Party, enterprise managers, and state bureaucrats from snapping up the shares of the companies under their control. Once an enterprise was corporatized, the ministry in Moscow lost any control over it. The top manager was freed from the ministry's supervision but constrained by the other board members, and found it expedient to cooperate with the workers to buy the enterprise.

Under corporatization, a company was registered as a joint-stock corporation whose shares were owned by the government through the Russian Property Fund. Since the value of the company was set at book value, the bureaucracy lost some opportunity to take bribes to adjust the valuation. Chubais's State Committee for the Management of State Property now controlled the future of the enterprises. Their boards of directors ran the companies. The rest of the government bureaucracy, especially the ministries that used to control enterprises, were left with reduced influence and rights to interfere in the enterprises.

How the Program Worked

In a general meeting at each enterprise employees chose one of three options, which transferred 40 to 51 percent of ownership to managers and employees. In most companies, the shares were divided in proportion to the workers' wages, their seniority, or a combination of the two. The remaining 49 to 60 percent of shares were to be sold later at a series of auctions.

Option 1 resulted in minority employee ownership. It allowed 40 percent of the shares to be sold to workers, while 60 percent would be sold at auction or held by the state for later sale. Workers got 25 percent of the shares free, and these shares were designated nonvoting to prevent workers from controlling the enterprise. Workers could buy another 10 percent of shares at a 30 percent discount from book value, and managers could buy 5 percent of the shares at a nominal price. Some additional shares could be bought by the pension plan.

Option 2 provided for majority employee ownership. It allowed 51 percent of the shares to be sold to workers, and the other 49 percent were to be sold at auction or held by the state for later sale. Workers would have to pay 1.7 times the book value. Some additional shares could be bought by the pension plan.

Option 3 was a management buyout by a group that promised to restructure the firm. Option 3 applied only to medium-sized enterprises. With the approval of all the workers, a managing group made up of managers, workers, or others would take responsibility for implementing the privatization plan while ensuring the enterprise's financial stability and employment for a year. Under these conditions, the managing group could buy 30 percent of the shares and workers and managers could buy 20 percent. If the managing group did not fulfill its privatization plan, their shares would later be sold at auction. This option was seldom chosen.

When voucher privatization was over, the results showed that 25 percent of the enterprises chose option 1, 73 percent chose option 2, and 2 percent chose option 3.

The shares were sold to employees under quite favorable terms. Managers and workers could use part of the enterprise's profits and the vouchers they received from the government to pay for them.

The price they paid was based not on what the market value of the enterprise would be if it were in Western Europe, say, but on the original cost of the buildings, equipment, and assets of the enterprise in Russia (the land was not included in this price because private ownership of land was not yet legal), which was a very low price indeed. This basis is called the "book" value of the enterprise. Employees were allowed to buy their shares before anybody else laid hands on the enterprise. Managers and employees did not have to compete with anyone to buy this initial package of shares. They simply decided what they wanted and bought the shares in their company on the basis of the low value assigned to it. No outsiders, no Mafia, no foreigners, no former Soviet bureaucrats had any formal role in the process at this stage. Managers and workers could secure initial control and allay their immediate fears. On average, the general directors surveyed in 1994 and 1995 said that they paid 40 times less than the enterprises were worth.

After employees chose an option and bought their shares, the region ran a voucher auction (large firms were sold at interregional auctions organized from Moscow). The law specified that at least 29 percent of the shares had to be sold to bidders, who could include citizens, companies, and the employees and managers. The auctions often left 10 to 20 percent of the shares in the state's hands to be sold at investment tenders or cash auctions later. An investment tender is a competition between investors to buy a package of shares. Investors must agree to give additional assistance to the company in the form of capital investments and technology. A cash auction of shares likewise produces capital for the enterprise. This arrangement was important because the enterprises received no capital out of the privatization process.

The management lobby and the trade unions were not satisfied with a government commitment that they would get virtually half of every major Russian company. Until 1994 they continued to fight for 100 percent employee ownership, though they did not try to stop the privatization process.

In a series of conversations throughout the country before privatization began, managers and trade union leaders indicated that they were terrified that some unknown outsider, perhaps a Mafia figure or a foreign investor, would come to the auctions after the initial employee purchases and buy a majority of the shares in their firm.

But there were only 17 million workers and managers in the big and mid-sized firms, and there were about 149 million citizens in the country. These initial purchases left out the many groups of citizens who were not employees of enterprises: people in the military and the KGB, many medical and educational professionals, pensioners, workers in agriculture and public transportation, students, and government bureaucrats. The privatization program gave each citizen, whether classified as a worker or not, a voucher worth 10,000 rubles, which he or she could use to buy additional shares in any enterprise, including the one where he or she worked. The accelerated schedule for distribution of the vouchers indicates how important speed was to the government. In view of the slowness with which the Russian bureaucracy normally worked, the fact that the schedule was nearly met was surprising. On August 14, 1992, the president issued a decree saying that all vouchers were to be distributed by October 1 by the Russian Federation Savings Bank, which had branches throughout the country. Citizens had to pay the equivalent of about 8 cents for a voucher. By the end of January 1993, 98 percent of the vouchers had been picked up.

Each voucher was worth about $84 when the law was passed in June 1992; the average monthly wage was then about $50. A citizen could come to the auction of an auto company and request 10,000 rubles' worth of shares in the enterprise. No one had to figure out how much an auto company was worth. Once the market price was established, the auction mechanism was designed so that bids by individual citizens were filled before those of banks, corporations, or foreign companies, and individuals could compete with each other by bidding specific share prices. Unfortunately, little evidence is available on what citizens actually experienced when they went to a voucher auction as individuals. (How much ownership citizens actually acquired and how many dropped out of the process are described in Chapter 2.)

In theory, anyone—a rich person, a new business started by a smart entrepreneur, a Mafia front organization, a foreign company —could buy vouchers and come to a voucher auction. In practice, privatization officials in the various regions we visited reported, they tried to prevent unsavory characters from participating. It is hard, however, to differentiate between an "unsavory character" who was a Mafia figure and an "unsavory character" who was simply an unwanted competitor of a factory manager whom the regional bureaucrat wanted to help maintain control over his enterprise. Some managers also told of maneuvering to prevent legitimate outside investors from participating. The state, either the Russian Federation or the regional government, held back 10 to 20 percent of the shares for future sale. This stake was held until it appreciated and became a "golden share," which the state could, in theory at least, sell to a strategic investor and make a profit. In some cases, 5 to 10 percent of the total shares were reserved for future sale to the employees and managers. After the initial privatization program was completed in 1994, the government's new privatization program emphasized further auctions for cash of any shares that were left in the state's hands.

The vouchers were printed in brown ink with a picture of the Russian parliament building, the White House, in the center. They looked like currency, and because they did not bear the names of the owners, they functioned much like securities or shares of stock. They could be bought or sold, traded or given away. In fact, the voucher was meant to be used like a share of stock. It could be traded, but the government prohibited stores from accepting vouchers in exchange for goods and services. Critics in the Supreme Soviet actually blamed vouchers for causing Russia's hyperinflation; they argued that they increased the money supply. Family members could give all their vouchers to one person to bid. A citizen could also go to people who did not believe in privatization and offer money for their vouchers, say 5,000 rubles for a 10,000-ruble voucher. The trading of vouchers allowed people who did not want to bother with the program to get money fast, and it was most Russians' first experience of a share that could be freely traded and whose price was determined by what the market would bear. Indeed, the prices offered for vouchers in Russia's first "stock exchanges" in 1992, 1993, and 1994 became good indications of public confidence in the program. When confidence was low, one could buy a 10,000-ruble voucher for less than 10,000 rubles, and when confidence was high, one had to pay several times 10,000 rubles for a voucher. It is important to remember that at all times, citizens could buy shares at the low 1992 prices (before hyperinflation hit Russia) by using vouchers distributed in 1992. Inflation did not increase the prices of those shares. The voucher program will be subjected to more analysis over time. On the one hand, on our weekly visits with factory directors during the months of the voucher sales we found that share prices remained fairly low, so vouchers really could be used to acquire shares. On the other hand, it might have been possible for the government to issue additional vouchers as the program continued in order to increase citizens' access to shares.

The architects of the privatization program wanted to encourage the creation of core shareholders, blockholders who would own more than 5 percent of an enterprise's shares. The hope was that these big investors would take a more serious interest in the enterprise, push to get on the board of directors, and monitor the performance of the old Soviet management closely. In order to jump-start the formation of such blockholder investors, the government licensed voucher investment funds to function like mutual funds. A citizen could hand over a voucher to the fund, and the fund would select the companies and group the shares in order to pressure management for performance and demand board seats. At least 29 percent of every company was supposed to be sold for vouchers to ensure widespread citizen participation and keep the value of the vouchers high. The average block of shares sold—actually 20 percent, as shown in Table 3— provides a measure of bidders who participated in the voucher auctions.

Two groups were hit very hard by this privatization plan, and they opposed it from the beginning. They were top managers and government bureaucrats in the branch ministries that had previously controlled groups of enterprises for the Communist Party. The program was able to weather their opposition because they were not numerous and because they were clearly fighting in their own self-interest against 99 percent of the population. Our extensive interviews with top managers around the country in late 1992 suggested that the managers wanted to move forward with privatization, but they opposed many of its features. The top managers, who were in virtually complete control of their factories after Gorbachev removed the power of the cabinet ministries to fire them, had expected the government's privatization program to treat them more liberally. They resented the power of an enterprise's employees to make decisions about converting it to a corporation and choosing a privatization option. They were insulted that in option 1, the 40 percent employee ownership option, only 5 percent of the shares in the enterprises were reserved for management, while in option 2, the 51 percent option, the general assembly of all employees could decide how to apportion the shares among all people who worked in the factory. They reacted loudly as privatization continued. Government bureaucrats were also unhappy that the rules prohibited the arbitrary establishment of holding companies, associations, and conglomerates that could simply take control of large chunks of enterprises. The design of the privatization program was supposed to make it difficult for government officials and managers in the large bureaucracy simply to set up a company and transfer state assets to themselves.

The progress of privatization was to depend on the pull of incentives and not the push of bureaucracy. The key question was who actually had the incentives. The managers of the factories had large incentives, as did enterprise employees. Entrepreneurs who quickly figured out how to benefit from the system had incentives. Citizens who correctly identified the valuable enterprises or realized that voucher investment funds could effectively choose enterprises for them had an incentive to participate. However, given the value of the vouchers provided to them and the sizable shares allotted to insiders, the incentive of citizens was smaller than that of managers, employees, and entrepreneurs. The impact of this inequity would become clear when the results of the program were examined. Despite a significant public relations campaign to explain the use of vouchers —the president himself even explained it on TV—it would later become clear that many citizens neither understood nor appreciated the program.

Once the process started, no significant central or regional government approval was required. The regional government just made sure the simple procedures were being followed, and Moscow monitored the regions. In theory, employees had a substantial incentive to schedule the meetings to convert their companies into corporations, determine their value, and choose a privatization option quickly— and in theory, management wanted to encourage employees to complete the procedures. In theory, citizens had an incentive to support the program, to pick up their vouchers at the state savings banks so they could get part of the national wealth. Entrepreneurs, rich people, newly emerging banks, small business people, and foreigners had an incentive to assess the relative values of companies, buy up other people's vouchers cheaply, and try to purchase many shares in companies they favored. Federal and local government officials had an incentive to support the program because a percentage of the funds collected went to their budgets.

The passage of the privatization program by the Supreme Soviet in June 1992 did not stop the controversy surrounding it. That summer and fall, harsh criticism of the program continued. The economist Tatyana Koryagina, a former colleague of Gaidar who would later become a key economic adviser to Gennady A. Zyuganov, the Communist presidential candidate in 1996, said, "Whether the government likes it or not, the privatization program will be beneficial only to foreign business and domestic shadow business [the Mafia]." This situation, she predicted, would eventually lead to social unrest and even armed clashes. A *Pravda* writer called it a boon for the *nomenklatura*. Russia's procurator general announced that he had lodged appeals against 600 decisions by government agencies that had been illegally trying to appropriate public property in eight regions. The economist Pavel Bunich wanted the program to go further and include a free transfer of land and housing to each Russian citizen. The labor union Unity, representing 3 million workers, argued that the state had to continue to control the companies after they were privatized. They did not want the new owners of retail stores to be permitted to turn those stores into video clubs and commercial offices. "It may well be," they said, "that tomorrow there'll be no place to buy bread or milk." Aleksandr Yakovlev, Gorbachev's key adviser on perestroika, opposed this old thinking. He wrote, "This country is the only one in world history to have for decades forbidden its people to earn as much as they are able to." Vladimir Isakov, a leader of the opposition in the Supreme Soviet, argued that the program deprived workers of the right to own what they deserved, and predicted that it would lead to massive violations, embezzlement, soaring inflation, an increase in social tensions, and a further slump in production. This would not be the last time that privatization was seen as the main cause of economic misery. Privatization's birth was taking place amid harrowing attacks on the overall economic program. Georgy A. Arbatov, head of the influential Institute of the U.S.A. and Canada in the Russian Academy of Sciences, wrote in the *New York Times* on May 7, 1992: "The price liberalization has wiped out savings, wages, and pensions, and virtually devastated the economy, all in the hope that foreign investment will pour in as production falls. The prospect of a flood of investment is increasingly dim."

One newspaper sharpened the conflict over the program with the headline "Chubais Wants to Give Factories to the People, Parliament Deputies Want to Hand Them Over to the Workers." Yeltsin argued that any drop in production made sense because "two-thirds of what our industry produced was channeled either directly or indirectly into defense. We had to stop manufacturing military products in such quantities." In October 1992, just before the privatization of larger enterprises began, he answered some questions sent in by readers of the conservative newspaper *Trud*. He said that he pinned great hopes on privatization, and that Russia would have to form a stock market of its own. But *Pravda* called privatization "a crime against the nation" and said that it emerged as a result of the Yeltsin government's links to the new rich. *Pravda* accused the government of deliberately impoverishing people. "In a situation where 80 percent of the citizens don't have enough money to buy meat and butter, it's easy to suggest that the vouchers will end up in the pockets of rich tycoons."

Petr Filippov, the pro-reform chairman of the Supreme Soviet's privatization committee, looked at the same reality and saw a different story. The managers of the companies, he said, "have been offered a bribe of sorts, so that they can turn from government bureaucrats into genuine proprietors." Chubais said that Communist factions opposed privatization only because they knew it would put an end to total public ownership as the essence of the Communist state, and he stressed that speed was its salient feature. A Public Opinion Center poll in September 1992 showed that almost three-quarters of the population now looked upon privatization with indifference or negative views.

Foreign observers severely criticized the program from their own perspectives. The privatization experts Roman Frydman and Andrzej Rapaczynski questioned whether giving insiders so much control amounted to real private property ownership. They doubted that workers would be more interested in profits than in safeguarding their employment and wages, and whether a manager would be more interested in restructuring than in continuing the search for subsidies. Meanwhile, foreign investment banks encouraged the Russian government to auction the companies one by one. The American management consultant John Simmons, debating Chubais on Russian television, accused him of not emphasizing employee ownership enough; employees, he argued, would actually restructure the companies more efficiently. Another view was that the government should focus only on freeing all prices completely, so that state-owned firms could compete with one another; privatization could come later. Andrei Shleifer articulated the bottom line for the government's advisers at this time in the *Wall Street Journal:* "Without private ownership there can be no market economy."

Would managers of the plants actually do an accounting of the value of all the plant's assets? Would workers push for the meetings to convert the enterprise to corporate status and choose a privatization option? Would the bureaucrats in the eighty-nine regional offices of the Privatization Ministry monitor the procedures and the paper flow? Would voucher investment funds and other investors start buying up vouchers and go to auctions? Would regional governments schedule auctions and would citizens go to them? Between June 1992 and November 1992, Chubais and his aides and advisers went to work at the Committee for the Management of State Property in Moscow wondering whether 150 million people would actually implement these plans. Every week elements of the press and the parliament called for Chubais's firing, his resignation, the suspension of the program, and amendments to give more to managers and holding companies. In those months, our research team was quietly visiting enterprises and talking with managers. Despite the public outcries and the heat of the moment, they were delivering a clear message: the workers were scheduling the meetings, the companies were corporatizing; they were implementing the privatization program.

The Bolshevik Biscuit Company was chosen for one of the model first auctions. The staff for the eighty-nine regional offices had been hired and supplied with training, computers, and achievement targets. Teams from Moscow went to the most reform-oriented regions to help with the first auctions. Then officials from regions that had successfully implemented the auctions trained those in other regions. A respected accounting firm was chosen to audit the "returns" of the auctions as they flowed into Moscow. After a slow beginning in December 1992, with only 18 auctions in 8 regions, the number of auctions surged in January to 108 in 26 regions, and privatization then took on a life of its own. Eighty-three regions auctioned 959 large enterprises in October 1993, the month of the violent struggle between Yeltsin and the Supreme Soviet. The number increased in the next two months and grew to more than 1,000 a month in 86 regions until June 1994, when the program ended. Table 1 shows the progress of the privatization of small shops and retail outlets from 1991 to 1995 and how new small businesses were developing at the same time. Table 3 shows the progress of the auctions. The privatization of small stores and retail shops had already begun in 1991 and was well over a third completed by the end of 1992, when the privatization of the larger enterprises began. The privatization of apartments began slowly in 1989, picked up speed in 1992, and continues today. The bulk of the privatization of the mid-sized and larger enterprises slated for the voucher privatization program was completed between December 1992 and June 1994. Privatization had taken nineteen months. How did what really happened match the theory and the design?

2

Ownership

Almost every Russian city and town has a monument to the father of the Soviet state, Vladimir Lenin, in front of the local administration building. In Tula, capital of the region of the same name south of Moscow, a towering metal statue of Lenin still dominates the central square. A favorite town of Peter the Great, who established an armament industry there, Tula has recently been a hotbed of privatization and economic activity, and early one morning in 1995, groups of local officials and general directors of enterprises were gathering in front of the administration building. Black Volga sedans pulled up one by one. Men and women with black briefcases, the general directors of Tula's big enterprises, talked, smoked, and made plans for lunch. One top director, Vladislav Nikolaev, could be heard saying, "We keep building capitalism behind Lenin's back."

Capitalism behind Lenin's back was precisely the result of privatization. By 1996, over three-quarters of Russia's large and mid-sized enterprises along with almost 90 percent of its industrial output had been privatized and were out of state hands. The type of private ownership was open to question. The objective described in the privatization law was to form a group of private owners who would contribute to the emergence of a socially oriented market economy by making the enterprises more efficient and attracting foreign and domestic investment. The goal was not merely to switch the title of the enterprises from the name of the state to the names of private citizens. When Boris Yeltsin introduced the program to the Russian people in a television address in August 1992, he said that his goal was to achieve broad-based property ownership, "a million property owners rather than many millionaires."

Yeltsin seemed to be describing a thin layer of stock owners spread across the entire population; other interest groups looked for different results from the legislation. Some observers believed Yeltsin's scenario would change little, since diffuse ownership spread across many small shareholders would leave the old Soviet-style managers essentially in control. That was the classic shareholders' dilemma: the multitude of shareholders attracted by a moneymaking concern left them with too little ability to make sure management used the corporation to return profit on their investment. Another frequently envisioned result was that a single large Russian outside investor or a foreign corporation would buy up a majority of the shares, install a new board of directors and a new management team, and completely transform the enterprise. Some Western proponents of employee ownership believed that the employees would take majority owner-ship and that they would then have a direct incentive to choose the right managers, work harder, and establish problem-solving teams that would begin to change the enterprise. The Russian managers envisioned taking over all the companies by buying up the shares immediately or by gradually buying employees' shares. They had been running the enterprises since Gorbachev and Yeltsin disbanded the ministries that supervised them. They had spent years worrying, planning, solving problems, and carrying the weight of the enterprise on their shoulders, and they had come to view the enterprises as actually belonging to them. Then there were people in the holding companies and financial-industrial groups who did not believe that managers, employees, or outsiders should own and control those en-terprises. In the leadership circles in Moscow, various officials and their aides and advisers believed that privatization should be con-trolled by them in one way or another, with managers returning to the status of their staff.

The Initial Division of Ownership

How was the ownership divided in the large and mid-sized compa-nies that had already been privatized by the first quarter of 1994, just over one year after the program started? (See Table 4.) All em-ployees owned a majority share in most of the companies, all outside shareholders owned about a fifth share in them, and the state continued to own just over a tenth. The top managers reported that they owned just under a tenth share in their companies, while all managers together owned just over three times that amount, but these estimates were based on very early and preliminary reports. Details on the outside owners during this early period are not meaningful because many of the companies were just in the process of organizing the auctions to sell shares to outsiders. Initially the most common outside shareholders were voucher investment funds, Russian commercial firms, and Russian citizens, in that order. The common prediction that holding companies would emerge to control most privatized enterprises was not proving true. The general directors were quite suspicious of giving over control to any entity, be it a majority outside investor or a holding company made up of their former supervisors in a cabinet ministry. In fact, there was virtually no role for holding companies, for related enterprises that were suppliers or customers, or for foreign corporations or banks. They would increase their influence later in the guise of financial-industrial groups.

These initial outcomes were to be expected, given the huge preferences granted to employees and the clear resistance of these insiders to outside ownership. Share prices were so low that many employees had money left over after paying for their shares, so they went as individuals or in groups to the voucher auctions and bought additional shares with their personal savings, their vouchers, and the vouchers of family members, friends, or other sources. One manager told of employees who went to the subway stations and nascent Moscow stock exchanges to buy up vouchers. The general directors of the enterprises made it clear in interviews that they opposed the sale of their stock to unknown outsiders, and some top managers admitted that they worked closely with the local privatization officials to block the participation of outsiders. In fact, in the winter of 1994 about a fifth of all the firms we visited had no outside ownership whatever.

The push for ownership by managers and employees had been an initial success. Fully nine out of ten companies that had passed through the privatization program had majority employee ownership in the winter of 1994. At this time, top managers were far from celebrating the broad-based ownership to which these numbers point, despite their public and aggressive calls for precisely that ownership just a year earlier. They had hidden behind "broad-based employee ownership" in the early debates on privatization as a kind of Trojan horse that would carry them through the gates of privatization. In 1992 and 1993, many managers admitted when pressed that their enthusiasm for employee ownership was based on the hope of fending off outside shareholders and allowing experts—themselves —to control the destiny of the firms. The manager of a sprawling machine tool factory outside of Moscow and a leader in the Russian Union of Industrialists, a managerial lobby organization, was deeply resentful that he did not personally own a more significant portion of the shares. He was still suspicious about any future outside owner-ship. He had been a vocal public defender of employee ownership, but in private he opposed the creation of a broad group of property owners, which would prevent a small group of insiders from corner-ing ownership.

Many managers have been responsible for their enterprises and the well-being of thousands of workers for years. The manager of a Belgorod trucking company with 600 employees observed, "The psychology of the employees is that they simply cannot understand that they are now the owners of this company. They're afraid the privatization program will stop and it will all be taken away from them. We're doing everything possible to keep control of the shares inside the enterprise. We're afraid that new businessmen who made a lot of money in some commercial deal will try to buy shares from the employees. If that happens, the employees will finally under-stand that it's not good to sell their shares."

These managers had strong opinions about how the enterprises should be developed and controlled after the passing of communism. At the same time, many, such as the manager of a furniture company who had twenty-five years' experience in the plant, reported feeling powerless: "I feel it's wrong that managers can't buy a significant amount of shares. I myself have no capital to buy shares. And if I were to do it, it wouldn't sit well with the employees. And now there's an auction for 29 percent of our enterprise's shares and I don't think the employees will have enough vouchers left to buy a significant amount of these shares. If an outside investor buys 20 percent of our shares, this investor will pay the money to the state and never really bring capital into the enterprise. And I don't want a foreign investor to take part in privatization because the relationship between the ruble and the dollar is so disjointed. If a foreign investor agreed to give us all the capital we need for control of the firm, I'm not sure I'd take the offer."

Ownership in 1996

No one expected that after the property of Russia was initially di-vided up, the apportionment would stay frozen. One hundred fifty million people had different attitudes toward privatization and each enterprise had its own chance of success. Our surveys revealed some notable changes in the composition of ownership between 1994 and 1996. Ownership by all employees went down; ownership by outside investors went up significantly to account for a third of the shares in the average company; and the state continued to own about a tenth of the stock. In 1996, all employees owned an average of 58 percent of the stock, outsiders owned 32 percent, and the state owned 9 percent.

Employee ownership declined 7 percent between the two years; more significant, the proportion of majority employee-owned firms fell from 90 percent to 65 percent. (Tables 4, 5, and 6 offer a deeper analysis of this division of ownership.) Outsiders had majority ownership of many more firms in 1995 and 1996 and a large number of companies continued to have no clear majority owner. On average, in 1994 and 1995 employees sold about 4 percent of the stock they bought at the time of privatization. The main buyers were outside investors and managers. Perhaps employees and managers were less aggressive about buying up stock in the privatizations that took place after 1993. They may have observed that most enterprises were not taken over by outsiders and that rampant loss of control never occurred, and it may have become more expensive to buy vouchers from other people as the value of the vouchers crept up and the funds the enterprises saved to compete with outside investors were tightly stretched. At the same time, outside shareholders gained experience and became aggressive about buying shares as privatization went into full swing.

Top managers reported that their ownership remained roughly the same. All managers together owned 18 percent of their firms and the rank-and-file workers as a group owned 40 percent. Of all groups of outside investors, the Russian commercial companies, investment funds, and citizens obtained the most shares. A commercial firm could be a new private company set up by several people or another privatized corporation. There was a widespread rumor that some general directors set up such firms, with their friends and family serving as fronts for their own ownership. Some openly disclosed that they had done so, and their holdings were counted as employee ownership. Owners of these commercial firms might be among the hundreds of thousands of new small business entrepreneurs who were emerging in Russia, or citizens who had built up savings over the years, or former members of the *nomenklatura* who appropriated state property as the Communist state came apart, or organized

crime interests. No one really has a clear idea. In general, the ownership roles of holding companies, companies that were suppliers or
customers of the enterprises, and Russian banks were small, and
foreigners had virtually none. Over a tenth of the enterprises still
had no outside ownership in 1995 and 1996.

In 1996, however, we found some surprises. Employee ownership
seemed to be on the rise—at least there was no evidence of an across-
the-board decline in average employee ownership or in the number
of firms whose employees had majority control. In the second phase
of privatization, scheduled for 1995 and 1996, the Russian government planned to sell the shares held by the state to outsiders through
cash auctions and investment tenders. In 1993, as the tension between Yeltsin and the Supreme Soviet rose, the parliament simply
never approved this new phase of privatization. The president issued
a decree, but public support for privatization had changed since
1992. At the end of 1994, when Chubais was promoted to first deputy
prime minister to take charge of the entire economic reform and a
new deputy prime minister, Vladimir Polevanov, was appointed to
oversee privatization, the parliament had significant Communist
and nationalist factions. Within weeks Polevanov said that the privat-
tization program was deeply flawed and that Russia should renationalize some firms. Before the president fired him, Polevanov helped
initiate a freeze on privatization. The freeze was a result of the rising
conservative political environment and the continuing vocal opposition of general directors to outside ownership and control of the companies. In 1996, nine of every ten privatized companies had never
held an investment tender, and three of every four had never held a
cash auction. Worse, many top managers admitted that they had
their company buy back shares originally purchased by outsiders
and resold the shares to managers and employees, or that they simply issued new shares to employees either free or at a nominal price.
Either way, the result was the same: a brake was put on the movement of shares from insiders to outsiders.

Outsider ownership is less a force than the averages suggest (Table
6). The figures for 1996 suggest that there is 32 percent average
outsider ownership nationwide; but a quarter of all privatized companies have less than 13 percent outsider ownership. A tenth of the
companies have no outsider ownership, and well over a quarter of
the companies have much less than the large national average of
outsider ownership. Majority outsider ownership is concentrated in
a small group of companies, and increasing management control of
the firms is a stronger force than the relatively modest average for

ownership by top managers and all managers suggests. The number of companies with big concentrated stakes—20 to 40 percent—by top managers and all managers grew substantially between 1995 and 1996. In 1996, top managers admitted that they owned more than 30 percent of 5 percent of all Russian companies and more than 23 percent of 10 percent of all Russian companies. They reported that managers at all levels together owned more than 48 percent of more than 5 percent of all Russian companies and more than 39 percent of one-tenth of all Russian companies. (See Table 6.) Finally, Russian commercial firms, voucher funds, and citizens play small roles in half the companies. The other ownership groups don't even have a presence in more than half the companies. But ownership is becoming concentrated. Financial-industrial groups own more than 49 percent of 1 percent of all Russian companies; Russian banks own more than 28 percent of 1 percent of all Russian companies; and foreign corporations own more than 51 percent of 1 percent of all Russian companies.

Russian Ownership in International Perspective

As the transition to privatization peaked in 1996, four competitors appeared in the race for Russian riches: the employees, the managers, the outsiders, and an odd combination of the three in which no group owned a clear majority. (See Table 5.) Consideration of the state's role in ownership has been put aside because it clearly declined. The line-up was as follows: the companies reported that employees of all kinds had majority ownership of 64.7 percent of the corporations, rank-and-file employees had majority ownership of 30.5 percent, managers had majority ownership of 5.4 percent, and there was no majority owner among the employees of 28.8 percent of the companies. Outsiders had majority ownership of about 19.8 percent, the state had majority ownership of about 3 percent, and there was no majority ownership group in 12.8 percent of the corporations. Some perspective is in order on management ownership. The large private corporations under discussion are not small family-owned businesses or sole proprietorships. Nevertheless, in conversation after conversation, Russian general directors spoke as confirmed capitalists by saying that "the enterprise has to have an owner." They meant one person, one capitalist who determined its fate, and many of them made it clear that they meant themselves. They had not understood that thousands of large and mid-sized firms in the United States and other countries are not owned by one person.

Institutions own significant stakes in firms in the United States, Japan, and Germany (Table 7), but institutional ownership is still developing in Russia. Most of these Russian firms are similar to the 7,000 or so U.S. corporations whose stock is traded on the New York Stock Exchange, the NASDAQ, and the American Stock Exchange and to the several thousand large corporations owned not by the public but largely by a variety of stockholders who know each other and have close ties, such as family corporations and small local corporations. In the United States about 50 percent of all the corporate shares—those traded on the stock market and closely held by corporations—are owned by households. Russian citizens' holdings, whether in voucher funds or in individually held shares, are fairly small in comparison. In 1996, on average all citizens owned 6 percent and all voucher funds owned 5 percent. These comparisons simply suggest that Russian ownership patterns will change. Internationally, both the size of public stock markets and the extent of individual citizen ownership varies.

Outsiders do play a big role in the flagship companies of free market economies. Twenty percent of U.S. shares are owned by public and private pension funds. About 30 percent are owned by all financial institutions, including mutual funds, and 5 percent are owned by foreigners. No shares are owned by banks, which are prevented from holding stock in the United States, and about 5 percent are owned by insurance companies. Investment and mutual funds have not yet attained this degree of influence in Russia. The holding companies of Russian banks can own corporations, but their holdings are still rather small nationwide.

The 50 percent owned by households in the United States can be differentiated in a way that is especially important to any comparison with Russia. On average, top managers—board members, CEOs, executive vice presidents down to the level of unit manager—own about 10 percent of the stock of all U.S. public corporations, although in larger companies the figure is generally under 5 percent and in huge companies closer to 1 percent. In the United States, rank-and-file employees own about 15 percent on average of a fifth of the public companies traded on the stock market. Their holdings are small in the others. The ownership of major corporations is dominated not by management but by institutions—pension funds and mutual funds. Nonmanagement employees of U.S. corporations own about 5 percent of all stock. The rich, the top 10 percent of households, own 90 percent of the stock. For obvious reasons, figures on Mafia ownership in the United States are not available. Russian top management is starting off where top management ended up in the United States, and Russian employees own much more stock than American ones do. And the United States represents only one point of comparison. The specifics of corporate ownership vary across nations, as do the laws that guide them.

Majority Employee Ownership

Employees own the majority of the stock in about 65 percent of the large and mid-sized Russian companies, although rank-and-file employees are a majority in only 31 percent of these companies. Such a concentration of employee ownership of the core of an economy is unprecedented in world economic history. Important Russian economists and politicians, such as the former deputy prime ministers Grigory Yavlinsky and Boris Fedorov, had warned that a privatization program that offered employee ownership as the incentive would lead to disaster: workers would vote themselves high wages and bleed the profits of the company. Nevertheless, the initial stage of the privatization program proceeded principally through the exchange of employees' vouchers for shares, the free and discounted shares employees received, and the shares employees bought with cash. Insiders are now the majority owners of most firms, although we cannot always say what proportion of the ownership is accounted for by top management.

Do such companies bear out the pessimistic predictions? Do they pay higher wages to their employees and spend more on employee benefits than other companies do? We have found no evidence that they do. By virtually every possible measurement, payments to employees are not significantly correlated with the identity of the majority owner. Majority employee-owned firms do not spend significantly more on either wages or social services. They do not have more employees working in the kindergartens and day-care centers; they do not provide more apartments and other amenities for employees. They do not use more of their loans from banks for employee compensation, nor do they receive more subsidies from the government or owe more taxes. They do not have fewer employees on temporary layoff. The explanation is not that Russian companies do not have high employee expenditures. Rather, workers in majority-owned firms do not seem to have substantially more power than workers in other firms because they have such weak trade unions and so few shareholder rights.

Other implications of this form of ownership are not easy to fore-

see, but some managers were already experiencing some ramifica-
tions. The manager of a thriving bakery, whose 1,000 employees
owned more than half the company, confided, "There's a hidden story
in this company. The son of a local government official with serious
conflicts of interest is none other than the owner of the private commercial firm that's desperately trying to take over the enterprise.
This firm opposes top management's policies and they tried unsuccessfully to elect someone to the board of directors, which is made up
entirely of senior managers who report to me. I'm negotiating with
equipment suppliers in two foreign countries, but our company
doesn't have the money to pay for the machinery. The favored son
meanwhile has hired an investment company to approach our employees to sell their shares. I've been matching every offer to buy
shares from employees with a higher offer."

The manager of an automotive plant that manufactures special
vehicles reported in detail the company's struggles to increase efficiency, including massive employment cuts. In addition to these battles, he must fend off investors who might take control. "About 70
percent of the stock is owned by the employees," he said, "and I own
5 percent myself. Among the outside owners, two investment funds
bought 5 percent of our shares each. The activity of this one investment company is rather dangerous. In our city, they took over a
chemical plant and fired the top management. To prevent this, we
set up a trading company that's owned mostly by our company and
partly by one individual. This trading house buys up employees'
shares. It's accumulated about 12 percent of them by now." His company desperately needs to modernize. "In Soviet times the state constantly gave us money to develop new products, but now we have
only our profit for capital investment." Outside investors are the only
other source of capital, but if they come in, they could seize control.

The general directors of these companies resent the fact that the
official privatization program forced them to be publicly traded open
corporations. When the managerial lobby tried to oppose the reformers between 1992 and 1996, the issue of turning Russian companies
into closely held corporations always came up. A closely held corporation, like a family corporation or a private corporation in the United
States, is controlled by a small number of insiders and their associates, and the buying and selling of stock is often restricted. Yet the
future of majority employee ownership will probably depend on how
desperate the companies are for capital.

Majority employee-owned firms are not bigger or smaller than
firms dominated by other owners, and there is no evidence that they

are financially weaker than firms whose majority owners are outsiders or companies that have no majority owner. There is some evidence that insiders fought harder because they secured majority ownership in the more valuable firms. A close look at employee majority ownership indicates that that majority is large in very few Russian firms. With 10 to 20 percent of these firms' shares still in the state's hands, ultimate control probably depends on who wins out at the auctions of those shares. A fifth to a third of majority employee-owned firms are within one auction or one modest stock transaction of losing majority insider control. This is one reason why the privatization of those state shares became so politically controversial in 1995 and 1996.

Russian and foreign investors are going to have to find a way to negotiate with the employee owners if they are to enter the market. Majority employee ownership is going to drop dramatically, though it may be a meaningful part of the economy for some time to come. Employee ownership will fall because employees will be tempted to sell their valuable stock in the more successful companies. In the less successful companies, they will lose their majority stake because of bankruptcy or because they will be forced to sell majority control to an outside shareholder who has the capital necessary to restructure the firm. Only five of Russia's top fifty firms have majority employee ownership, but employees seem to own an average of 36 percent of those fifty firms. Majority employee-owned firms that are profitable enough to finance their restructuring out of their profits and bank loans are likely to continue to have meaningful employee ownership, unless the workers and managers accept generous offers from investors, who will probably be interested in giving the insiders big premiums on their shares. The prospects for continued employee ownership are bleak in those companies that are very unprofitable and need restructuring and those that are on the edge of bankruptcy. Employees will probably lose most of their share ownership in those companies unless they move forward with a draconian restructuring soon. Because of the increasing value of the more successful firms, employees and managers may well be tempted to submit voluntarily to a friendly takeover by a serious investor. Aggressive investors will have every incentive to persuade employees to sell them shares in those companies. In some companies the employees will seek mechanisms to protect their ownership. They may finance investments with bank loans rather than issue new shares, or they may sell shares to remaining and new employees as older employees leave the firm. One meaningful indication of the future of employee stockholding is the structure of ownership in the fifty largest Russian corporations (see Table 8). Five of the top fifty admit to being majority employee-owned. The average employee ownership in this group of fifty corporations is 36 percent. But the information the giant companies release is often vague and may be hiding much larger insider ownership. Of the top fifty corporations in Russia, clear figures on insider ownership are not available in eleven, clear figures on outsider ownership are not available for twenty-eight, and clear figures on state ownership were not disclosed by eleven.

Majority Management Ownership

One of the most hotly debated perceptions is that the top managers really took over the enterprises and own most of them. If this is the case, most employee ownership is really management ownership. Some astute observers have made this claim, but none has offered evidence. On January 28, 1996, a front-page story in the *New York Times* claimed that the owners of many of these firms are the old Communist managers or the former *nomenklatura*. Marshall Goldman of Harvard University's Russian Research Center agrees. In a *Wall Street Journal* op-ed piece he wrote that 60 percent of the owners of the newly privatized enterprises were Party officials or former factory managers.

These analyses conflict with the popular view that the Mafia controls these companies. It is very hard to find more than impressionistic evidence for the more extreme estimates. On the *nomenklatura* there is some hard evidence. In 1993 a team of researchers interviewed 1,000 people in each of Russia, Hungary, and Poland who had been connected to the Central Committee of the Communist Party in their country in 1988. When they compared these groups with 600 members of each country's economic elite—the managers of the most successful state-owned or privately owned companies—they found the least continuity between the former *nomenklatura* and the private business elite in Russia. There the overlap between the two groups was 19 percent, whereas it was 28 percent in Poland and 30 percent in Hungary. But Russia had the greatest continuity between its *nomenklatura* and persons in high political, cultural, and state-sector economic posts, with a 48 percent overlap (compared to 18 percent in Hungary and 27 percent in Poland).

More digging will be necessary to resolve this important question. It is not unusual for a visitor to Moscow to hear this claim from critics of reform, and it is common to hear about managers who completely took over the ownership of their companies. Top managers admit to owning a majority interest in about 1 percent of the firms that are majority employee-owned, and managers in general admit to owning a majority interest in 4 percent of these firms. So the charge of management ownership has some basis in fact. Since 1993 only a handful of accounts in the Russian press have supported this notion. A famous story in the regional press tells of a beverage plant in Penza whose managers were put on trial for somehow gaining control of all its stock through a legal entity they set up. A day before the trial began, a strange thing happened: all the employees of the plant executed a legal document and thereby became members of the legal entity controlled by the top two managers and the general director. When the managers appeared in court for trial, the case was dismissed because the cause for the legal action had disappeared. There was broad-based employee ownership. The next day all the employees requested that the general director and his two managers cancel their membership in the legal entity that owned all the firm's stock.

The fact that top management controls the records of shareholders contributes to the difficulty of getting to the bottom of this issue. When we asked the general director of a large firm in Belgorod about the amount of top management ownership, he said, "I simply wouldn't tell you the answer." The question made him furious. Later he conceded that the entire top management of his firm owned about 50 percent of the company "or something close to it."

The general director of a large firm in Lipetsk answered the same question in a friendly manner, as though he had nothing to hide. "Yes, I own a rather big share and it keeps growing and nobody is against it. And I hope it increases considerably because it only helps my work with this enterprise. You see the people here trust me, and that's quite enough, and you can see for yourself that we're quite successful." He personally owned 15 percent of the company, he said. Other managers at the same firm professed to be strongly in favor of his large ownership stake.

One senior manager in the Moscow region resolves the problem of securing employees' shares with a human resource policy. An employee who resigns voluntarily must surrender his or her shares in exchange for 10,000 rubles per share (about $2 in 1996), though the market value is 50,000 rubles. An employee who is fired receives nothing. Where do these shares go? Top managers may well step in and buy them. With company control of stock ownership registration in many firms, there is no way to know.

The authorities in the Mordovia region tried to establish a committee to defend employee shareholders against pressure exerted by general directors to sell their shares to top management. An employee who resigns is likely to be instructed to sell his or her shares to the boss. Most workers do not know their rights and do as they are told. General directors in this region strongly opposed the creation of such a committee, just as some advisers to members of the government with ties to general directors opposed a provision in a draft law on corporations in 1995 protecting employee shareholders against any attempt by a boss to use the employment relationship to coerce them to relinquish their stock.

The general director of a large plant in the Astrakhan region told us that 30 percent of the shares in his firm had been resold by the employees in the last year. When we asked who the main buyer was, he acted confused and avoided a straight answer. Later a local government official told us that his office had received complaints that the general director had bought all the shares himself. Top managers seldom admit to participating in other companies that serve as fronts for their ownership of their own firms.

A 400-person construction company in southern Russia had been part of a conglomerate of nineteen enterprises before the government forced them to be privatized as separate companies. Fifty-one percent of the construction firm's shares were distributed among the employees; the rest went to outsiders. Little by little the managers bought all the outsiders' shares. Many of their employees sold shares in the secondary market in 1993. Employees were uncertain how much the company was worth. One worker astutely bought a lot of shares for 1,000 rubles in 1993 (about 90 cents at the time) and two years later sold them for 30,000 rubles (about $6.50 in mid-1995). The management was very open about the fact that the general director and his wife now owned about a third of the company. There seems to be less of a flap about management ownership when top management acquires a majority stake in a small firm as a result of open trading. Employees seem to regard this as responding to opportunity rather than robbing employees. Most of the firms whose top management openly admits significant share ownership have fewer than 500 employees.

A meat processing plant with 130 employees in the Moscow region had such a high value that it was privatized as a mid-sized firm. Its general director is forthright about his goals: "This plant is my home, it's all I have. I handled the privatization personally. The employees initially got 51 percent and management 15 percent. All the employees trust me and feel my positive attitude toward them. In a written agreement they gave me control over the votes of their shares. The mentality of the Russian people is not ready for privatization. It's really impossible to pass from feudalism to capitalism immediately. It's against all the laws of human history. I started buying shares from employees, and they continue to sell them to me. Most employees are women. They got the shares for free and don't know what to do with them. I want to be the owner of this entire company, and the fact that I own 60 percent of the shares is no secret. Can people disagree with me? No. Of course, employees have the right to criticize me, but I've never made a wrong decision."

When we began to talk about the ownership of shares in a huge metal company in southern Russia whose 11,000 employees presumably owned all its shares, the top manager became very vague. He assured us that all the stockholders were employees but refused to say precisely who owned what. Who owned more than 5 percent of the shares? He would not say. But he did say that the shares had tended to be redistributed because the company had had two new public offerings of shares, and that the number of stockholders was diminishing while the blocks of stock they owned were expanding.

When managers evaded our questions about stock ownership, we sought to uncover evidence by asking them how they would design the ownership of their companies if they could do it themselves (see Table 4). Top managers who had shied from telling us how much they personally owned did not hesitate to tell us how much they wanted to own. We had asked this question every year since 1992, and the results were quite stable. The top managers said they wanted almost 70 percent of the firm to be employee-owned—but their definition of "employee" was quite narrow. They wanted virtually half the firm to be held by managers, with a large chunk of ownership for the general director personally and a significant amount for other top managers. Ironically, their own reports indicated that the general director owned a sizable amount of stock held by all top managers, and that managers other than his top deputy owned very little. Top managers had complained loudly since 1993 that they did not get enough shares, and these complaints were widespread and emphatic enough to require some attention. We were most struck by the virulence of the complaints in February 1993, when the managers' frustration took on an alarmingly political character. The lengths they went to are the best evidence that they had not succeeded in gaining what they wanted.

In February 1993, about two hundred large and mid-sized enterprises had been sold off. The managerial lobby in the Supreme Soviet offered an amendment to the privatization program to create an additional option: every enterprise could create close to 100 percent employee ownership by getting a low-interest loan from the Russian government to buy back the shares that the privatization program had systematically sold off to outsiders. Since inflation was very high that year, the low interest rate made the loan essentially a gift. The option was a front for managerial control of privatization. It allowed 90 percent of the employee stock to be voted by one person, the general director, who would receive dividends on the employees' stock, and its passage became the cause célèbre of the *nomenklatura* for several weeks. The government managed to defeat the legislation by publicly embarrassing those who raised the idea. In view of the government's choice to make privatization a populist cause, going public with such a program was a remarkable demonstration of Soviet bravado. Finally, the KGB, the Ministry of Education, and the Ministry of Defense, which had millions of employees who would get nothing if the workers in the enterprises secured the wealth of Russian industry for themselves, came out publicly against the proposed new option and turned it into a question of patriotism.

The proposed option surfaced again in another guise in the summer and fall of 1993, when the main opponent of reform in the Supreme Soviet, Speaker Ruslan Khasbulatov, was preparing legislation to bring the American employee stock ownership plan (ESOP) to Russia. To no one's surprise, Russian ESOPs would be set up as management-controlled trusts that could borrow money from the state to buy shares from outsiders. Who would vote the stock in these trusts? The general director. One should note that Russian managers did not simply dream up this idea. Most ESOPs in the United States are in fact controlled by a bank trustee if the company is large and by a management trustee if the company is small. The trustee's control of employee ownership would be more problematic in Russia than in the United States because Russian companies need more restructuring. A few weeks before the violent struggle against the government, one of its leaders, Khasbulatov, lost interest in the ESOP law.

Top managers were complaining so loudly and trying so hard to secure majority management ownership that they could not have already had it sewn up as tightly as some observers claim. They were too nervous to have been the victors. Although there is evidence that some of them are lying about the way the employee ownership is apportioned, it is probable that if the abuses were truly widespread, the workers would have protested. Employees all over the country were told by the president, the media, and their regional government officials that they would get 40 to 51 percent of the stock in their enterprise and that they could decide how to divide it up among themselves. If the top managers of most firms in the country had succeeded in robbing the other employees of this right, one could have expected widespread protests, lawsuits, and demands for government investigations. We are aware of only a few public demonstrations. One took place in front of the government's privatization offices near the Kremlin. The demonstrators were the employees of the Moscow machine tool factory whose general director we quoted earlier. He was openly trying to buy up all the shares in his huge plant for himself. The employees later voted him out of his job.

It is possible that some top managers bought up stock without the employees' knowledge, and there is surely reason to be a bit suspicious of "outside shareholders" in Russian companies. Some managers reported using "pocket companies" to buy up such shares quietly.

In many firms, however, top management has not been able to buy employees' shares because the value of the shares has risen so rapidly, because outsiders have competed for them, or because employees have simply refused to sell. If the top managers are to be believed, they are successfully preventing many employees from selling shares to outsiders. But employees, who understand the principle of passive resistance, do not seem to be trying to sell in droves. Managers say employees sold 4 percent of their shares on average in 1995 and 6 percent in 1996, and the heavy sales were concentrated in a small number of companies.

Taken as a whole, the evidence from stories in the press, lawsuits, complaints from regional government officials, confessions, and the impressions of researchers who spoke to managers repeatedly over four years suggests that the number of enterprises dominated by management is indeed much larger than managers report—majority shareholding in about 5 percent of the enterprises and ownership of more than 76 percent of the stock in 1 percent of the enterprises we studied in 1996—but probably much smaller than some observers have guessed. In all likelihood the claim that Russian industry is totally owned by the *nomenklatura* is exaggerated. Members of the Russian research team singled out this issue as the one they expected to elicit inaccurate answers, but no one had the impression that top managers owned the majority of shares in most firms yet.

Though top management ownership is likely to continue to increase, the prognosis for its domination in Russia is not very good. Even in the "employee-owned firms" that are really owned by management, the managers are likely to be forced to give up control to get capital to restructure their firms if they are to have any hope of preserving them as going concerns. Not one of the fifty largest firms in Russia reports that its top management or management as a whole owns a majority of its shares. Very few companies report management ownership separate from employee ownership, but when they do, it is always exactly 5 percent—the amount that option 1 allowed for sale to management. The average number of workers employed by these firms is 41,000. Anyone who asserts that the managers own the majority of the stock of most of these companies is obliged to explain how they accumulated all those shares from employees and outsiders.

Majority Outside Ownership

Our 1996 statistical averages indicating that outsiders own an average of about a third of Russian industry and that they own at least some shares in nine out of ten Russian companies is extremely misleading. Outsiders are majority owners of only 19.8 percent of Russian companies. True, top managers are known to hide their ownership by using outside shareholder fronts, but this ruse is not possible in the 50 percent of firms that have no outside commercial shareholders. The Russian press has devoted much space to companies that are dominated by outside shareholders, such as the Bolshevik Biscuit Company. In 1993 and 1994, overoptimistic observers of privatization cited these firms as if they indicated the way privatization would develop over the next few months.

The Lubyatov Cookie Factory in Pskov is controlled by a voucher investment fund called Alfa Capital. The price of shares was low because there was little competition for shares and they sold at close to the minimum bid price, and the speed of privatization left no time for financial analysis. Investors liked the enterprise because it was quite young and had imported equipment. Western companies showed great interest in this enterprise, and they started purchasing its shares from the employees and local citizens. By December 1993, Alfa had 55 percent and gave the new deputy general director, 24-year-old Valery Kabakov, wide authority. He was impressed by the first scene he encountered at the plant: the whole workforce turned out to celebrate the general director's birthday. But the company's financial situation was dire. It owed a great deal of money to its suppliers, it had borrowed from a local bank to pay employees' compensation, and the top managers were paying twice the market price for some raw materials so that they could preserve their business connections with particular suppliers. Bookkeeping was in chaos, and the top management had funded numerous additional companies.

Kabakov did a complete audit and discovered that some cookies were being sold for less than the ingredients that went into them. The bank loan was repaid, Alfa Capital loaned the enterprise money, the cost of production was cut, and suppliers were paid the moment they delivered their goods to the plant. Customers were asked to prepay. By the autumn of 1994, the company started advertising on TV and radio and then switched to a new form of packaging. It drastically increased its prices and developed a network of regional offices to replace middlemen and lower its costs. The new general director said that employees understood the development program. Wages were not very high, but the plant was maintaining its social programs. Alfa's goal was to make the enterprise healthy and auction it off to a Western company.

Another outsider-dominated company is Baltika Beer, in St. Petersburg. With 700 employees, it is the largest brewery in Russia and a winner waiting to be noticed. Its profits increased sixfold between 1993 and 1994. In 1995, its sales per employee rose from $53,000 to $105,000. The plant was built in 1990 by a Czech contractor and has modern equipment. Brunswick Brokerage, a major brokerage in Moscow, offered this report: "High-quality beer, good product marketing, and a well-developed distribution system contribute to Baltika's overall competitiveness. It is the only company with increasing sales, as total industry sales are declining. Baltika produces seven brands of beer and provides bottling services for the Coca-Cola Company. Baltika's market share in St. Petersburg and the northern region is 70 percent. The brewery currently operates at full capacity."

The Swedish company VVN bought three-fourths of Baltika's shares and took control of the company. To gain control the Swedes bought up shares from employees, first slowly, then rapidly. They asked the shareholders to issue new shares, and they bought some of those so it would be clear that they were the dominant owners. The Swedes invested more than $21 million in the plant to upgrade equipment, storage, and refrigeration facilities, and they decided to continue investing the company's considerable profits in more equipment and more buildings. They made Baltika the first enterprise in the St. Petersburg region to work a twelve-hour day through a seven-day week. The company ships beer to seventy towns in Russia and is moving heavily into the big Moscow market.

There is no magic in having a dominant outside shareholder unless that owner has deep pockets, or connections to deep pockets, and can finance a restructuring of the firm. At the cookie factory, for example, the employees received shares free and used vouchers, savings, and cash to buy more shares. Any money paid for shares went to the Russian government, not the factory. Alfa paid cash to citizens for their vouchers, then exchanged the vouchers for shares of the cookie factory held by the government. No money went to the cookie factory because the vouchers were only pieces of paper that were exchanged for shares, and anyone who paid for the shares at this stage gave the money to the government as the seller, not to the company. Only later was the factory able to sell a modest package of its shares for capital that went into the company.

Because of the speed of privatization and the fact that the enterprises' financial documents either were not disclosed or were made meaningless by hyperinflation, outside investors were not so shrewd in picking the best companies as one might assume. There is no correlation between most potential indicators of an enterprise's financial condition and substantial ownership by outside shareholders. Given the lack of financial disclosure during the privatization auctions and the fact that management did not even want to meet with many potential outside shareholders before their bids, it is likely that outsiders were able to collect only some cursory but accurate data on exports and downsizing. But there is no evidence whatsoever that they were able to get enough information to identify which enterprises were winners and which were losers. Since most Russian firms needed extensive restructuring, the outside shareholders either had to invest in the limited number of companies that were proved to be strong and profitable or had to take a chance on getting in the door for a low price at firms that might be somewhat promising.

A preliminary study of the companies in 1994 and 1995 showed that outside shareholders bought enterprises that had significantly more exports and more downsizing than other firms in the years preceding privatization. Firm size, as indicated by the number of employees, did not seem to influence majority outside shareholder ownership, but outside shareholders did establish majority stakes in companies whose sales were slightly lower than those whose employees took control. Half of majority outside shareholder stakes are concentrated in firms that seem to be in need of far-reaching restructuring. In weaker firms that do not have access to bank loans, outside shareholders will have an opportunity to buy more shares. In stronger firms that can issue new shares and continue to restructure, their investment will increase. If they cannot lead the restructuring and cannot buy the enterprise out of bankruptcy, they will probably lose their entire investment. Only four of the top fifty companies report being clearly majority owned by outside shareholders. The average outside shareholding is about 32 percent. If outside shareholders bought another 18 percent of the stock, they would be the majority owners in six more of the giant companies. Clearly, outside shareholders have not taken majority control of Russian companies in general or of the blue-chip corporations. They have not seriously challenged management in most companies. They are probably biding their time until the managers of the companies became keenly aware of the need to restructure their firms and desperate for the capital to do it. From this point of view, outside shareholders may have a bright future, but they will not necessarily be the same outsiders who now hold the companies' shares. Many managers complained that Russian commercial firms that currently own their stock have given no indication that they have sufficient capital to turn the corporations around. Therefore, just as employee ownership will change, the identity of the outside shareholders may also change.

No Majority Ownership

In 12.8 percent of the companies visited in 1996, neither employees nor outsiders nor the state have a majority interest (the remaining 2.6 percent of companies have majority state ownership). In most cases outside shareholders hold over a third of the stock, and in almost every case they could become the majority shareholders if one or several of them bought out all or just part of the amount left in state ownership or a reasonable proportion of the employees' shares. The struggle for property was fought in these firms in 1995 and 1996 as general directors blocked further auctions to sell their shares and issued and bought back shares for insiders. At the same time, in these companies the possibility of cooperation between insiders and outsiders is very real. This is what eventually took place at the Food Factory in Nizhny Novgorod. In 1993 employees and managers bought just over half the company. The company had a young management team led by Boris Sidorov. They had visited foreign plants and were determined to be a success, and they were focusing on acquiring new foreign food-processing machinery in exchange for a quarter of their profits. This barter deal allowed them to upgrade their equipment without taking out high-interest loans or selling their shares to foreigners. Management was against employee ownership. "Our basic view is that the plant has to have one owner. . . . All we have to do is finish equipping the enterprise with new machinery. After that we'll have no problems. We just need financing." By 1994, employees held less than half of the company's stock, and by 1996 the firm was largely owned by a Russian bank. Its business was booming.

The senior managers of the large firms are very concerned about who will own those firms. They have been used to the visible hand of the command economy and do not like the invisible hand of the potentially anonymous capital market. A senior manager at a 10,000-employee motor plant in Siberia expressed reservations about "anonymous capital" investment: "Our outside shareholder is an electricity company. They own 10 percent of the shares. They wanted 40 percent, then 50 percent, and we worried a lot about their attempts to control us. . . . We want a friendly bank to buy these shares because we're interested in having a bank as our shareholder." Conversations with factory managers suggest that they simply do not like the idea that someone can buy shares anonymously in the capital market and then walk into the enterprise the next day and identify himself as a new owner. The fact that the factory manager has had no previous relationship with the new owner is very worrisome: how is he going to control a person he doesn't even know?

Our estimates show that a sizable number of Russian corporations have no clear majority owner but large state stakes, and that such firms probably account for twenty-five to thirty-five of the top fifty Russian companies. In this situation, the state's shares become prizes worth fighting for. The average share of these companies owned by the state is 37 percent. As the future Du Ponts and AT&Ts of the Russian Federation, with the price of their undervalued stock poised to rise dramatically in a stable political environment, they are highly unlikely ever to fall under the control of their employees or managers. Insiders will probably do everything they can to keep the state from selling its remaining stake if they cannot afford to buy it themselves. They will try to get friendly firms to buy those shares. If they fail in that attempt and the company is profitable, its top managers will try to buy the shares. If the company desperately needs capital or a thorough restructuring to avoid bankruptcy, insiders have two choices: they can welcome outside shareholders and increase the value of the company while losing control, or they can push for a reversal of privatization and an increase in state subsidies.

The Struggle for Ownership

The end of voucher privatization of mid-sized and large firms in July 1994 was not the end of privatization. One of the goals of the program was to subsidize the federal and regional governments' budgets with the proceeds of the sales of shares for cash. The program made some contributions to government budgets, yet it was not so successful as had been expected. At the end of voucher privatization, some state ownership still remained among the 15,000 companies included in that program. In 1996 the average state ownership among mid-sized and large firms was 9 percent, but it was still more than 20 percent in a quarter of privatized companies and more than 32 percent in a tenth of them. (See Tables 4 and 6.) As we have seen, state ownership in the fifty largest Russian corporations was about 38 percent, and many other firms had not been privatized, because enterprises with more than 10,000 employees could not be privatized without government permission. The government devised special rules for these larger firms. In the oil and gas sector, the government kept 38 percent of the shares for three years and allowed the others to be privatized. It retained majority voting control over these key strategic firms.

There was still much more to be done before Russia was transformed into a market economy. With significant Communist and nationalist factions in parliament, there was no hope of actually passing a program of privatization. On July 22, 1994, President Yeltsin issued a decree on the second stage of privatization: the remaining state holdings were to be sold for cash at competitive auctions, with part of the proceeds going to the companies as capital for their restructuring and the rest going to the government. The land under the privatized enterprises was to be sold to the enterprises. The government hoped to raise many billions of dollars to finance its budget deficit in a noninflationary way. And it wanted to allow outside investors to build up larger blocks of shares so that they could increase their role in corporate governance. Some companies that had not been privatized were also slated for sale, but the benefits to insiders were reduced.

This second stage of privatization was a failure on many fronts. In early November 1994 Yeltsin promoted Anatoly Chubais to the position of first deputy prime minister in charge of overall economic reform. The man Yeltsin chose to replace him at the privatization ministry, Vladimir Polevanov, scared off potential investors with talk of renationalizing companies and criticism of privatization before he was fired. In the first nine months of 1995, 7,000 companies were slated to sell their remaining shares. The government expected to raise about $2 billion. The procedures for the auctions were issued late. Little information about the enterprises was made available, and few investors were interested in buying shares. Plans to sell the shares through nationwide auctions and the stock market did not live up to expectations. By November 1, shares in only about half of the companies had been sold for about $500 million, because of a depressed stock market and opposition from enterprise management and regional government officials to introducing outside owners. Privatization officials expressed concern that shares would be sold too cheaply in the depressed market.

The 1995 Russian National Survey detected this failure. In late 1994 and 1995, only 9 percent of the enterprises had investment tenders for their shares and only 24 percent had cash auctions, at which smaller stakes were sold. The privatization ministry later found that the shares were bought very cheaply by commercial firms that had little capital to invest. Many of these firms promised additional investments that they were not able to deliver. And the sale of land under privatized enterprises accounted for only a tenth of 1 percent of the cash sales because the right to own land was still not clearly established. The voucher auctions had at least attempted to make the shares of companies openly available to the broader public, but these "auctions" were wide open to domination by insiders and back-room deals. That may be one explanation for the surprising increase in average employee ownership and majority employee ownership in Russia between the 1994–95 survey and the 1995–96 survey.

The government had planned to sell 136 large companies, but the minimum prices set were too high and the sales were postponed. Finally, it attempted to rescue cash privatization with a program called INVESTINFORM, designed to provide information on potential share sales over the Internet, but various conflicts in the government prevented this plan from getting off the ground. On May 11, 1995, President Yeltsin issued a decree that increased the proportion of privatization proceeds that was to go to the central government at the expense of the regional governments. Where earlier the regional

governments had seen cash privatization as an opportunity to increase their incomes to cover their budget deficits, now they lost a
key incentive to schedule more auctions. The Russian government
also tried to sell 25 percent of Svazinvest, a holding company that
holds 38 percent of the stock in the eighty-five regional telecommunication firms across the Russian Federation. The intent was to raise
upwards of $1 billion and develop a model international auction of
a major firm. N. M. Rothschild & Sons worked with the Russian
Privatization Center to ensure a fair and objective auction process.
The winner was STET, the Italian state telephone company. Dis-
agreements arose between the government and STET, however, and
the deal was not closed.

The Russian government needed seriously to increase revenues
from privatization in 1995. Earlier, a consortium of commercial
banks suggested that they lend the Russian government funds and
take large blocks of shares in the country's giant companies as collateral. The banks would manage the shares. An additional objective
was to prevent a continuation of the drop in prices on the emerging
Russian stock market by restricting the release of large numbers of
state-owned shares into the market. The banks also wanted to restrict the involvement of foreign investors in buying up Russia's strategic companies. Many members of the reform team raised serious
objections to this proposal and offered amendments to make it more
competitive, open, and transparent. On August 31, 1995, President
Yeltsin accepted a version of the plan that came to be known as the
loans-for-shares scheme. Twenty-nine blue-chip companies would be
auctioned separately to banks. The auctions would be open to all
interested bidders, even foreigners, and the bank that offered the
largest loan to the government would win each block of shares. The
banks were required to hold the shares until September 1, 1996.
After that date they could sell the shares and take a third of the
capital gains. The bids of loans to the government appeared to be
offers of assistance, but in fact the banks were simply looking for a
way to acquire control of some of Russia's largest companies. It is not
likely that the Russian government will be able to repay these loans,
and the banks will end up as the owners of the companies.

The implementation of the loans-for-shares scheme had many
problems and it created a public uproar over privatization. The list
of companies participating was repeatedly shortened, sometimes as
a result of political pressure and lawsuits by managers of influential
companies who opposed the sale of their shares to either the banks
or other outsiders. The Duma repeatedly called for the suspension of

the program. The participation of foreigners was seriously restricted. So many Russian banks were weak that only a few were able to participate. The banks were allowed to organize the auctions themselves and participate in them as both bidders and depositors for bids, a clear conflict of interest. In the end, only twelve companies were auctioned. The first firm auctioned was Surgutneftegaz, the eighth largest company in Russia, with oil reserves of almost 11 billion barrels. An offer of one bidder was disqualified on technicalities and the auction was won by the pension fund of Surgutneftegaz. The LUKoil Group, the largest corporation in the country, joined with Bank Imperial to win its own share auction after excluding foreigners and Russian corporations that cooperated with foreigners. Both deals helped secure insider control of the companies. Oneximbank organized the auction for Norilsk Nickel, the sixth largest Russian corporation, and won the auction. Its bid of $170.1 million was just $100,000 over the starting price. Oneximbank disqualified a competing bid for $350 million on a technicality. Oneximbank then took control of Norilsk, fired its managers, and settled a strike by offering to pay workers' back wages. Acting on a petition by the fired managers, Communists and nationalists in the Duma supported a nonbinding resolution to reverse the results of the auction and return control of Norilsk to the state. At the end of the loans-for-shares "auctions," in which only a handful of bidders participated, Russia's banks were openly feuding. The banks that organized the auctions repeatedly disqualified their competitors and won the bids; most bids were fairly low; foreigners were completely excluded; some banks and companies used front companies to bid; and banks that were bidders, auction organizers, and bidding competitors helped each other with loan guarantees. In the end, the government did acquire over $1 billion, but the repeated public fights and recriminations over virtually every auction gave privatization a black eye. To Communists and nationalists in the Duma, the loans-for-shares scheme symbolized the whole privatization program, and they called for an investigation. The Communists appointed a special "Committee to Investigate Privatization and Punish the Guilty," and Russia's public prosecutor announced he was investigating these transactions along with the privatization of the gold producer Lenzoloto and the chemical giant Apatity. In June 1996, the Moscow Arbitration Court annulled the results of the loans-for-shares auction of the oil giant Sibneft. Some observers feared these investigations would turn into a political witch hunt against the original 1992 privatization program. By the time of the Russian presidential elections in the summer of 1996, little had happened on either front. One reason was the Communist Party's effort to reassure the public that it was not planning wholesale renationalizations if its candidate won the presidency. Another Duma committee, this one headed by a member of Prime Minister Chernomyrdin's party, was also planning to review privatization between 1992 and 1996. The broad public participation in voucher privatization was scarcely remembered.

How Much Property Did Citizens Get?

The attitude of Russian citizens toward voucher privatization was documented by a number of Russian polling organizations throughout the process. The main conclusion that we draw from these polls is that the Russian public became more cynical about privatization as privatization itself became more concrete. Public support for a move away from the Communist system was obvious before 1992, but as time went on, Russians increasingly questioned privatization. The negative views remained fairly stable in a series of polls conducted from June to September 1992 by the Russian polling organization VSIOM as the details of the voucher privatization plan for larger companies were being aired. Before the program was implemented, 43 percent of the persons polled thought it was a deception that would make some people richer and the rest poorer; 22 percent thought it would not change anything; 8 percent said it was a program to make people owners; 6 percent viewed it as an attempt to provide people with material assistance; and 21 percent had no opinion. Then the voucher privatization program began in December 1993. By September 1994, nine months later, when voucher privatization was half over, 30 percent of respondents thought privatization was necessary at their enterprise; 26 percent thought it was unnecessary; 6 percent were against privatization; and the rest had no opinion. At the same time, 1 percent felt that privatization had improved the economic performance of their enterprise; 20 percent believed it had made the performance worse; 69 percent saw no change; and the rest had no opinion.

Citizens were then asked how they were personally affected by privatization at their enterprise. Sixteen percent felt they won, 15 percent felt they lost, 50 percent felt they had neither won nor lost, and 19 percent had no answer. Each group was then asked to give more specifics about their win or loss. Multiple answers were permitted. Of those who said they had lost, 48 percent believed—correctly, as events would later determine—that the danger of losing their job had increased; 49 percent reported—correctly, as the downward fall of real wages in Russia would later determine—that their income had gone down; 4 percent felt they would have to work more; and 29 percent said that the working environment had become worse. Indeed, downsizing, declines in real wages, and poor working environments also emerged in nonprivatized firms. Of those who said they had won, 55 percent said their wages had increased significantly, 24 percent felt the enterprise was more stable, 19 percent believed working conditions had improved, 3 percent said they worked better and harder, 3 percent felt that the psychological climate had improved, and 4 percent had no answer. When the pollsters examined the status of these winners, they found that the managers of the enterprises were nine times more likely than their employees to find their situation improved.

In late 1994, according to another VSIOM poll, three-fifths of workers said they wanted to own their enterprises, yet only one-fifth said they thought they would end up doing so. About a tenth said they wanted top management to own the enterprise, whereas three-fifths said they thought the top managers would indeed end up as the owners. Only 5 to 8 percent thought that new Russian businessmen would own the enterprises in the end, and even fewer—3 to 4 percent —hoped for that outcome.

This mixed review raises the question how exactly the vouchers were used and who the owners of the enterprises' stocks actually were. Russian citizens at large, who were not favored with incentives for extensive stock ownership, were consistent in the way they planned to use their vouchers before the program began in December 1993 and the way they ultimately used them. Of the roughly 149 million citizens, about 12 million, or 8 percent, said they used vouchers to buy shares at their place of work. About 9 million, or 6 percent, said they used vouchers to buy shares in other enterprises. About 58 million, or 39 percent, said they either sold their vouchers or gave them away. And about 45 million, or 30 percent, said they invested their vouchers in voucher investment funds, which then bought shares for them. No information is available on the remaining 17 percent, so these figures must be viewed with caution. And some people doubtless made these decisions for children and other family members.

What do these figures mean? Employees of enterprises have reported that they used the enormous advantages offered to insiders the way—according to this poll—21 million employees of enterprises

say they used their vouchers. They feared a redistribution of ownership to managers. Despite the great publicity accorded the voucher
program, doubts, lack of information, or cynicism led 58 million people, or almost 40 percent, not to participate in the program. Where
did these vouchers end up? In fact, the *New York Times* reported that
one investment banker, Boris Jordan, working for CS First Boston in
Moscow, acquired 17 million vouchers on the secondary market for
various clients. Most of this ownership probably went to large shareholders. And there is some evidence that workers themselves bought
other people's vouchers so that they could increase their share of
ownership in their own firms. Some enterprises told us that they
bought vouchers to use to purchase their own stock at voucher auctions. There is one large discrepancy, however: whereas the poll indicates that 45 million people turned their vouchers over to voucher
investment funds, the funds report that only 23 million people actually opened accounts with them. It is possible that some people invested 22 million vouchers for other members of their families. But
since we have no reliable explanation for the discrepancies, the figures must be interpreted very conservatively. A final conservative
estimate is that around 17 million employees of enterprises and 24
million other adults—41 million in all—became shareholders in enterprises. In 1990, adult shareholders in the United States made up
just over 20 percent of the U.S. population. Forty-one million adult
shareholders is equivalent to 28 percent of the Russian population, a
solid achievement for a program that lasted less than two years. This
evidence further suggests that two extreme claims about the voucher
program are open to serious question. Any claim that the program
was wildly popular clearly exaggerates the extent of public support
and public participation. But any counterclaim that Communist bureaucrats or the Mafia hijacked the entire privatization program
seems inconsistent with the evidence currently available from both
the polls and our own investigations.

The final report card on citizen ownership sheds light on why
privatization, which was so popular in theory before reform began,
was so unpopular by the time of the presidential elections in 1996.
Employees of the newly privatized enterprises, who made up about
10 to 15 percent of the population, owned 58 percent of the stock
of those companies in 1996. All the other Russians got ownership
of only 11 percent of the stock, 6 percent as individuals and 5 percent through voucher investment funds. (See the figures for 1996 in
Table 4.) On the other hand, the very small group of citizens who
control Russian commercial firms, certainly less than 1 percent of the

population, ended up with 11 percent of all the stock by 1996, while Russian bank holding companies and financial-industrial groups have taken substantial stakes in one in ten of all privatized companies. Since a substantial number of the enterprises in which citizens and workers own stock may go bankrupt or have to restructure in a way that significantly dilutes the stake of existing shareholders, many citizen investors face additional disappointment. The attitude of some citizens toward the program may be influenced by these unfortunate choices. Voucher privatization certainly represented an unprecedented change from state ownership to private property rights, but it is easy to understand why some Russians, whether or not they participated in this historic event, took so little interest in it.

These limits on citizen participation in the new economy were supplemented by a host of other problems that complicated the public's perception of privatization. The economic reforms of 1992 and 1993 caused enormous pain to the majority of Russian citizens. Privatization was designed mainly to change the system of ownership quickly. Because privatization and the freeing of prices in the marketplace were the two elements of economic reform that the individual citizen concretely experienced in 1992 and 1993, they came to be identified with each other in the public mind. Ira Lieberman, a privatization expert for the World Bank who advised the Russian government during this period, notes: "Every time we polled the Russian population on privatization, it was clear that their responses were colored by the overall anger at inflation and the broader economic reforms. Privatization served as a lightning rod for other angers. Beyond this, citizens in their own minds even thought that privatization had caused the inflation and the bad things happening to them."

The hope was that privatization would be part of a coherently applied economic reform plan for the whole economy that would benefit citizens rather quickly. In the end, privatization went forward and the overall economic reform plan faltered until 1995. During this period, the Russian government spent billions on subsidies for industries, low-interest loans for incompetent managers, tax breaks to the oil and gas industry, and the disastrous war in Chechnya without ever considering the need to construct a reasonable safety net for ordinary citizens. The share of property given to citizens in the privatization process must be viewed in the context of the declining living standards of many Russians. In 1992, as the *Financial Times* reported in March 1996, "the then state-owned Sberbank's

70 million depositors in effect had their life savings wiped out as hyper-inflation destroyed the value of the ruble. The government is working on a plan to compensate these depositors but the sums are colossal." Citizens saw privatization in the context of all these events. Finally, the reformers had not been able to persuade the government to include all companies in the program of rapid privatization, so the program excluded a large number of controversial companies in order to get the process moving. The loans-for-shares scheme demonstrates that elements in the government and in the society were committed to structuring the later privatization of many of these large and valuable companies in a way that did not benefit ordinary Russians. This is one reason why the loans-for-shares scheme served as such a lightning rod for public criticism of privatization. Indeed, 43 percent of the Russian stock market is accounted for by oil and gas giants, 21 percent by electric utilities, 13 percent by metals, and 11 percent by telecommunications firms, many of which were held back from voucher privatization yet constitute the 100 most valuable companies in the country. (See Table 8.) These are precisely the companies that were privatized by the loans-for-shares scheme, without citizen participation. Whether the privatization of the companies that remain in state hands is conducted under a loans-for-shares program remains to be seen. If it is, public criticism of privatization will only increase.

While citizens got a smaller portion of the assets of large and mid-sized companies, their participation in private ownership of smaller businesses and apartments should not be overlooked. In 1992 nearly all firms with fewer than 200 employees were slated for privatization. The privatization offices in the country's eighty-nine regions held auctions and sold food stores, barbershops, beauty parlors, clothing shops, cafeterias, and bakeries for cash to the highest bidders. Because the local and regional governments retained the proceeds from the sale of these shops and stores, they had a powerful incentive to complete the sales quickly. Each region was given a monthly quota of enterprises to be sold, and they had to report their progress to Moscow. Table 1 shows how rapidly small-scale privatization moved forward and how Russian citizens took advantage of the freer economic climate and founded hundreds of thousands of small businesses each year of the economic reforms.

By late 1995, 105,111 retail stores—six of every ten stores throughout the country—had become privately owned. About 1,000 small businesses a month were still being privatized in 1995. Usually the stores' employees bought them, though outsiders gained ownership of some of them. The greatest progress has been made in St. Petersburg and Moscow and the Saratov region, the site of one of the big research centers of the Russian Academy of Sciences and a region with many firms in the military-industrial complex. In these regions almost all stores have been sold. The least progress has been made in North Ossetia and the Bashkir Republic. The Ossetians, an Aryan people of the Caucasus, are in the midst of a civil war ignited by the division of their region between Russia and the former Soviet repub-lic of Georgia. Only about a quarter of their small establishments have been privatized. In Bashkiria, in the southern Ural Mountains, only about a third of small retail stores have been privatized. The Bashkirs, under Russian domination since 1556, have rebelled nu-merous times over the centuries, and they have been wary of privat-ization for fear that Russians would come and buy up all the property in the region. The same forces are at work in the Tatar Republic, which has privatized only half of its stores.

Privatization of housing has moved more slowly. By early 1995, only a third of apartments had been privatized—about 11 million apartments—and about a half-million apartments were still being privatized each quarter in 1995. Citizens must apply to receive title to their apartments. The cost is negligible, mainly the time and bother of filling out the forms and dealing with the local bureaucracy. Under communism, rents were very low, representing a minuscule percentage of the tenant's monthly income. Utilities were also heav-ily subsidized, and the state paid for insurance on the apartments. The main incentive for ownership is the ability to sell the apartment, turn it over to a son or daughter, or rent it. One government study finds that many tenants fear that private ownership will require them to pay heavily for maintenance and insurance and subject them to discriminatory property taxes. Since the typical apartment house still contained unprivatized apartments in 1996, the state continued to pay the building's operating and maintenance costs. Half of the apartments and houses were already privately owned before rapid privatization of housing began in 1993.

Several million citizens gained ownership in the privatization of small businesses and about 12 million in the privatization of apart-ments. Little is known about how the ownership of these shops and apartments changed hands after the property was privatized. Citi-zens obtained retail shops and apartments practically free. But how many retained them and used them as a source of income, how many sold them at a profit, how many sold them at a very low price, and how many were cheated out of their properties are questions yet to be answered. In any event, there is evidence that a vibrant housing market is starting to develop in Russia. In 1994 alone 15,000 unoccupied apartments were sold, and in the first part of 1995 that number almost doubled.

Next Steps

The formal change from state property to private property has taken place and the enterprises have become legal entities separate from the state. To get the job done quickly, the process was designed to transfer ownership mainly to employees and managers, and that is exactly what happened. Managers took advantage of the process to build up their own power. Top managers captured control of the firms far in excess of the share of ownership they gained. As we shall see, firms whose employees own a majority of their shares are not controlled by rank-and-file employees. Like most corporations around the world, they are tightly controlled by management. From this perspective, privatization created normal companies. Some observers may be confusing management's control with the notion that top managers own most of the shares; other observers are confusing majority employee ownership with some kind of workers' democracy. So far, there is no solid evidence to support either claim.

Inside owners and outside owners have begun a tense battle in Russia because the managers who have day-to-day control no longer have anyone to supervise them. Oddly, because managers have more power now than they ever had before, the prospect of any outside interest seems all the more threatening to them. The government has lost any legitimate basis for authority over most of the enterprises. The workers are passive and the trade unions are generally bankrupt. According to the original agenda for privatization, the private owners would start to govern the companies and change their management and operations. In theory, these were necessary steps if the firms were to survive in a market economy that rewarded them with profits rather than subsidies. The plan for reform was now hobbled by the fact that after privatization the managers—in the name of all employees—continued to dominate both the formal ownership and the reins of control of the very firms the government hoped would change with privatization.

While insiders had the upper hand under the rules of the privatization process, they were not able to dominate it completely. Two years after the main privatization program had ended, outside shareholders had established a beachhead in Russian firms. The average percentage of outside ownership and the number of firms that were majority owned by outsiders were slowly if erratically going up. The loans-for-shares program can be considered a key event in the insider-outsider struggle. Despite the low public participation in stock ownership under the loans-for-shares scheme, one new propertied class in Russia, the bankers, had finally succeeded in pushing the government to design a privatization scheme that did not uniformly favor insiders. Some voucher investment funds, however, were disappointments. Ideally the funds would collect the shares of individual citizens so that they could act in unison as big outside blockholders, but the overall influence of voucher investment funds seems to be peripheral. Whereas all financial investment funds in the United States—mutual funds, pension funds, and insurance companies—control 43.5 percent of corporate stock, voucher investment funds control 5 percent of the stock of Russian firms and own no stock in half of them. No one really knew how much capital and know-how the Russian commercial firms that got 11 percent of the ownership actually had to offer. And the program resulted in very little foreign ownership, an odd turn of events, since foreign capital had played such a large role in Russian economic development before the Bolshevik coup in 1917. Citizens, meanwhile, were sour on privatization and unwilling to risk their own funds to enter the stock market. Certainly, a comparison of Russia in transition with the United States alone can be very misleading and it ignores the ownership traditions of other free-market economies.

The jury is still out on exactly how ownership will evolve after the transition period. Privatization started to slow in 1995, and Communists and nationalists in the Duma have been calling for some of the biggest enterprises to be renationalized ever since. Is the Kremlin finished designing ownership? We do not yet know. It would seem difficult and complicated for the state to attempt to reassert its authority over so many thousands of enterprises and millions of shareholders. Yet it might not be so hard for the state to nationalize or renationalize the top few hundred firms that represent the real industrial, oil and gas, and utility powerhouses of the nation, or to keep the current large state holdings in many of these companies. Any further privatization programs are bound to bring the struggles between insiders and outsiders into the open again.

The beachhead that outside shareholders have established may expand or it may not. The ownership picture is incomplete and the implications of the new ownership structures are not fully clear. The rate of change will be influenced by how much inside owners feel they need the capital and the skills of outside shareholders, how Russian politics evolve, and how welcome outside investors are made to feel. Right now, the process of restructuring the ownership and operations of the enterprises is only in its initial stage. Ownership will probably become concentrated as it accumulates in large blocks controlled by financial-industrial groups, banks, corporations, and perhaps mutual funds and pension funds. The notion that top managers have already taken over all the firms or will take them over—essentially a management buyout—is simply not proving to be true. The number of insider-dominated firms will decrease despite fierce struggles in some companies. Other companies will rush headlong to bankruptcy in their efforts to protect their majority employee ownership from an outside capitalist who could turn them into valuable investments. In the long run, outside ownership will dominate most Russian firms. At the same time, the view that employee ownership, having been useful in getting the transition done, can now be dispensed with is very shortsighted. Majority employee-owned companies that are successful and profitable have a chance of surviving without being taken over by someone else. Employee ownership is so extensive, even in the giant companies, that many investors will have to learn to live with it.

We can glimpse the complexities of the ownership puzzle by examining the bellwether metal industry. Of Russia's 400 metallurgy firms, only 12 remain in state ownership, although the government still holds veto power over certain decisions in 55 others. The deputy chair of the State Committee on Metallurgy, Vsevolod Generalov, has complained that privatization has not led to the influx of investment that Russia's metals plants urgently need. Foreign traders, he charged, have bought up blocks of shares in order to control lucrative exports in the Sayansk aluminum works, the forty-third largest company in the country. Generalov urged the firms to issue a fresh batch of shares to raise new capital—although they would dilute the value of the existing shares. Thus, while insiders are bound to lose their monopoly in many companies, the identities and power of some of the key outside investors may also undergo a change.

Once the ownership is redistributed, Russian companies will need a new internal government other than a dictator in the person of the general director. Top managers may continue to dominate some firms. This solution is less common in free market economies, where the truly large companies have many owners and therefore require a board of directors to harmonize the interests of all shareholders and stakeholders. Is a way of running these firms emerging that will allow the infant corporations to do well, to hire and fire the right managers, to be run for the profit of shareholders, and to hasten their own restructuring and that of the country at large? That is the story of the next chapter.

3

Power

When Russia formally became a democracy, the state relinquished its power over enterprises. After privatization, Russia's large and mid-sized enterprises found themselves with strange new identities. Each had become a corporation owned by its shareholders. Property rights went to the new shareholders, but what happened to the control that had been exercised by the state? This abrupt shift in power left many people disoriented. At the huge Ordzhonikidze machine tool factory, near Moscow, the new owners were slow to recognize their power. Five years earlier, in 1989, the employees had used the power transferred from the Gorbachev government to elect Andrei Soloviev, the plant's senior engineer, to replace an ineffective general director. At 35, Soloviev was considered an innovator and a democrat. He could talk to employees. He liked to walk around the plant and make promises and predictions in each department. With privatization the employees gained ownership of 51 percent of the shares. Soloviev had prevailed against an attempt to fire him during the Gorbachev era, but now many employees believed that Soloviev had not improved the economic performance of the plant in his years as general director. Experienced workers began to leave the plant, and the workforce fell from 4,500 people to 1,500. Soloviev had fulfilled none of his promises, and employees viewed him as being motivated by self-interest. In 1993 and 1994 the plant fell deeper and deeper into debt. Wages were paid from the proceeds of mortgages on the plant's equipment and from the rents on its buildings. There were rumors that some of these rents were so low that they did not even cover the factory's cost to maintain them.

In 1993, Soloviev prevented a shareholder meeting from taking place and for the second time avoided being fired. The employees were passive, but other shareholders were growing angry. Two commercial firms that specialized in investment projects and technical advice to factories, Orgservis and Tis-trust, bought stock at the voucher auction and had seats on the board of directors. By 1994 these outside shareholders were impatient with management's neglect of marketing, advertising, and financial accounting. The warehouses were full of unsold machinery and the sales department was not even trying to find buyers. Management was considering a move to divide the plant into subsidiary companies, each to finance its own activities. It was obvious that the two outside shareholders alone could not fire the general director, but then the unexpected happened: the head of an investment company in Moscow was elected chairman of the board. Now other managers, employees, and outsiders formed a coalition to fire Soloviev. His career was over. "Our optimism has run out," explained Irina Sedotova, a new manager. "Rich guys come. They want to give us salaries to work. So we'll work for them now."

Under law, power in any corporation is distributed among the board of directors, top managers, and shareholders. Though the shareholders are the ultimate owners of the corporation, their power to intervene in day-to-day management is limited, so that the company can function efficiently. This arrangement is the source of the classic principal-agent problem: shareholders are the principals of a moneymaking company, and top management is the agent designated to make a profit for them. How do shareholders make sure that management is working for the profit of shareholders rather than for their personal profit? How can shareholders—many of whom live far away and who do not manage the company from day to day—monitor management's performance?

In a free market economy, top managers can work at cross-purposes to shareholders by taking salaries and bonuses that are not justified by their performance, trying to expand the company even if it is not profitable, failing to run the company efficiently and profitably, or pursuing a faulty long-term strategy. One way to resolve the principal-agent problem is to have top managers own a substantial number of shares in the company, so that their profit depends directly on the amount of money they make for the other shareholders. Shareholders face a bit of a dilemma in their suspicions about top management, because top managers really are—or at least they need to be—the most important and competent leaders in the enterprise. They need some monitoring, but not too much. Another very common way to resolve the principal-agent problem around the world is for shareholders to concentrate their ownership in large blocks in order to compensate for the fact that many legal systems are not very protective of outside investors.

The Initial Transition, 1993 and 1994

No one was expecting enterprises to change from the Soviet system to a smoothly functioning system of corporate governance overnight; after all, many big corporations in the Western democracies and Japan still struggle with governance issues. But in Russia the transition from government to governance began at a crawl. Each enterprise prepared for the transition by converting to a stock corporation, appointing a board of directors, and adopting a model corporate charter that designated the powers of the board of directors and the shareholders to oversee the general director and other top managers. The Privatization Ministry stipulated that until an enterprise was privatized, it would have an interim board of directors with five members. Two seats would be controlled by the general director, one by the local government, one by the federal government in Moscow, and one by the employees or their trade union representative. This interim arrangement preserved the power of the general director, who needed the vote of only one other board member to retain control. Once they realized that they would not be given a major ownership interest, most general directors settled for the knowledge that they would probably be able to maintain control over the board of directors until the company was privatized. Many, however, reported being nervous and worried during this period. Until the company was privatized, the general assembly of employees still had the power to dismiss the top manager. The average general director wanted just to get through privatization without being fired by the employees or ending up under the control of a large outside shareholder.

Five conditions had to be met if Russian shareholders were to have power in the companies, the motivation to invest in them, and the capital to restructure them: (1) open trading of stock, (2) independent shareholder registers, (3) accurate financial disclosure, (4) democratic boards of directors, and (5) fair issuance of new shares.

Open Trading of Stock. Open trading of stock allows shareholders to buy and sell shares according to their view of the stock's prospects. When a company is openly traded, an anonymous outsider can buy stock from a broker or another shareholder, and a current shareholder can sell to the public at large. Investors can buy into companies they see as promising or exit companies with disappointing performances.

Closed or closely held companies are typically family-owned corporations or are controlled by a few shareholders who know each other. They are often the smaller firms, but that is not the case everywhere. In some countries, closed companies are the norm. Most free market economies have some open and some closed companies.

The 1992 Russian privatization program mandated that all companies should be open because its aim was to create a market for companies and to open them as wide as possible to investments after privatization. The general directors and their lobbies in the Supreme Soviet and industry associations bitterly opposed this concept because they realized that even if insiders dominated the initial stage of privatization, outsiders could eventually enter their companies.

Open stock trading is the "market for corporate control." Top management's opposition to open trading of shares at the beginning of privatization should not be viewed as completely self-interested. The managers pointed out that they were trying hard to run a company under difficult conditions when the government was allowing outsiders to get the company's shares for vouchers, and these transactions yielded no capital for the company. The companies' short-term need for capital conflicted with the overarching goal of rapid privatization.

The general directors did not stand still for what they saw as forced perestroika. In 1992 and 1993 they repeatedly pushed government officials to declare their enterprises "closed joint-stock companies," but only 3 percent of the general directors said they succeeded. In the end, they essentially lost the battle to define their companies as closed. But for the time being, since nine of ten companies were majority employee-owned and many companies had no outsider ownership at the end of 1993, it made no difference whether the company was called open or closed.

The general director of a machine tool factory with 2,700 workers argued vehemently against open trading of stock in 1993. "If the government wants to create a new class of owners, their program must be supported by the existing general directors, who were really left with nothing in this privatization process. The current program will lead to a majority of the shares in the hands of some new private businessmen who don't understand production. They'll be in the hands of people who got money by making fast trades in commodities under Gorbachev—Mafia. I'm against the idea of an open stock market setting the prices of our shares. Some rules must be set and the prices of the shares must be set. The market has to influence the share price but it must first be under government control. There must be rules to govern this process or it will go out of control. The leaders of the enterprises must be taken into account. They're all at the creative age of fifty-five and they started out under Khrushchev's perestroika. They got heart problems because of the brutal realities of our system and now they want to reap the fruits of their efforts. I could be rich. I could be a trader, but I can't abandon my enterprise. I know my abilities and I am doing my best."

Independent Shareholder Registers. When the enterprises were privatized, the proof of share ownership was not a share certificate but the record of the owner's name in an official book called the shareholder register. If your name was not there, you did not own stock. Period. At first the general directors were determined to keep the shareholder records on the company premises, sometimes in their own offices, under the control of a trusted staff member. In 1993 and 1994 several general directors told us that they did not even trust other managers or employees to see these lists. By keeping the lists confidential, they reserved several kinds of power to themselves. If an outsider they disliked bought shares, they could simply refuse to register the new ownership. An employee who wanted to sell shares had to get management's approval before the transaction could be registered. This requirement put a chill on sales to outsiders and increased the chances that employees would sell to other insiders. If an outsider wanted to start accumulating shares with the hope of gaining control of the company, the general director could simply refuse to reveal the current owners' names. Outsiders had to go to a lot of trouble, buying newspaper ads or radio time or even parking a bus outside the company grounds, to find people willing to sell their shares. Even if a company's stock was openly traded, the general director had only to guard the shareholder register to stamp out the market for corporate control and protect his or her own position. In 1993 and 1994, most shareholder registers were closely held secrets.

Accurate Financial Disclosure. Thousands of firms were technically "public" companies whose stock was to be openly traded, but no financial information about them existed outside the companies themselves. Most of the companies were not audited by an independent accounting firm, so no one had any means of judging what they did disclose. At the beginning of privatization there was no equivalent of the Securities and Exchange Commission to compel companies to issue regular financial reports, and the companies could decide themselves which outside shareholders should receive financial information and which ones they wanted to boycott. Furthermore, hyperinflation made most company financial information virtually useless. If in 1992 the inflation rate is 2,323 percent, for example, what is the dollar value of sales of 1 million rubles in 1992? In 1992 the price of a dollar rose from 198 rubles to 415 rubles. Thus good financial information was not only improbable, it was impossible. Since investors could not tell whether a stock was a good deal, only favored investors had much incentive to buy it. In 1993 and 1994, many managers echoed the general director Marina Tikonova: "Our financial statements are commercial secrets."

Democratic Boards of Directors. Although outsiders owned 21 percent of the stock of the average firm in 1993 and 1994, they were denied seats on the board of directors. Insiders used their control of a majority of shares to outvote the outsiders. In a few instances outsiders and insiders compromised on board representation for the minority shareholders, but in most cases the board of directors was really a management council, made up of the general manager and his or her senior management staff plus a representative of the local government that controlled shares not yet auctioned off or otherwise distributed. This member almost always voted with the general director. We found no widespread evidence that rank-and-file employees used their shares to elect representatives who would be independent of top managers. If Russian trade unions had wanted to do so in 1993 and 1994, they could have taken over nearly every board of directors in the country; yet workers wielded no influence on the boards. In fact, the one employee or trade union representative mandated by the privatization ministry in the transition period was dropped from most boards as soon as privatization was completed. An occasional trade union official was kept on the board as window dressing. The assembled managers of a huge road construction firm sat in stony silence when the trade union president asked one of the authors if he would be willing to become the labor collective's representative on the board.

Even outside shareholders who owned a significant block of shares were unlikely to be represented on the board. In 1993 and 1994

Russian companies selected their boards of directors according to the system used by most U.S. companies: management and other shareholders proposed slates of directors, each share had one vote, and the members of the slate that received more than 50 percent of the votes were elected. The minority shareholders or those who lost out in the election had no representation on the board. Since nine of every ten companies were majority employee-owned in early 1994, the insiders virtually always elected the general director and his or her top assistants as the entire board. Most general directors simply did not understand the need to share representation with the minority shareholders, the rank-and-file employee shareholders, or anyone else.

One alternative to this situation is cumulative voting. Cumulative voting in corporations is very uncommon around the world. In the United States it is practiced in only a few states. Under cumulative voting, each candidate for a seat on the board runs as an individual, and each share of stock entitles the holder to as many votes as the number of board members to be elected. If a company's board has ten members, each shareholder has ten votes per share owned. The ten nominees who receive the greatest number of votes succeed to the board. Under this method, the insiders still elect most of the board of directors by spreading their votes across the candidates they want. It is possible for the minority shareholders to concentrate their votes on a few outsiders and elect them to the board. Typically, outside shareholders do not know one another and do not organize themselves and coordinate their voting efficiently. Still, the possibility is there: they might elect one or more members to the board, creating a diversified body. That's why cumulative voting is opposed by corporate leaders around the world. In 1993 advisers to the government began to consider this alternative because of mounting evidence that managements were receiving virtually no input from anyone outside their companies. Even if outside shareholders could get financial information without representation on the board of directors, they could not protect their money by monitoring the company's management and performance. So why invest? On December 24, 1993, the president's decree 2284 mandated cumulative voting. But cumulative voting is only one protection for investors, and its potential impact cannot be exaggerated.

Fair Issuance of New Shares. Occasionally a corporation will need to raise capital by selling new shares rather than developing the business only with profits or with proceeds from bank loans. This is a special concern in Russia, where many companies are not very profitable and need outside capital desperately. Theoretically a bank loan may be a solution, but since companies do not own their land, they cannot offer it as collateral; the interest rates have been very high; and banks have been more interested in speculating in currency and government bonds than in lending money to enterprises. Furthermore, Russian bankers are only gradually developing the skills to help restructure weak firms. When a company sells new shares, the buyer of those shares gains control over that portion of the company. Because sales of shares involve the trading of power, they are a key element in corporate governance.

Throughout 1993 and 1994 Russian managers spoke openly about a tactic to thwart outside ownership. The trick was to issue new shares to managers and other employees but charge them only a minimal amount. Often the general director and the board looked the other way while the insiders delayed paying for the shares until the rate of inflation reduced the price to practically zero. This tactic effectively reduced the power of the outside shareholders. If a voucher investment fund owns 20 percent of your company and you issue enough new shares to insiders, the fund managers wake up the next morning to find that they hold only 10 percent of a company that received no new money for the shares that reduced the fund's ownership. Obviously, the new shares had never been offered to outsiders.

In 1994 the first well-publicized serious violation of shareholders' rights in a new issue of stock took place at Komineft, one of Russia's largest oil companies. Komineft has reserves of over 2 billion barrels of oil and is the country's thirty-sixth largest company by market value (see Table 8). Without giving adequate notice to its outside shareholders, the company called a meeting, and the shareholders present approved a very large issuance of new shares. Several key outside shareholders were not notified of this action and were not allowed to buy the new shares if they did hear about it. The result was that the outside shareholders' ownership in the company was diluted by a third. The outsiders were a virtual *Who's Who* of Russian portfolio investors: Brunswick Brokerage, Credit Suisse (CS) First Boston, the Grant Financial Centre, Bank Menatep, Gambit Securities, and Troika-Dialog. Top management was unavailable to the press for a week. The share issue was registered only with the Ministry of Finance of the Komi Republic, not with the federal government in Moscow, as the law required. The company's offer of a new issue of stock was illegal, too, because three-quarters of its shares were not yet in private hands. Presumably the shares went to insiders and to companies friendly to Komineft's management. It was impossible to determine whether and how they had paid for the shares. The outside shareholders threatened a lawsuit. The Federal Commission on Securities and the Capital Market has repeatedly demanded that the company reverse the share issue. But the share issue has not been reversed, and the outside shareholders have not been able to resolve the issue privately or in court because the laws were unclear.

In the spring of 1995 the Primorsky Sea Shipping Line found the same trick equally successful. Primorsky, in the Far East, ranks eighty-second among Russian firms by market value. The company set up a subsidiary called PRISCO-Stocks and gained its insider shareholders' approval to double the company's shares, which the subsidiary was then allowed to buy for $43,000. This ploy effectively diluted the 12 percent stake of CS First Boston by half. At the current market price of $2 a share, the daughter company should have paid $22 million for the shares. The Sakhalin Sea Shipping Line, a major Far Eastern shipping company, engaged in the same maneuver.

Other firms have achieved the same effect by using the company's funds to buy back its shares from outsiders and then selling them at a very low price to managers and employees. In other words, the company uses other shareholders' money to increase its employees' ownership.

It is impossible to know how widespread these practices were. Technically, they were not against the law, because Russian corporate law was still evolving. There was no law requiring new share offerings to be offered equally to all shareholders, not just to insiders, or requiring immediate payment for shares. The solution to the stock buyback trick would be to prohibit a company from using corporate funds for a buyback without the approval of a majority of shareholders or to require insiders to pay a fair market price for any shares they buy. Even if an outsider freely bought shares, somehow gained access to the shareholder register and financial information, and secured a seat on the board of directors, other directors could still vote for a share issue or a stock buyback to reduce that outside shareholder's power.

During 1993 and 1994 many general directors spoke openly about their views of governance. While their comments did reveal stratagems to manipulate governance to serve their own interests, they also reflected reasonable concerns about the fate of the enterprises they managed. The average general director, in his or her fifties, had been working for several decades under the Soviet system, in which the enterprises were controlled by a known group of bureaucrats who developed bonds of trust among themselves and coordinated their efforts to make the system work.

The manager of a chemical factory in Volgograd told researchers in 1993, "We believe the board of directors should include only top managers. The employees don't need to have representatives on the board of directors because the general director himself was an employee of the plant for many years and he knows all the employees' problems. Our employees are passive. If we temporarily raise their pay, they'll support us. The enterprise needs to be managed by specialists, not by people who don't understand production."

To the manager of a Belgorod trucking firm, the dangers of outside influence on governance were real in 1994: "The major outside investor, who owns 4 percent, came to the company two days after he got his share certificates and told the employees he was going to become the sole owner of the company. He promised to fire the entire senior management team. For the past four years this person has been selling sugar and vodka." The manager's sneer made clear his contempt for such activities. "He has put ads in local newspapers several times, saying he wants to buy our shares, but he had failed. He wants to buy them because the price is so low. He knows their real value. We have a small company, and he can see who the shareholders are. He'll have the right to vote at the shareholder meeting but he won't influence the decision making."

It would be a mistake to think that only Red directors practice these tricks. In a steel company with about 12,000 employees near a major Russian city, the managers are aggressive free marketers. One described their system of corporate governance in 1994 this way: "In our company the rules on rights and authority can be summarized in two sentences. Sentence one: The president is always right. Sentence 2: If the president is not right, see sentence one. This fact has nothing in common with the legal documents of the enterprise. A problem we have is that because of our size, the employees and managers can't buy a majority of shares. We have an investment fund that deals in our shares. Its office is below mine but it's not technically part of this enterprise. We have a brokerage subsidiary that buys our shares on the Moscow Stock Exchange. We have a solution to the problem of majority ownership. We announced three new issues of shares. A lot of investors heard about it and said they were afraid their ownership would be diluted. We decided to sell seventy percent of this new issue of shares to our own employees very cheaply. Some of these were preferred shares with special rights. Then we did a second and third issue of shares. These issues diluted the outside investment funds that had our shares. Our president controls this situation very well."

No high-profile case of share dilution has been reported in the press since the 1994 and 1995 controversies.

Governance in 1996

As 1993 ended, it was becoming obvious that rank-and-file worker ownership would not interfere with corporate governance. As we indicate in Table 9, summarizing our surveys on corporate governance, the companies still have open trading in name only; the managers want strict control over who buys their shares; most companies do not use independent shareholder registers; and most managers say they oppose financial disclosure and majority ownership by an outside investor with enough capital to turn the firm around. Top management is well entrenched. This is a principal-agent problem typical of corporations everywhere, but the Russian version has had higher costs for society because Russia's corporations were not functioning well to begin with and needed massive infusions of capital and determined restructuring. Ignoring shareholders' rights is not the way to encourage reinvestment in Russian industry. The depth of management entrenchment began to terrify observers of the privatization process, particularly Dmitry Vasiliev, then deputy chairman of the privatization ministry. If Russia were rich in capital and had a developed banking system that would lend funds for restructuring, perhaps most companies could succeed as closely held firms. If there were overwhelming evidence that most companies were financially stable and well managed and that all they needed was capital, perhaps it would have been easy to attract minority investors who would sit back, shut up, and wait for the dividends. But no outside investor, domestic or foreign, was going to risk a significant amount of money in Russia until the situation of enterprise control had changed. Until power accrued to investors in proportion to their investment, firms were not going to get the management or the capital they needed. Because of the weakness and unpredictability of the Russian court system, the reformers sought to emphasize regulations that gave citizens incentives to enforce their own rights and economic interest. The investors did not put their faith solely in legal rules. By 1996 they had begun to concentrate their ownership in large blockholder stakes. (See Tables 6, 9, and 11.)

From 1993 to 1996, the Russian government took a series of actions to reduce the barriers to outside shareholders' power, and it continued to stand by the principle of open trading. Despite these actions, some companies managed to maintain the status of closed joint-stock corporations. In late December 1993, the government moved swiftly and decisively to reduce the power of employee-dominated boards of directors. A new regulation instructed all privatized enterprises to reelect their boards of directors by means of cumulative voting by the end of April 1994, and no matter who owned the stock, no more than one-third of the board members could be insiders. Our small preliminary investigation in the spring of 1994 indicated that the mandate for cumulative voting was being ignored by 97 percent of the companies. As it turned out, all the companies that complied were controlled by one large outside shareholder.

Then there was a surprise. About a third of the companies, mostly those with high outside ownership concentrated in few shareholders, added one outside representative to their board of directors. When pressed to explain, managers said that they met with the outside shareholder and informally offered the person a board seat even though they had no intention of using cumulative voting at the shareholders' meeting. When Alliance, an investment arm of Bank Menatep, tried to take over the Red October Chocolate Company in the spring and summer of 1995, the Russian public got a peek at just this kind of management compromise. Alliance was attempting a hostile takeover of the chocolate maker and tried hard to buy up employees' shares. The top managers resisted the takeover successfully, and in the end they offered Alliance some board seats and the possibility of cooperation in restructuring the company.

Most companies continued to say that they were open, but trading of shares was very limited. Neither employees nor outsiders were selling many shares in 1994. Although there is evidence that employee selling may have increased in 1995, most such sales were concentrated in a small number of corporations. In fact, the number of majority employee-owned firms apparently rose between 1995 and 1996. With the freeze on further sales of state-held shares in 1995 and 1996, very few companies sold their shares in investment tenders or cash auctions.

Russia's "pink-sheet market" is much like the over-the-counter (OTC) market in the United States, comprising thousands of smaller companies whose stocks are too thinly traded to be listed on a major stock exchange. Brokers trade them mainly by phoning each other, and prices are based on a regularly circulated list printed on pink sheets. Obviously, these stocks have little interest for the Moscow and international stock brokers, who concentrate on the top 100 firms. Table 9 gives a detailed picture of all the evidence that follows.

In January 1996 a new corporate law came into force. Drafted by a team at the International Institute for Law-Based Economy in Moscow, it attempts to exert a determining influence over corporate governance. Every corporation was required to bring its corporate charter into compliance with the law by a certain date; if it did not, its charter became invalid. The law requires all companies with more than fifty employees to be openly traded. Open trading, however, is not necessarily active trading. Many managers want strict control over the buying of their shares. About a fifth of managers believed someone outside the firm was trying to accumulate their shares, and the corporate law provides some protection for insiders and current shareholders against surprise takeover attempts. Anyone who intends to acquire more than 30 percent of a corporation must notify the company of their intent and offer to purchase the shares of other shareholders at a fair price. Any company that intends to purchase more than 20 percent of another company must make this information public immediately. These provisions are designed to balance the interests of workers and managers and current shareholders against those of anyone who aggressively seeks corporate control.

Both the privatization ministry and the Federal Commission on Securities and the Capital Market repeatedly mandated that an independent third party maintain the shareholder register of every company with more than 1,000 shareholders. Evidence from the most recent survey indicates that many companies failed to comply with this provision, so the new corporate law of December 1995 mandates independent shareholder registers for all companies with more than 500 employees and requires the registrar to enter newly purchased shares in the register within three days of a shareholder's request. It was virtually impossible, however, to determine from public documents disclosed to a Moscow broker by the 100 largest companies in Russia whether those companies used independent registrars. The Russian Securities Commission is now considering the licensing of share registrars.

The corporate law requires companies to distribute to their shareholders the firm's annual report, the auditor's evaluation of its financial statements, information about board candidates, and any draft amendments to be considered at the shareholders' meeting—all information that most managers were loath to disclose—thirty days before the annual meeting. It remains to be seen whether companies will comply.

The new 1996 corporate law mandates cumulative voting in companies with more than 1,000 shareholders. The law also says that
senior managers may not constitute a majority of the board of directors. By 1996 almost 40 percent of Russian companies had adopted
cumulative voting. But of the 60 percent that were still ignoring the
cumulative voting regulation, many had made deals with outside
shareholders in exchange for board seats, so that 76 percent of companies had outside representatives on their boards of directors. Cumulative voting is practiced in twice as many companies with
majority outside ownership as in companies with majority employee
ownership. By 1996 the typical board, once consisting of top managers only, had two outside shareholder representatives, one state representative, and four managers. Since five board members are
required to make a decision, the significance of the two outside board
members should not be exaggerated. All decisions of almost any
board of directors in the country can still be made without the support of the outside directors. Nevertheless, the gradual increase in
the number of outside representatives on boards and the increasing
compliance with cumulative voting are visible cracks in the barriers
to corporate governance. Every 1 percent increase in outsider stock
ownership significantly increases the probability that an outsider
will sit on the board. The number of companies with no outside
director is dropping, and the percentage of the boards controlled by
outsiders is increasing.

Under the new corporate law, any shareholder who owns at least
2 percent of a firm's stock has the right to introduce two proposals to
the agenda of the annual shareholders' meeting and to nominate
candidates to the board of directors and the audit committee. If 10
percent of shareholders are dissatisfied, they can call a special shareholders' meeting by their own authority. For the first time in Russia,
conflicts of interest are regulated, and the law requires board members and managers and their families to disclose any possible conflict
of interest.

Evidence in 1996 showed the issuance of new stock still to be a
serious problem, and the new corporate law deals decisively with it.
An alarming number of companies admitted to such maneuvers as
giving new shares at low prices to insiders or buying back shares and
giving them to managers and other employees. The creation of new
shares must now be approved by more than three-quarters of the
shareholders, and at least half of the voting shareholders must be at
the meeting. Shares must be sold at market value, and purchasers,
who have no voting rights until they have paid for the shares, must

pay in full within a year. Most important, whenever new stock is offered, current shareholders have a right to buy new shares in proportion to the percentage of the company's stock they already own. If enforced, this law will prevent the kind of dilution of ownership engineered by the Komineft management. Compliance may improve now that the Federal Commission on Securities and the Capital Market has established branch offices in most of the country's eighty-nine regions and has a clear corporate law to enforce nationwide, a law that actually has the support of both parliament and the president.

Are outside shareholders getting more board seats in one industry than in another? Does majority ownership determine whether outsiders get board seats? Are the companies with good governance more financially successful and more likely to restructure? Fortunately, the Russian National Survey provides insights into all these issues (Table 9).

About three-fourths of the large and mid-sized companies across Russia had outsiders on their boards of directors in 1996, as compared with two-thirds in 1995. The presence of outsiders on company boards is stable when adjustments are made for differences related to the size of the company or, in general, industry group. In 1995 about 14 percent of the typical board was made up of outsiders, and that number rose to 31 percent in 1996 (Table 9 shows which blockholders have the least board representation).

For every 10 percent increase in employee ownership, the number of outsiders on Russian boards declines 7 percent, after adjustment for the size of the company or its industry group. Generally speaking, the more inside owners dominate, the less willing they are to share board membership with outsiders; conversely, an increase in outside stock ownership significantly raises the probability that outside representatives will appear on the board of directors. Here we see why general directors are so anxious to have strict control over employees' shares and further auctions of their stock.

The association of outsider representation on the board with some initial indicators of restructuring is very strong. Significantly more companies with outside representatives on the board have downsized substantially, engaged in joint ventures, and sacked the general director. This finding may reflect outsiders' preference for stock in companies that have made large cuts in their workforce and appointed a new general director. The less competent general directors are correctly perceiving the potential effect on them of the market for corporate control. Yet, as our interviews bear out, top managers—even those in majority outsider-owned firms—do not have to learn to like life with outside shareholders. There is a significant relationship between the number of outside representatives a company already has on its board and the amount of outsider ownership *and* management's willingness to agree to outside investor control if that investor will bring all the cash needed to restructure the firm.

In 1996 we gave all Russian corporations corporate governance scores based on the number of outsiders on their boards, cumulative voting, the use of independent shareholder registrars, the degree to which owners of concentrated blocks of stock (over 5 percent of shares) had board seats in proportion to ownership, and maneuvering to keep new share issues and stock buybacks within the firm. Thirteen percent of companies engaged in bad practices so systematically that their corporate governance was graded as horrible; 46 percent received bad corporate governance grades; and 39 percent, who engaged in only one or two questionable practices among generally good ones, were graded as good. Two percent of the companies attained excellent scores. This is not encouraging news, since even those companies with reputations for good corporate governance engaged in at least one practice that might make a serious outside investor think twice.

Some perspective is needed on these corporate governance scores. A recent Harvard study of corporate governance systems in forty-nine countries found that the laws in place to protect investors vary a great deal from country to country, in accordance with the legal tradition that inspired those laws. Countries whose corporate governance systems originated in the common law tradition (such as Great Britain and the United States) protect investors more than countries whose systems originated in the French Civil Code tradition (such as France, Italy, and Spain). French Civil Code countries also have the worst enforcement of investor protections and poorer accounting standards, which govern the information provided on the financial condition of the companies. Better law enforcement partly reflects higher income levels in a country. Countries that operate in the French tradition often have fewer companies that go public, smaller stock markets, and thus less access to external finance. In countries with weak legal protections for investors, extremely concentrated ownership develops as an adaptation: such shareholders can devise some alternatives to legal rules to protect themselves. Indeed, countries that protect shareholders against manipulation of their voting and other rights have lower concentration of ownership.

The Russian system of corporate governance is still evolving. Some progress has been made. The new corporate law of 1996 laid down some strict legal rules to protect investors, but in many respects the realities of enforcement in Russia—the inefficiency of the judicial system, corruption, and the general poor attitude toward the rule of law—suggest that concentrated ownership may be one critical way investors adapt to these problems.

What role do core investors—the blockholders who own more than 5 percent of the company's stock—play in the governance process? (See Table 9.) Seven of every ten companies have blockholders, and the average blockholder owns 16 percent of the company. Domestic commercial firms are the main blockholders, followed by citizens, investment funds, and domestic holding companies and banks; foreigners play a very small role as blockholders. The voucher investment funds created by the privatization program to concentrate ownership represented an important economic force. In the summer of 1995, each of the approximately 600 voucher investment funds in Russia concentrated the shares of just over 30,000 citizens. The presence of blockholders in a company is very strongly associated with a substantial proportion of outside directors: 38 percent of the board members of corporations with blockholders are outsiders, whereas outsiders account for only 14 percent of the boards of corporations that have no blockholders. On average, the proportion of outsiders is 24 percent higher on the boards of blockholder companies than on the boards of companies that have no blockholders, when the industry group and the size of the company are taken into account. A 10 percent increase in blockholder ownership is associated with a 6.5 percent increase in outside board representatives as a percentage of the total board. Citizen blockholders, foreign corporations, holding companies, Russian banks, and, surprisingly, voucher investment funds are doing a poor job of getting board seats in proportion to their ownership stakes. The Harvard study found that dispersed ownership is a myth in world stock markets. The average ownership of the three largest shareholders in the largest public companies in forty-nine countries is 46 percent. Russia may be moving in this direction.

While the emergence of outsider ownership is associated with some change in corporate behavior, the attitudes of the general directors have remained very rigid in most companies, no matter who owns them. The manager of a majority employee-owned plant in the metal industry with 21,000 workers sees outsiders as a problem to be managed: "I expect that about fifteen percent of the company's shares were recently sold by employees, mainly to outsiders. Many Moscow banks are interested in participating, and two, Alfa Bank and Inkombank, have been very successful. I suspect they're representing foreign financial institutions, such as Credit Suisse First Boston. Outsiders own thirty percent of our company today, but I assure you that management is going to take dissuasive measures to prevent further shares from flowing away. Our current outside shareholders are very helpful and cooperative, and we'd prefer to keep this ownership structure without serious changes."

The manager of a majority employee-owned diversified machinery plant with 8,000 employees realizes that the firm needs outside capital but does not make the connection between his attitude and the lack of investors: "Three voucher investment funds own five, four, and two percent of our shares. The Petrov voucher investment fund is rather dangerous. They bought control of a chemical plant in our town and changed top management, including the general director. The workers struggled against this but were defeated. A defense against this buying of our shares was one of the reasons we founded our own trading company. This trading firm is a closely held company that we mostly own. It has bought twelve percent of the shares from our employees. We have two outside members on our board of directors. One is a bank we've known for twelve years and one is this Petrov voucher fund. We've been searching for an outside investor for three years because the company needs enormous capital investments. But we just cannot find a domestic investor." The general director of another company is more straightforward: "Yes, we need investments, but we would never agree to get them in return for our shares. We don't need anything outside shareholders have to offer. We have not given our share register to an independent registrar and we're simply not going to."

Even the general directors of firms with lots of outside ownership are having a hard time adjusting. The general director of a company in the Vologda region that has 78 percent outside ownership says, "We'd rather be a closely held company than have problems with all these different outside shareholders today. Of course, we wish we could find a really efficient strategic investor. But there's no reason to try to sell our shares to several groups. We need one partner, a serious one." Many general directors were concerned that a broad range of diffuse outside shareholders who bought the stock at low prices might not really add up to significant capital to renovate their companies. Some outside shareholders are taking over completely, installing their own general directors, and radically changing the firms. A Moscow bank that owns 85 percent of a steel company in central Russia with 8,400 employees got the support of the employees to appoint a deputy director as the new general director and fire the entire old management team. He says, "This is the second biggest steel rolling mill in Europe, with an annual production of about a million tons. The previous general director made the workers hostages to the former top management's mistakes. I have worked here for sixteen years. Now we have reorganized into a true holding company, with twenty-seven daughter companies responsible for their own production. It's very efficient now."

Other managers are learning to live with outsiders, as the general director of a transport company in Volgograd with 11,000 workers reports: "Thirty-two percent of our firm is owned by foreigners, the biggest of which is a British securities firm, with eighteen percent of the company. They got to be a big shareholder simply by concentrating shares sold by employees. The British firm showed no interest in the board of directors until a month ago, when their general director and I decided that a representative would enter our board. We have increased employment by five percent and exports are growing. There's no decline in demand for our products." And managers with large blocks of outsiders are very preoccupied with the issue of their power and position. The general director of a 10,000-worker Siberian mining operation confesses, "The intense acquisition of our employees' shares by foreign and domestic firms began last year. Now all employees have three percent. A big financial-industrial group owns twenty percent, a South Korean company owns ten percent, two Russian commercial firms own ten percent, and thirteen other firms have less than one percent each. Nobody has much and nobody should have much. This is better than another aluminum plant where the new owners changed the management. The price of our shares has increased from four dollars and eighty cents to six dollars in the last year, and once it went up to ten dollars."

In companies that have no majority owner, the ownership structure creates uncertainty. The head of a 16,000-employee machine building plant in the Bryansk region says, "We lack cash. There are delays in paying wages. The state owns just over a tenth of our shares. We're looking for a foreign investor to buy it, but if we don't find an investor ourselves, the state will auction the stake and we'll lose more control. Our largest outside shareholders are a local bank and a Moscow investment fund. They don't interfere with our life and they're not going to make serious changes here."

The general director of an electric and heating utility in central Russia with 6,000 workers is afraid of the Mafia: "We depend entirely on the tariff policy of the state. We don't need an investor. We could be a great company if our customers just paid us for the services we provide. The state owns forty-nine percent of our firm through its holding company, United Energy Systems. Nobody knows what will happen to those state shares. Investors won't buy our shares without knowing what the tariffs will be. Some ask why the shares of the energy systems in some of Russia's big metropolitan centers are being traded actively on the market. The purpose of this share buying is to launder the money gained through dirty channels. The goal of this buying is to take over the energy and fuel industry, as having such control means having overall control."

The general director of a small but valuable 600-employee Moscow construction firm finds that the various shareholders' interests do not yet add up to a sense of order for him: "Our employees were too passive. They bought shares with vouchers but wouldn't use their savings, so the managers were forced to save the situation in this way. A group of officials that were involved in our former Soviet cabinet ministry formed a corporation that founded a voucher investment fund and bought fifteen percent of our shares. Actually, we are shareholders in this corporation. They are our adherents, so we have a control stake in our company together with them. The second big outside owner is from Moscow and has just over a tenth of our shares. They knew us because their affiliate leased our premises. Our relationships with them are good but very formal. Many other firms own less than one percent of our shares. We don't like it that some investment funds bought our shares and don't find some way to cooperate with us. We consider them as making wrongful claims on our profits. Three outsiders are on our board. We did everything according to the law except for cumulative voting."

The managers are desperately searching for an ownership structure that makes sense to them, provides them the capital they need to modernize, and is nonthreatening. Rank-and-file employee shareholders are the largest insider blockholders in the companies, yet they have no corporate power. Even so, the blockholder effect on governance partly explains the resistance of managers to open trading of stock.

Workers as Shareholders and Employees

Privatization of industries affected about 20 million workers, 18,000 general directors, and about 100,000 other top managers. These groups are not formally involved in a traditional labor-management relationship, in which shareholders own, managers manage, and workers work; and employees have very little of the power we have come to expect of workers who belong to formally recognized trade unions. They also have very little of the power one might expect them to demand when they own a significant amount of stock in the firm.

Workers supported privatization and a respectable number believed they influenced it. In 1992 a survey of about 5,000 rank-and-file workers in four cities—Moscow, Ekaterinburg, Voronezh, and Smolensk—found that 40 to 50 percent of skilled and unskilled workers supported the privatization program, and approval was highest among skilled workers. Almost half wanted privatization to proceed more quickly, and less than a quarter saw no need for privatization. Managers, however, supported the program at almost twice that rate, perhaps a reflection of their belief that they had the most to gain by it. There was disagreement between workers and general directors, particularly over how much influence workers had in the decision to privatize. Fewer than a tenth of the workers believed they were the primary decision makers, yet a third of unskilled workers and almost half of production workers believed they did have a great deal of influence. Most top managers, aside from the general directors, agreed with the workers. This evidence suggests that workers recognized that they did indeed have some power in the beginning stages of privatization, when they could choose the privatization option and the manner of distributing shares.

After privatization, the workers' role in the companies weakened. Employees and their trade unions were required to have one representative on the board of directors during corporatization. Many of these members were removed, ironically, after the rank-and-file employees gained almost half of the stock in their companies. Once the companies were privatized, the general directors were elected not by the workers, as they had been under Gorbachev, but by the shareholders. Since the workers were the shareholders, top management understandably moved swiftly to gain control over their votes. Insiders were represented on the board predominantly by top managers, who were dependent on the general director for their senior positions, and top managers took control of the shareholder registers. Throughout the country, general directors described for us the way they involved employees in shareholder meetings. Before a meeting, managers met with workers in the various departments and asked them to sign proxies transferring their voting rights to the managers. On average, a third of the workers in the country signed such proxies in 1995. In fact, however, the number of workers who signed over their votes to managers may have been significantly higher, for most managers refused to respond to questions about this practice. Most employees who did vote their own shares found it impossible to hide their identities, for over a quarter of the companies voted by a show of hands, and those that used paper ballots required a signature. The boss was watching.

Employee shareholders were not completely passive in the face of efforts to discourage them from exercising their rights as shareholders. In almost half of the responding companies, the managers themselves reported that fewer than a fifth of the employees gave proxies to managers. Some observers had expected the companies to set up employee stock ownership plans (on the order of American ESOPs), which would collect workers' shares under a top management trustee. Very few companies report having such trusts today, partly because managers have demonstrated that they can control employees' share voting through less formal means, and a large number of managers reported that it would be difficult to persuade the workers to set up such a trust. Theoretically, groups of workers and their trade unions could have meaningful independent power on these company boards. As large blockholders in their own right, they could nominate their own candidates and use cumulative voting to elect them. They could choose respected lawyers, public figures, or business people to represent their interests on the board. Yet we have not recorded one case in which they did so. This finding reflects the fact that Russian trade unions are heavily dominated by management; they cannot be viewed as independent organizations. In what traditional free market economy could workers in most large factories belong to trade unions, own the majority of their companies' shares, yet never elect an independent representative to the board of directors? The Russian trade unions have no tradition of independence; they have always been creatures of the companies, which in turn were once creatures of the Party and the state. Now the managers rule supreme.

The weakness of trade unions during economic reform was predestined by their past. Trade unions appeared in Russia only in the early part of this century. They were subordinated to control by the Communist Party after the Revolution. The Communists purged independent trade unionists in 1929 and eliminated any discussion of worker self-management from the operation of the factories. The unions, however, were the largest public organizations in the Soviet Union. Their job was to keep workers working and administer their welfare benefits. They helped discipline workers, collected contributions, and distributed social benefits. For 1 percent of their pay union members got access to a broad range of social, medical, cultural, and recreational benefits. They coordinated the construction and assignment of enterprise apartments and food catering in the factories. Labor-management agreements existed in many enterprises, but the union's role was mainly to specify working conditions, help resolve disputes between workers and managers, and help management rather than defend workers' rights. Throughout the Soviet period, various attempts were made to increase the unions' involvement in the enterprises. Gorbachev tried the most radical change in June 1987 with the State Enterprise Law, which determined that a general assembly of all workers was the sovereign power in the enterprise. The law was not universally implemented, and the general assemblies tended to be dominated by management. In 1989, strikes in the coal industry—which is still largely unprivatized—stimulated the development of free trade unions, and the movement has slowly spread to some other industries. In 1992 Yeltsin set up a commission consisting of representatives of the government, the trade unions, and the employers to encourage a partnership of the three parties. The government promised to soften the impact of free market reform, employers said they would reduce the impact of closures, and the unions said they would support privatization and price liberalization and refrain from strikes. The government clearly did not keep its side of the bargain. Laws to support the rights of workers as both employees and shareholders are still extremely weak.

Still, in a few cases (such as the Ordzhonikidze machine tool factory discussed earlier) employee shareholders and outside shareholders, often with the acquiescence or leadership of senior managers, have used their shareholder power to vote general directors out of their jobs. At the end of 1994, dissatisfied outsiders and insiders at the large Kuznetsk metal works, in the town of Novokuznetsk, formed an alliance. Insiders owned 47 percent of the stock, and neither outsiders nor the state held a majority. The voucher investment fund Neft Almaz Invest played a key role in the affair. The employees, the deputy general director, and outside shareholders voted the general director out of his job. A Russian paper called it the "revolt of the gray collars."

Like workers everywhere, Russian workers care most about bread-and-butter issues. Real average wages fell by almost half between 1991 and 1992, when prices were liberalized. In 1996 they were still almost 27 percent below what they were in 1992, when the economic reforms began. None of the information on wages even comes close to reflecting the incomes of citizens in the informal or underground economy, which Prime Minister Chernomyrdin estimated to account for one-quarter of the economy in August 1996. And the government statistics bureau claims that industrial enterprises are under-reporting their wages in order to escape taxes. In March 1996 the average monthly wage was 740,000 rubles, or about $152. That is about half the wage of the average Czech worker. Obviously, the average wage is not what everyone actually earns. Workers in the gas industry, for example, earned $437 a month in 1995. Late that year, workers in industry earned 111 percent of the average wage, workers in construction earned 131 percent, and workers in transportation earned 152 percent. Workers in education and health—under the control of the state—earned about 80 percent of the average wage, and workers in agriculture earned only 47 percent. The differences in wages are actually an indication that the free market is beginning to work, as the wages of employees start to follow what people are willing to pay for the goods they produce.

Wages have clearly not been closely indexed to inflation. The general directors we interviewed reported that they largely ignored collective bargaining agreements, yet they did attempt to increase wages regularly to keep pace with inflation, and sometimes to prevent conflicts with workers. Certainly, the national picture does not seem to indicate that most managers in majority worker-owned firms catered excessively to workers by wildly increasing their wages. In 1992, the consumer price inflation was 2,323 percent, while the average wage had risen only 1,245 percent at year's end. In 1993, consumer price inflation was 844 percent, while the average industrial wage had risen 775 percent at year's end. (See Table 2.) Yet managers in many companies reported that they continued to support both the ownership and the expenses of extensive social services for employees, such as apartments, kindergartens, day-care centers, vacation retreats, and cultural, medical, and sports centers. Michael Andrianov, manager of a building materials plant in Krasnoyarsk, described how he managed compensation in 1994: "Our average pay is equal to about twenty-five dollars a week. We increased it four times this year. When the minimum wage is increased by the government, we raise our wages proportionately. And sometimes we feel that employees become concerned about the value of their wages after prices go up. Once, to prevent conflicts with the workers, we increased wages two months running, though we hadn't really planned to. Payroll accounts for twenty-two percent of our costs. But we have social programs for employees that account for about twenty-five percent of our costs."

The picture of what has happened to real wages does not accurately reflect the actual spending power of Russians. For example, it would be wrong to assume that because the output of privatized factories declined about 50 percent and real wages have fallen, living standards have simply been dropping. (See the real income index in Table 2.) The gray economy is enormous. To offset this loss, Russians are moonlighting in part-time jobs and engaging in various small business ventures on the side. Some have dividend income from shares of stock. Whereas wages made up 60 percent of household income in 1992, they made up only 40 percent of household income in 1995. Surveys of household expenditures by Goskomstat found that household consumption actually rose by about 8 percent between 1993 and 1994, and a real expenditure index of what Russians actually spend indicates quite clearly that spending has gone down less than wages.

The hardest hit are the pensioners, who carry the disadvantage of falling real wages with them into retirement, and some pensioners find it difficult to supplement their income. In January 1996, the average pension was 113,250 rubles a month—about $50. Like the average wage, the average pension varies from industry to industry, and in May 1996 President Yeltsin signed a bill to increase the minimum pension to $14 a month. To make matters worse, a large proportion of the country's 36 million pensioners are not paid their pensions on time; in January 1996 pensions were paid on time in only fifty of Russia's eighty-nine regions. In 1995 real average pensions were 15 percent lower than they had been in 1994.

In 1995, one in ten employees in a privatized firm is officially employed but on temporary furlough, receiving less than full pay. Almost a third of such people are getting no pay at all, and over half are getting 40 percent of their usual pay. And as we mentioned earlier, it has become common for firms simply not to pay their workers. Large and mid-sized enterprises began to run short of cash to operate as inflation rose during the first years of market reform. Many consumers and industrial customers lack the cash to pay for products, and many enterprises continue to "sell" their products without receiving payment. The government has been running low on funds because of low tax receipts and low privatization revenues, and it stopped paying its bills in a timely fashion. This has been called the "mutual nonpayment problem." (See Table 2 on trends in real overdue wages and real interenterprise arrears.)

Confronted with this situation, managers asked workers to come to work and consider their pay as "owed" to them. One coffin factory actually sent workers home with coffins so that they could sell them for their wages. By 1996 this problem had reached overwhelming proportions. The State Statistics Committee reported that total un-paid wages owed to transportation, agricultural, and industrial workers amounted to $4.5 billion. The amount had doubled in the first eight months of 1995. Wages go unpaid most often in those industrial sectors where wages are already low. According to the government's figures, by the third quarter of 1995 about a third of all enterprises owed wages to their employees. In our 1996 survey, the companies reported that they owed their workers on average 7 percent of their annualized sales.

By April 1996, enterprises' overdue debts to the government bud-get and to one another came to just over 14 percent of the entire gross domestic product of Russia, the highest figure in eighteen months. The wage arrears of privatized companies increased by 12 percent. The most indebted sectors are defense, energy, and machine building.

Nonpayment of wages was the first labor issue to break on the national scene. One of our research visits to a factory manager was interrupted by an elderly woman who was distraught because she needed 5,000 rubles (about $1) for medicine for her son; she had not been paid in months. The manager told her there was no money and sent her away. In 1995 and 1996, news reports of worker protests and conflicts with managers poured in from all over the country. The newspaper *Trud* (Labor) reported that 12 million workers—every sixth worker—had not been paid on time and a third of them had not been paid for two months. At the beginning of 1996, Yeltsin fired a number of senior government officials to demonstrate to the voters in the upcoming presidential election that his government would not tolerate nonpayment of wages. Teachers and other workers in the public sector and in state-owned enterprises were staging more and more troublesome strikes and protest demonstrations, and in March the government released almost $2 billion to pay their back wages. The president publicly criticized certain general directors for paying themselves high salaries while they withheld workers' wages, and fired several governors whom he accused of tolerating high rates of nonpayment of wages in their provinces. The situation with em-ployee benefits was not much better. (See Table 10 on social services provided to employees.) The companies were transferring their kin-dergartens, day-care centers, and health-care facilities to the munici-palities. This move may have been necessary to restructure the enterprises as profit-making companies, but it was hard on workers. Workers' apartments were being sold to them, and companies started charging fees for many services that used to be free.

One slightly brighter spot in this picture was the unemployment rate: it was only about 8 percent in 1995, despite the fact that production had dropped by half since 1991. Nevertheless, the average enterprise fired about a quarter of its workers during this period, and the unemployment figures do not include the "hidden unemployed"—people who remain in their company's records but are working reduced hours or are on unpaid leave. Observers were predicting that official unemployment would rise to a tenth of the population by 1997; unofficial unemployment would of course be higher. Since most enterprises offer more extensive social benefits to employees than the government does, the reluctance to downsize has been bad for the enterprises' efficiency and for the values of workers' shares, but good in the narrow sense of allowing employees to adjust slowly to the restructuring of the economy. If they stay with the factory, workers continue to get housing, health care, day care, and other benefits. The unemployment benefit is very low, and inflation has driven it lower. Fewer than 5 percent of laid-off workers receive retraining.

An analysis of news reports of worker action over unpaid wages in 1995 and 1996 suggests that trade unions mainly organized protests against the central and regional governments, but did not seek to disrupt production in the workplaces. They cannot sue for back pay. And short of giving subsidies to the private corporations, there was little the government could do about the unpaid wages of employees who did not work in the public sector.

Lenin once said that the trade unions were to serve as "transmission belts from the Communist Party to the masses." If one substitutes "enterprises" for "Communist Party" and "employees" for "masses," Lenin's pronouncement accurately describes the views expressed by several hundred general directors we interviewed. Employees still view trade unions as adjuncts of management or distributors of social wealth (apartments, consumer goods, foodstuffs) and only secondarily as representatives of their interests. Employers still do not consider trade unions equal partners in the negotiating process, or as organizations able to uphold somebody's interests. A nationwide survey of 2,000 Russians revealed that less than a fifth of trade union members said they trusted national trade union leaders, and half believed that the leaders did little or nothing to help them. A recent study by Russia's International Confederation of Free Trade Unions found that trade unions formally existed in only one of ten enterprises. One story of an abolished union was told by Aleksei Bondarenko, manager of an equipment plant in Krasnoyarsk: "I had a lot of trouble with our labor union. Instead of coming and discussing problems with me, they go to the workers and badmouth me. Then they ask me to do everything for them. They have their car, their office here, and I even collected employees' dues for them. And I decided it was too much for people who didn't want to collaborate and told them to collect their money themselves. They did that for six months and then wrote articles in the newspapers saying I ask too much of them. After that we abolished the union, since their only job was to do nothing and criticize me. They had no constructive ideas. We provide our employees with various services. We sell them food and consumer goods at discount. We finance the hospital, housing, and schools. We have property in the Crimea for their vacations. We do everything—we have pigs and we grow mushrooms for them. I can't feel good if all the children in town stare at me because I'm not paying their parents' wages."

The manager of a machine building plant in the Pskov region decided to get rid of the union by creating one. "The trade union here was in opposition to us. So we organized a company trade union. We gave them millions of rubles for a start and now we wait and watch."

Top managers of privatized enterprises speak with ease of their employees' lack of influence on virtually every issue. A group of deputy directors of a fertilizer plant in northern Russia spoke bluntly: "The general director conducted privatization, and even we know nothing about it. We raise our employees' wages after neighboring enterprises raise theirs, so we won't lose our employees. The decisions are made by the general director. In a way the employees do influence the process, because the general director knows that if he doesn't raise wages this month, employees will leave the plant."

A manager in a chemical plant with 1,800 employees in Novosibirsk describes her approach to negotiation: "I don't think the employees influence me very much on matters of wages and working conditions. Two or three times a month we raise wages [to offset inflation]. The compensation system is systemless. I'm joking."

The general director of a 7,000-employee steel plant describes how employment is expected to fall: "We have reduced employment every year since 1991. In 1991 we had ten thousand employees, in 1992 we had eighty-five hundred, and in 1993 we have seven thousand. But the reduction was not proportional to the decline in our output. Our output decreases more slowly. We could fire five hundred people right now. Our output will decline further. We'll fire a lot of employees, and we're waiting for that now. The labor union has no influence over the workers. The general director and managers run this factory."

The head of a road-building company in Tver with 3,500 employees is trying to kill unions with employee ownership. "We don't have any common trade union for the whole enterprise. Each department has a board of shareholders, as we call it. It fulfills the mixed function of the trade union and the shareholders' meeting."

Only one general director, a woman who ran a textile factory, spoke respectfully of trade unions. Her analysis illustrates the difficult position of Russian workers in inefficient and unproductive companies. "We make clothing. We have nine hundred employees. If we had modern equipment, we would need only twenty to a hundred employees. We built a large apartment building for our employees this year because we needed the support of the most skilled workers. Trade unions are a social part of the economy. They should become independent structures. They shouldn't be inside enterprises. They must be objective structures with the duty to defend employees."

This picture of worker passivity must be balanced by the fact that strikes have increased. In the first nine months of 1995, the number of work days lost to strikes was nine times what it had been the previous year. But during that period 95 percent of the strikes, 55 percent of the strikers, and 31 percent of the days lost to strikes have been in public sector education, where unpaid wages are a most serious problem. Industry, which most closely tracks the sector of privatized large and mid-sized firms, accounts for 3 percent of strikes, 38 percent of strikers, and 57 percent of days lost to strikes. So, at least, it appears; but it is not yet possible to differentiate with confidence the teachers and miners, who strike frequently and are not privatized, from workers in fully privatized firms. Strike activity seems to increase when the problem of unpaid wages plagues a particular sector of the economy. Nevertheless, strikes appear mainly in the state sector; industrial action is still much rarer in Russia than in Western Europe and the United States.

Safety is another aspect of industrial life that is deteriorating. The accident rate has increased as equipment deteriorates and enterprises cut spending on labor safety by almost two-thirds. One worker in 14,000 is killed on the job in the United States; in Russia the figure is one worker in 9,000.

In sum, neither the workers nor their unions have much power after privatization.

The Mafia as a Corporate Power

Is the Russian Mafia the "gray eminence" behind most or all large and mid-sized privatized companies? Several estimates of the Russian Mafia's influence have been published, but their definition of "control" is vague. After August 1991, the police charged that organized crime controlled banks, stock exchanges, hotels, and commercial enterprises in most Russian cities. There was a report in 1993 that every one of the thousands of kiosks in Moscow pays protection money, some 5 to 10 percent of earnings. The Russian government's Analytic Center for Social and Economic Policies reported on January 17, 1994, that gangs owned or controlled about 40,000 businesses, including 2,000 in the state sector. On February 19, 1994, the *Economist* quoted this report to the effect that three-quarters of private enterprises are forced to pay 10 to 20 percent of their earnings to criminal gangs, and that 150 such gangs control some 40,000 private and state-run companies and most of the country's 1,800 commercial banks. In 1995 the head of the Academy of Sciences' Institute of Sociology said that the government believed that "criminal structures in the state now control over 50 percent of all economic entities." The institute reported that 40 percent of all entrepreneurs and 66 percent of all commercial structures were then involved in criminal relations, and that the Mafia had established control over 35,000 economic entities, including 400 banks, 47 currency exchanges, and 1,500 enterprises in the state sector. Quoting calculations by the Academy of Sciences' Analytic Center, the report states that the practice of exacting tribute from commercial structures in the form of stock had transferred 35 percent of all capital and 80 percent of all voting shares into the hands of criminals. The Russian Mafia exports its capital to foreign bank accounts and then reintroduces it into the country as foreign investments in the names of foreign companies. Others have claimed that the former Communist Party elite and organized criminal groups have purchased a majority of state assets through the privatization program.

Any credible analysis of power and governance in Russian firms must deal seriously with these estimates and with the fact that, despite a recent drop in the number of crimes reported, the crime rates in Russia have risen dramatically since 1991. The Mafia threat cannot be dismissed. To what extent do these figures refer to the 17,937 mid-sized and large privatized enterprises that are at the center of the Russian economy?

The Mafia had deep roots in the Soviet Union before privatization. Mafia influence is most evident in the small business sector. Most larger companies were not even privatized when these estimates were made. With the exception of the expensive commodity industries, such as metals and oil, where corruption began before privatization, there is little hard evidence that the Mafia owns these companies, although they may be targets of protection rackets and other crimes. (Table 1 shows the development of new small businesses, new privatized small businesses, and the larger privatized corporations. It must be read closely to interpret these various Mafia estimates.)

When the 1991 estimate of widespread criminal influence in commercial businesses—those not owned by the state—appeared, the privatization of mid-sized and large enterprises had not even begun. This estimate specifically referred to new businesses and places where criminal influence was widespread, such as small retail businesses and hotels. The main new commercial structures were the small cooperative banks and restaurants started during the Gorbachev era. This estimate then applies primarily to smaller enterprises, and it appeared at a moment when elements in the Academy of Sciences sympathetic to the old Communist order were regularly issuing press releases condemning privatization. Under the Soviet state all profit making was "profiteering." Making a profit was immoral and illegal, and business people were suspect simply because they were engaging in business free of state control.

The 1994 estimate of 40,000 businesses under criminal control and 2,000 in the state sector must be examined carefully. By January 1994 about 89,000 enterprises had been privatized. More than 90 percent of them were small retail shops. More than half of all mid-sized and large enterprises had not been privatized by late 1993, when this estimate was prepared. The "40,000 businesses" referred to in 1994 were four times the number of mid-sized and large enterprises that were privatized at that time and twice the number of large enterprises in existence. Moreover, our surveys, reports streaming into the privatization ministry from all regions, and press reports indicated that a majority of the shares went to employees initially. If the 40,000 firms cited included most or all of the larger firms that had been privatized, organized crime would have had to take over the entire privatization process in eighty-nine regions; they had to have forced employees to sign their names to documents declaring a preference for majority employee ownership and subscribing for shares in thousands of enterprises with the collusion of Privatization Ministry bureaucrats in all of those regions—all in about eleven months. Clearly the 1994 estimate must refer mainly to small enterprises, and one must pay attention to the actual assertions in the government report cited by the *Economist* that criminal elements "controlled" these businesses and were demanding payments. If these estimates are correct, the reasonable assumption is that the "criminal control" took the form of the gangs' well-documented and widely reported practice of demanding protection money from start-up small businesses and recently privatized small shops. No doubt this number included some—whether modest or extensive we do not know—incursion into larger newly privatized enterprises. Many observers view this practice as a private attempt to offer protection that the police could not provide in a transitional period.

In 1994, when 2,000 state-owned enterprises were reported to be under Mafia control—whatever that means—more than 10,000 large and many thousands of smaller enterprises were still owned by the state. We cannot tell whether the 2,000 figure refers to the large companies—a fifth of all large businesses—or mainly to smaller firms, or to both. Even if the estimate is correct, the numbers do not bear out the charge that the entire privatization process was criminalized.

The 1995 report by the prestigious Institute of Sociology, however, is very specific and has serious implications. When it estimates that 40 percent of all entrepreneurs are under Mafia control, it is not referring to large privatized firms; the 66 percent of all commercial structures it estimates to be controlled by the Mafia clearly do include larger privatized firms. The authors of the report calculate that by demanding or accepting shares of stock as tribute and securing seats for their representatives on boards of directors, criminals have gained control of 80 percent of all stock and 30 percent of capital. But they stress that their conclusions are based on "estimates," not cold facts and not research.

Steven Handelman, the former chief of the *Toronto Star*'s Moscow bureau and the author of *Comrade Criminal,* has carefully investigated this situation. He points out that according to many serious studies, an extensive network of criminal gangs has grown up in the Soviet Union. The Vorovskoi Mir (Thieves' Community) reportedly grew up inside Soviet prison camps, which he calls their "university and parliament." In the later years of the Soviet system, he reports, some criminal leaders used the camps as bases for black market operations. When criminals interned in the Siberian camps were released, many reportedly settled in nearby towns. Under the strict state economic control of the Soviet system, black marketeers were one of the few nongovernmental groups capable of circulating goods and services freely. Their smuggling and trading introduced some flexibility into the Soviet industrial machine and had the tacit approval of some authorities. Other studies support the contention that enterprise directors did turn to the criminals to arrange access to scarce machinery and other resources.

In December 1991, the Vorovskoi Mir met at Vedentsovo, outside Moscow, to discuss their response to the economic transition. The group's trading activities at that time—they dealt mainly in spare parts, autos, caviar, and gems—were estimated to account for about $1.3 billion, or 15 percent of the volume of goods and services at the end of 1991.

To assess the role of the Mafia (also known as the Organizatsiya) one needs to distinguish between criminals outside the Soviet system, who were stealing, and citizens inside the Soviet system, who were corrupt or were taking advantage of a lack of clear rules. Handelman writes that as the Soviet Union collapsed, many officials tried to walk away with property. They found themselves guardians of a vast patrimony of buildings, factories, tanks, missiles, hotels, ships, and other products of the Soviet industrial state. Under Soviet management, these products had no intrinsic price, so it was fairly easy to enter all kinds of sweetheart transactions into the account books of the enterprises. Enormous amounts of Communist Party money were purloined and transferred to the control of commercial trading houses and banks. Parts of the intelligence community are reported to have invested millions in new commercial structures and banks. When the reform government relaxed export controls in 1993, many firms smuggled goods abroad and accumulated foreign currency. According to one report, 30 percent of the gold produced in one city evaded tax authorities and surfaced in world markets. General directors of large privatized factories started their own daughter companies and joint ventures, to which they transferred equipment or sold goods at low prices. Handelman found a case in which the managers of military-industrial enterprises in central Russia tried to smuggle twelve tons of copper across the border in a truck loaded with onions.

As communism was supposedly collapsing, existing criminal organizations, dishonest bureaucrats, and entrepreneurs all had meaningful incentives to pursue profitable schemes, legal, illegal, and borderline. Some commercial firms and citizens who own shares in privatized enterprises may have used money generated by such questionable activities to buy shares in companies. These commercial firms' capital had to come from somewhere, and it is likely that the criminal element, too, discovered that one could buy a 10,000-ruble voucher for 3,000 rubles and then exchange it for 10,000 rubles of stock in an oil company, say.

Is there specific evidence linking criminal elements or corrupt members of the *nomenklatura* to large and mid-sized privatized corporations? The report of the Academy of Sciences' Institute of Sociology refers to a finding by the Interior Ministry that 1,500 criminal associations have divided the country into spheres of influence, and that the sphere of commercial activity is expanding beyond small-time racketeering. "One can see a gradual transition from small-scale to larger operations. Recently criminal structures have gotten involved in some very remunerative spheres of legitimate business: finance, export-import operations in the fuel and power complex, etc." The Interior Ministry identified metals, weapons, and oil as the commodities most likely to involve larger privatized firms. A more recent report by the ministry specifies 49 criminal gangs operating in Moscow, with 4,000 members, 257 bosses, and 7 kingpins; with money invested in banking and financial structures they have opened stores, restaurants, casinos, and automotive service enterprises. Both reports point toward gradual infiltration of large companies but not yet domination of them. Several of the top 200 companies are reported to rely on criminal elements to prevent the buying of their shares. Several brokers who bought the shares of one firm were killed. In 1995 the Russian Business Roundtable lost nine of its thirty top officials to assassins. Forty-five business people were assassinated from 1993 to 1996.

Can it be true that 80 percent of corporate shares and 30 percent of capital are controlled by criminals? Not likely. Criminal elements are probably influential chiefly in three areas: first, smaller privatized businesses and start-up firms, where a lot of cash changes hands and a small amount of effort in the area of loan sharking and protection can lead to easy profit with little overhead; second, smuggling and transportation of valuable commodities, such as fuels and metals, and wholesale and retail outlets where the products can quickly be turned into cash; and third, some proportion of very profitable large enterprises that produce such commodities or have access to them. But the available evidence is simply insufficient to substantiate the assignment of 30 percent or 80 percent or any other figure to this trend.

It would be bad Mafia business for the figure to be very large, because many big privatized firms are unprofitable, and even organized crime wants a risk-adjusted return. It is hard to imagine why organized crime would want to control weak firms that are cutting employees, reducing capacity, confronting serious cash-flow problems, and struggling to supply the kindergartens, housing, and hospitals their employees need. Protection money and access to an enterprise's commodities may be all that is necessary to turn contact with the enterprise into less complicated profit. It may be true, as police reports indicate, that organized criminals want to move their money into legitimate businesses and to invest in undervalued Russian stocks, but the privatization program's strong emphasis on insider ownership and control has made entry to the larger enterprises costly. Indeed, management's maneuvers to keep out outside investors may have served to keep out organized crime in the early stages.

Whatever the current extent of the Mafia's infiltration of mid-sized and large privatized firms, organized crime does pose an extremely serious threat to such companies. As governance replaces government, the need for strong regulation of securities markets will continue, for without full disclosure of the ownership and financial condition of the country's new corporations, outsiders are unlikely to invest in them. Yet those outsiders, armed with cash and all that information, may well be members of the Mafia. In 1996 the president of the Russian Commodities Exchange, who also heads Russia's union of stock exchanges, said that "criminal organizations have acquired share portfolios." Another officer of the stock market association adds, "Some forces want to reshape the capital markets by intimidation so things remain in a state of lawlessness and fraud. We demand measures for the protection of Russia's capital markets." The Mafia may sink its roots as deep in Russia as it has done in Sicily, or yesterday's scam artists may seek to transform themselves into legitimate business people. The Mafia is growing. But the influence that has been ascribed to it is far in excess of the hard evidence. At a recent meeting organized by Britain's National Criminal Intelligence Service, Valery Serebryakov of Russia's Chief Directorate for Organized Crime said that extortion and money laundering still figure prominently among the Mafia's activities. Louis J. Freeh, director of the FBI, has said that Russian criminals are involved in money laundering, embezzlement, extortion, murder, drug trafficking, prostitution, and manipulation of banks. And John M. Deutch, director of central intelligence, cited the Yeltsin administration's "claim that some 70 to 80 percent of private businesses are paying extortion fees worth 10 to 20 percent of total retail sales."

As Russia negotiates the transition from one economic system to another, it needs to take a more determined and stricter approach to corporate governance. Shareholders need firmer and clearer control over corporations in Russia than they do elsewhere because many Russian managers still consider themselves to have a right to complete control. Both the creation and enforcement of investor rights and the concentration of large ownership stakes will play roles in determining Russia's ultimate system of corporate governance and the size of its public capital markets. When Crystia Freeland, Moscow bureau chief of the *Financial Times,* investigated a fight between outside shareholders and Soviet-era managers at the huge Kuznetsk steel mill in the Siberian town of Novokuznetsk in 1996, she concluded that the struggle was really over control of the Russian economy: "It is the showdowns on the factory floor that are likely to determine the role of private ownership in Russia for decades to come." As she tells the story, the former general director had allied himself with the outside shareholders, led by the top manager of Hermes-Metal-Invest, a local investment fund that owned 10 percent of the shares. The old general director entered the offices of the current director accompanied by armed guards to enforce a court ruling that the post of top manager was really his. The next day the other general director entered with a bigger contingent of local policemen and ejected the old director, who meanwhile had acquired authority to sign checks drawn on the firm's bank accounts. The outside shareholders accused the current general director and a local official of siphoning profits from lucrative metals exports, and they formed an alliance with a popular local Communist politician. The current director outlined his strategy for resolving the conflict: he wanted 10 percent of the plant to revert to state ownership so that the state would guarantee its operations. "Our problems will be the government's problems and our happiness should be the government's happiness. . . . A factory of this importance cannot simply be sold off with an auctioneer's hammer." Just for good measure, he announced that the plant would start to buy back its own shares. To ensure the success of this plan, he would penalize factory workers who sold their shares to outside investors: they would be deprived of the subsidized cars, housing, holiday packages, and other benefits available to loyal employees. The head of the local investment fund gave his opinion: "They are almost bankrupt but at the same time they are buying back their own shares. That's not right and it's not legal." Other local businessmen viewed the situation as the struggle of a corrupt quasi-feudal elite willing to do anything to retain economic and political power.

As shareholder meetings got under way in the spring of 1996, the new corporate law and the increased emphasis on informing shareholders of their rights were slowly raising public awareness of the governance issue. Shareholders' challenges to the managers and boards of directors of other large companies were less dramatic than the performance in Novokuznetsk, but they were no less serious.

4

Restructuring

The ultimate goal of the privatization program, after ownership rights in enterprises were redistributed from the state to citizens, was to improve the performance of the new private corporations. The designers of privatization expected that the withdrawal of government control would give citizen owners an economic incentive to effect the changes necessary to make their enterprises profitable. Unfortunately, the financial condition of the newly privatized companies and the forces of the world market have conspired to make the restructuring process far more complex than they anticipated.

Russia's managers are typically men and women (a very few women) of unusual technical competence. The average age of general directors was 50 at the time their firms were privatized, and only a quarter were under the age of 45. These managers came up through a system in which the state handled all allocation and distribution of products, transportation, and the hiring and firing of managers; the state appropriated the money generated by the firm, allocated money for the firm's operations, and set its production targets. There was no market research or advertising or pricing; there were no shareholders, no boards of directors, no independent public accountants, no stock markets, no private bank loans, no investment bankers. Soviet citizens were the state's resources; enterprises were mechanisms to transfer wealth from citizens to the state.

In 1992, as managers struggled with the unaccustomed tasks of finding their own suppliers, pricing and marketing their products, finding customers, and arranging deliveries, the Russian government's subsidies to enterprises accounted for almost a third of the gross domestic product. The World Bank estimated that in 1992 direct government subsidies to enterprises and Central Bank credits to commercial banks, which ended up as cheap enterprise loans, together accounted for about 32 percent of the gross domestic product. Most of the subsidies went to the agricultural and coal sectors; the rest went to enterprises in machine building, energy, food processing, and defense conversion.

The corporations will need management leaders who have the skills and understanding to make radical changes; then they will need the capital necessary to buy equipment, refurbish factories, develop marketing networks, do research, and so forth. Therefore, not all restructuring activities are equal. Setting up a marketing department or working on a new product may sound like restructuring, but these activities may simply be decoration if radical changes in management and a far-reaching modernization of the companies are not forthcoming. The restructuring of a corporation that was formerly controlled by a ministry in Moscow involves more than cosmetic changes or general plans. The principal ingredients of restructuring are human capital and investment capital. All other elements of restructuring are secondary to leadership and capital.

Most managers implemented spotty and cosmetic changes in their enterprises and have been unable to secure the capital to modernize. They cut their operations and employment and then relied on government subsidies, loans, and delays in paying their bills to survive. The government's policies in regard to creating a "hard budget constraint"—that is, controlling subsidies so the firms would truly be at the mercy of the market—were inconsistent in 1993 and 1994. In 1995 the government did have a consistent economic reform policy, but most enterprises continued to avoid restructuring. If they are to survive, they must confront strategic investors, takeovers, financial-industrial groups, banks, mutual funds, and the emerging Russian stock market. Each of these confrontations promises to restructure radically both leadership and capital in privatized enterprises and perhaps to transform some Russian corporations into powerful companies.

What Is True Restructuring?

To restructure a company is to introduce all the management skills
and investment capital necessary to enable it to design and sell at a
profit the products and services that customers want. True restructuring will obviate the need for further government assistance and
allow continued development of the firm and its workforce and community. The experience of KamAZ, Russia's largest producer of
trucks, is a case in point.

KamAZ, in the Tatar Republic, employs 117,000 people and turns
out 120,000 vehicles a year. In addition to trucks, it produces Oka
passenger cars, engines, and spare parts. It is the fifty-fourth largest
company in Russia by current market value (Table 9). In 1994 it
produced only about a quarter of its annual capacity, and the U.S.
firm of Kolberg Kravis & Roberts (KKR) began working with the
company to restructure it. The daily newspaper *Kommersant* announced the deal in 1995. KKR is known for its $31.4 billion lever-
aged buyout of RJR Nabisco; over the years it has purchased fifty
firms for $82 billion, mounting some of the largest buyouts and re-
structurings in the world. The goal of the deal was to make KamAZ
the world's largest truck producer, but the company is currently in
financial crisis.

KamAZ's general director, Nikolai Bekh, first began looking for
investors in 1991. When Yury Borisov, the company's vice president,
sent a volley of investment projects to major global banks, there were
no takers. Then in 1992 fire destroyed the company's engine factory.
KamAZ desperately needed cash to buy equipment, a thorough revision of its product line to increase customer demand, and marketing
advice to develop and sell its products. In 1994 KKR contracted with
KamAZ to line up $3.5 billion in investments over seven years.

Employees and managers reportedly own about 20 percent of
KamAZ's stock, which was trading at $2 to $3 a share in the fall
of 1995. If the deal goes as planned, at the end of seven years the
KKR-controlled KamAZ International Management Corporation will
own a majority of KamAZ's shares and control its board of directors.
Both KKR and KamAZ's management expect the price of the shares
on international markets to increase twentyfold. While the percentage of shares owned by KamAZ's managers and employees will decrease, the value of their shares should skyrocket. KKR said that
they "believe in owner-managers as the key links in effective management." Both the government of the Tatar Republic and the central

government of Russia will have an incentive to cooperate because together they retain about 15 percent of KamAZ's stock.

KKR planned to bring a large amount of capital along with governance. KamAZ's top management undertook a calculated risk. They did not have the necessary capital, management skills, or world contacts to change their firm overnight, so they sacrificed complete control of the firm in exchange for capital and expertise.

If the plan succeeds, the management and owners of KamAZ will own less than 50 percent of a more valuable and profitable company rather than a larger percentage of a firm that is declining in value. Yury Borisov found this trade-off was difficult to make. At first he objected to KKR's conditions. How could he agree to grant KKR working control of the firm, assign KKR seats on the board of directors, push a radical restructuring of the firm's products and markets, and concentrate unswervingly on profit? "We accepted the last condition immediately," he reported, "but we rejected the others because they did not agree with the Russian mentality." Ultimately, however, KamAZ's management tacitly agreed to the other conditions.

During 1995 KKR worked with KamAZ's general director, Nikolai Bekh, on restructuring $300 to $400 million of bank debt and helped recruit an international team of consultants, including experts from Deloitte & Touche and Cummins Engine to help KamAZ with its restructuring. The top managers realize that the state will no longer distribute their products and are beginning to consider how to use their 200 automobile centers inside and outside Russia. KamAZ's trucks will have the highly regarded Cummins engines, transmissions from the German firm ZF, rear ends from Rockwell International, and driver's cabs made in collaboration with DAF. The company plans to issue additional shares to the European Bank for Reconstruction and Development in return for $100 million to expand its production. KamAZ's success, if it comes, will have a ripple effect throughout the Russian metals sector. It will be closely watched.

Most restructuring is likely to be at least as dramatic as KamAZ's. Current Russian managers may not have the heart for such far-reaching changes, and it can be difficult to distinguish between restructuring and a spontaneous sprinkling of ideas and changes throughout the privatized enterprise. Radical restructuring involves serious changes in four areas: management and control, organization of the business, capital, and the social services the enterprise provides for employees. But again, management leadership and modernization through capital investment are the critical ingredients.

The Companies' Initial Responses, 1993 and 1994

In 1993, as the country moved rapidly to privatize companies, the state's role did not disappear. Now began a period of governments split between reformers and officials more interested in helping companies. Gaidar was fired as acting prime minister on December 12, 1992. On December 14, Viktor Chernomyrdin, a former minister for the gas industry and manager of a state-owned enterprise himself, was appointed prime minister with the strong support of industrial managers. Chubais remained deputy prime minister for privatization and the liberal economist Boris Fedorov was appointed minister of finance and deputy prime minister. He tried to bring government subsidies of all kinds under control. Subsidies dropped dramatically but still accounted for about a tenth of gross domestic product, and there is evidence that regional governments dramatically increased their subsidies to enterprises. Because half the subsidies were concentrated in only 2 percent of the firms, enterprises' situations varied. Some got huge subsidies, some got very little, and many got nothing. When an enterprise applied to the government for aid, it did not have to say whether it was privatized or not. The reform wing of the government wanted to cut subsidies more deeply, but conservatives, pointing out that Russia was privatizing its firms in the midst of an economic collapse that weakened their ability to produce, often won this argument in practice.

In the face of cutbacks in government aid and a shortage of customers able to buy their products, the enterprises' primary tactic was to cut both workforce and production. They shrank the firm to give it a chance to survive. Most of the managers we talked with expected the government to continue to assist their firms after they were privately owned, in a kind of communist capitalism. They privatized, though they were not happy with all the details, and then waited to see what would happen. From 1991 to the end of 1993, industrial production fell by about 40 percent. Many managers hoped for a change in government policy—or in the government itself—so that an influx of government aid would reverse their companies' decline. Just the same, according to the former minister of finance Boris Fedorov, so many parts of the government were issuing loans to industries during those years that it was impossible for his ministry to know the total amount. The Central Bank, headed by the conservative Viktor Gerashchenko, who answered directly to the increasingly antireform Supreme Soviet with its big industrial lobby, just kept printing money and shoveling it into commercial banks, which in turn loaned it to factories at a profit but at negative interest rates. The loans were tantamount to subsidies. By the end of 1993, the economy began to feel the effect of all these subsidies. The value of everything produced in the country again declined by about a tenth, electricity production continued to fall, inflation dropped but it was still just shy of 1,000 percent, and the budget deficit was very high, at almost a tenth of domestic production. Workers' wages rose but never enough to match the inflation rate, and unemployment was rising (see Table 2).

In October 1993, just ten months after voucher privatization began, the World Bank investigated newly privatized Russian corporations in the regions of Moscow and Vladimir to see whether they were restructuring. The managers reported that their orders from the government were dropping and that they were having a very hard time. About a third of the managers had lined up work for more than six months, but most of the others had work for less than three months, some for less than a month. The companies that produced consumer goods were doing better than the firms in heavy industry. Still, most factories were running short of cash, the prices of raw materials were rising, and as the companies increased prices to compensate for their rising costs, they found their orders falling. Just over a third of the enterprises did not have enough cash to meet their bills for raw materials and overhead or to pay salaries and wages, interest on their loans, and taxes. Many firms were unable to collect payment for goods and services delivered to customers. Firms simply stopped paying their taxes, in effect forcing a new kind of subsidy on the government.

In response to this situation, many corporations reported that they were taking out short-term bank loans, tightening up on slow-paying customers, and demanding partial payment before delivery. They were making little effort to cut costs. One reason may be that many firms had little competition. But managers were putting all their efforts into surviving from day to day. The enterprises had cut about a tenth of their workforce from 1992 to 1993. Some firms had transferred some of the extensive social services they provide their employees to the municipalities, but many continued to cover most of these expenses. About half the firms had introduced some new products. Just over half changed the way they paid employees by linking pay to performance and creating wage differentials between skilled and unskilled workers. About two-thirds began to rely on private firms rather than the government as their main customers. The managers were still hoping to keep their private companies solvent with money and orders from the government. They were making adjustments to survive, not thoroughgoing revisions. Our extensive interviews with managers in thirty-two Russian regions in 1993 uncovered similar trends.

Economists point out that managers will not change their ways radically if they feel no hard budget constraint: they will have no incentive to restructure if the government has not set a tough limit on the aid it will give. If the government is willing to bail out weak companies, why should their managers make difficult changes? There were glimmers of changes in most enterprises in 1993, but they did not amount to extensive restructuring. While the lack of a hard budget constraint throughout much of 1993 may partially explain the failure to make real changes, it is possible that managers might not have been sure how to go about restructuring their firms even if state aid had been cut off entirely. The managers had a totally new economic situation thrust upon them practically overnight. Their customers were running out of money, inflation was running wild, and the prices of raw materials shot through the roof. Many managers put off efforts to restructure in the hope that the political situation would change and their subsidies would be restored.

Our conversations with general directors at the end of 1993 reveal their strategies. The director of a large industrial plant in the city of Cherepovets said, "Our government predicted a threefold increase in prices and in reality it was many times more than that. So the government has to help the corporations, either by giving us subsidized loans or by passing a law to decree that our assets are worth more. Privatized enterprises are agents of the government in the various regions of Russia, but if the government won't support them, they'll become enemies of the government. What are my plans for the future? If Gaidar or Fedorov refuses to support this enterprise, we'll have no way out. Our plant is the biggest of its kind in the world. It's a monster."

The manager of a textile plant with 3,000 employees in the Krasnoyarsk region spoke of the subsidies he was getting. "We received one long-term loan at eighty percent interest from a government source. The regional government got subsidies and distributed them to the most reliable enterprises. Usually we get loans from commercial banks. The last interest rate was a hundred and eighty percent. I hear it's now two hundred and fifty percent." The manager was speaking in November 1993, when the annual inflation rate was 844 percent. The "loan" was essentially a gift. Throughout 1993, the reformers in the government tried to cut some subsidies, while they were prevented from touching others. But the enterprise managers wanted a clear and strong system of government support.

At the end of 1993, it seemed to many managers that their dreams of more government aid were about to come true. The splits in the government were becoming increasingly evident. On the one hand, Yeltsin brought Yegor Gaidar back into the government as deputy prime minister and minister of the economy in September 1993. The Supreme Soviet adopted a budget that would have led to a deficit estimated at a quarter of the gross domestic product. Fedorov abolished all subsidized loans in September. Yeltsin moved to dissolve the conservative Congress of People's Deputies and the Supreme Soviet, which had slowed his economic reforms and now firmly opposed them. On October 3–4, the speaker of the Supreme Soviet, Ruslan Khasbulatov, and Vice President Aleksandr Rutskoi led an armed uprising. Yeltsin ordered it put down by force and then called parliamentary elections and a referendum on a new constitution. A brief spurt of reform action took place between Yeltsin's victory over his opponents and the election. In November, the real interest rate on loans was positive—that is, greater than the inflation rate—for the first time since the beginning of economic reform. Fedorov liberalized more food prices and got the government out of the business of buying food. But the reformers failed again to get the free-spending Gerashchenko fired as head of the Central Bank. The Russian people showed their dislike of the pain of reforms by delivering a stinging defeat to the reformist political parties. Vladimir Zhirinovsky's oddly named Liberal Democratic Party received 22.9 percent of the vote, the new Russian Communist Party received 12.4 percent, and two conservative parties, Women of Russia and the Agrarian Party, got about 8 percent each. Yavlinsky's party, Yabloko, got 7.8 percent. Gaidar's party, Democratic Choice, received only 15.5 percent of the vote. Centrist and smaller parties received the balance of the votes. Under the constitution, only half of the 450 seats in the Duma were distributed according to the popular vote and the other half were distributed among deputies who won individual contests. In the end, Communists and nationalists controlled about 40 percent of the Duma.

In June 1993 the International Monetary Fund had approved another credit of about $1.5 billion to support the government's economic reform program. The central objective of the program was to reduce the *monthly* rate of inflation to the single-digit level by the end of the year. The Russian government also agreed to continue privatization and to limit credit extended by the Central Bank. The

IMF said the government was going to cut the budget deficit in half through a reduction of its expenditures and remove the restrictions on the privatization of land and the reorganization of state farms. By the end of 1993, it was evident that privatization had accelerated but the monthly rate of inflation never sank to a single digit. The country continued to struggle with its reforms.

As 1994 began, political pressures again created inconsistencies in the government's policy on subsidies, which then directly affected the attitudes of general directors toward restructuring. Yeltsin kept Chernomyrdin as prime minister, but both Gaidar and Fedorov resigned from the government in January. First Deputy Prime Minister Oleg Soskovets, another former enterprise manager, represented the metal industries in the government. Chernomyrdin himself represented the energy lobbies. Another deputy prime minister, Aleksandr Zaveryukha, represented the agrarian lobby and protected farm subsidies. Chubais continued as privatization minister and deputy prime minister, the only senior reformer left. Chernomyrdin began the year by calling for wage and price controls and large subsidies to agriculture, and made his famous comment that the time of "market romanticism" was over. In fact, however, the prime minister continued to cut direct support to enterprises, which sank from an estimated 32 percent of gross domestic production in 1992 to just 5 percent at the end of 1994. The bulk of subsidies were shifted to the large enterprises that had strong influence with the government. Hidden subsidies, however, continued: it is estimated that tax exemptions for enterprises amounted to 3 to 4 percent of GDP. Some international financial organizations believe that the various types of subsidies to enterprises are so numerous that no accurate picture of their extent is possible. Chernomyrdin continued to support a large tax exemption for Gazprom, the giant gas monopoly, and the oil and gas industries in general. And tax arrears by enterprises grew substantially in 1994. The government continued to transfer huge amounts of money to regional governments to help enterprises divest themselves of kindergartens and employee housing. The agricultural sector continued to be the largest recipient of government subsidies. And the Central Bank continued to believe in credits to enterprises.

At the end of 1994, there were some successes and some failures. The government had held the budget deficit at 10 percent of GDP, a slight increase over the previous year, and tightened the subsidy squeeze on many enterprises and the military-industrial sector. As a result, the inflation rate fell to 202 percent, a significant decline. In the first half of the year, foreign capital and Russian capital in other countries began returning to Russia, and the stock market experienced a boom in August 1994. Late that summer, government subsidies resumed with a large transfer of credits to agriculture and the northern regions. In the end, domestic production as a whole declined by 12.6 percent; industrial production fell 21 percent and agricultural production 12 percent. Unemployment rose. The government began to experience the severe budget difficulties that plague it still as a decline in tax revenues fails to be offset by cuts in spending. The Ministry of Finance reported that total revenues dropped almost a quarter from 1992 to 1994. The continuing generosity to some enterprises resulted in a decline in the proportion of the budget spent on education, health, and social services. The government favored industrial lobbies over citizens in need. On October 11, 1994, as a result of a zigzag economic policy, the ruble collapsed and lost 27 percent of its value and the stock market began a decline. Shortly thereafter, Yeltsin fired the head of the Central Bank and promoted Chubais to first deputy prime minister with overall responsibility for stabilizing the Russian economy. He assembled a group of reformers that included Yevgeny Yasin as minister of the economy; his deputy, Sergei Vasiliev; Vladimir Panskov, minister of finance; and Tatyana Paramova, who replaced Gerashchenko as acting head of the Central Bank. Maxim Boycko became deputy chairman of a commission that would guide the economic reform program.

In mid-1994, Russia received a new loan for $1.5 billion from the International Monetary Fund. The goal was to reduce the monthly inflation rate to 7 percent by the end of the year and to tighten both fiscal and monetary policies by further reducing the expansion of credit made available by government authorities and achieve a budget deficit of 7 percent. The government committed itself to encouraging more foreign investment and improving the functioning of the social safety net. Russia did not achieve these goals. The result of the government's efforts were a monthly inflation rate of about 16 percent at the end of the year, a budget deficit that was 10 percent of gross domestic product, and little over-all progress in efforts to encourage foreign investment and improve the social safety net. The IMF expressed disappointment in the Russian government's performance. The dominant trend among the new corporations was continued reduction in production. Between 1990 and 1995, the goods and services they produced had dropped by over half.

In the summer of 1994 the World Bank again examined whether Russian enterprises were restructuring in twenty-four regions. The news was still not good. Most privatized enterprises were doing what can be called negative restructuring: laying off workers, reducing work hours, and reducing wages in order to deal with the big drop in demand. The World Bank uncovered a widespread phenomenon that sheds light on the mind-set of the managers. Imagine a maker of machine tools called Kirov Enterprises. Say that Kirov's production sank from 1,000 machine tools to 500 machine tools, but its managers reduced their workforce by only a third, keeping on more workers than were necessary to produce 500 machine tools. So the productivity of Kirov's labor was dramatically declining: the company was now producing fewer machine tools with more workers per unit of production. The managers were also trying to protect workers, for they had no sensible social welfare and unemployment insurance system to depend on. This kind of restructuring was not going to make the privatized enterprises more competitive or rescue the Russian economy.

As 1994 ended and 1995 began, the predicament of Russian reform is best illustrated by the troubled giant Zil, the maker of trucks and the famous limousines that top Kremlin officials have always used. The company sits on prime Moscow real estate. The enterprise was privatized in 1993 with 40 percent employee ownership. With 118,000 employees, it was a potential Chrysler of Russia. Mikrodin, an investor now connected to the powerful Oneksimbank, bought about 20 percent of the shares very cheaply for vouchers. As usual, privatization resulted in no significant influx of capital to reequip the plant. Management's restructuring plan involved reductions in employees and output and reorganization as a holding company, so that the firm's far-flung individual units would have more accountability. Since its privatization Zil has received huge "restructuring" loans from the government, mountains of tax credits, extensions of past bank loans, special orders from the ministries of Defense and Agriculture, gifts of social and cultural facilities on its premises from the government, and emergency loans for workers' wages arranged by Mikrodin. The position of each player describes the restructuring crisis that industry faced in 1995. The plant's general director wrote President Yeltsin that the firm needed "to change its shareholders for new patriotically oriented ones." He proposed a new share issue. If the situation was not resolved, he said, the government should renationalize the company. There was talk that the city of Moscow would buy shares, and ultimately it did, in August 1996. Yeltsin asked Chubais to look into the matter. Chubais later said that the management did not even have a business plan. Mikrodin conducted an audit and found that the company's accounting was totally confused, that management made key agreements verbally, and that the company was selling products without specifying a due date for payment or a penalty for delay. Mikrodin said that Zil's management was incompetent, and no one would invest money in the company until that problem was addressed. Meanwhile, production plummeted and workers were not paid on time. Management shut down the plant for several weeks. Auto industry experts noted that Zil was not making the kind of light trucks the market now demanded. There was a plan for Zil to get control of the land under its plant so it could raise capital by selling it.

Restructuring in 1995 and 1996

The year 1995 represented something of a turning point in the Russian economy. Under the discipline imposed by Chubais in his new role as first deputy prime minister, the Russian economy began to stabilize for the first time since the inception of reform. The new economic reform team negotiated a sizable increase in IMF credits to $6.8 billion in 1995. The goal was to make decisive progress and bring inflation down to an average monthly rate of 1 percent by the second half of the year. They intended major cuts in the budget deficit and a much smaller decline in gross domestic production. The government again pledged to address the social costs of economic reforms. For the first time, the government would come close to achieving its goals on cutting inflation and the budget deficit.

As for the enterprises, Chubais sought to force them to stop looking to the government as a source of capital. Government aid was further restricted as the budget deficit was sliced to less than 5 percent. Inflation slowed, and the interest rate charged by the Central Bank on the money that commercial banks borrowed to lend to enterprises not only was positive, it continued to be much higher than the inflation rate, as had been the case since November 1993. The enterprises were now being squeezed to compete for capital on the supposition that they might make a profit. Now it was very hard for the top managers to borrow money to buy new equipment and restructure their factories. They were still withholding taxes and not making payments on their bank loans—essentially creating subsidies for themselves—but government policies were forcing them to think seriously of giving up some ownership and control in order to get capital through the only route left, by selling new shares to outside investors—who might take a long, hard look at the performances of the managers running the companies.

The annual inflation rate dropped to 131 percent from several thousand percent a few years earlier. At the end of the year, monthly inflation was 3.2 percent, and weekly inflation fell below 1 percent for the first time since the transition to a market economy began. Any financial advantage the managers derived from inflation disappeared. The fall in production, less than 5 percent in 1995, finally was brought under control. Foreign investment rose somewhat during the year, and the ruble was fairly stable in relation to the dollar with the successful implementation of a "ruble corridor" by Chubais. Unemployment continued to rise (Table 2).

Unfortunately, the situation was complicated by the government's decision to raise funds to cover its budget deficit by issuing securities at very high rates of return. Seeing an opportunity to make tremendous profits, Russian banks invested their capital in these securities instead of lending it to privatized enterprises, which were starving for capital to restructure their operations. Obviously, a loan to the government seemed like a better investment than a loan to an enterprise whose financial condition was uncertain and which probably had defaulted on other bank loans and tax payments. Furthermore, enterprise managers in key export industries complained that the good news of lower inflation and a more stable ruble made their products more expensive in other countries. Some claimed that reductions in exports would deprive them of earnings that might have financed their capital investment.

Did these developments lead Russian corporations to seek new ways to restructure? One general director gave us his view of restructuring: "I remember a tale my mother told me. Two frogs jumped into a can of milk. One of them decided there was no sense in struggling since it was impossible to get out, and it sank. The other one started swimming around, and it kept swimming until it felt butter under its feet. Then it jumped out of the can. This is my philosophy."

The tale describes the managers' situation quite well, but they are still waiting for the happy outcome. During 1994 and 1995 managers had flailed about, making some significant changes but undertaking very little capital investment and modernization. By 1996, one could no longer argue that the enterprise managers had not had time to come up with restructuring plans and begin to implement them. As 1995 ended and 1996 began, the fortunes of economic reform underwent more shocks. In the December 1995 elections, the Communist Party won 21.5 percent of the popular vote and Zhirinovsky's party took 11 percent. Prime Minister Chernomyrdin's party, Our

Home Is Russia, took about 10 percent and Grigory Yavlinsky's reform party, Yaboko, won 7.2 percent. Communists also won most of the individual contests for Duma deputies. President Yeltsin angrily fired Chubais and positioned himself to deal with the lack of public support for reform. He replaced Chubais with the general manager of AvtoVAZ, the troubled automobile producer. Prime Minister Chernomyrdin publicly denounced the privatization program. The president strongly criticized enterprise directors' practice of failing to pay workers' wages, a favorite tactic of survival restructuring. For a year, however, the country had the lowest inflation since reform and a relatively stable ruble.

Restructuring Management and Control

By 1996, managers were being fired and replaced. (Details are provided in Table 10, under "Management and control.") Thirty-three percent of large and mid-sized workplaces had replaced their general director since 1992, and 12 percent replaced the general director in 1995 alone. In about 80 percent of those firms the general director was replaced by another manager from within the company. So few of the old general directors were replaced by outsiders that it was impossible to gauge the impact of outside managers on efforts to restructure the firms. Since insiders were still the majority owners of most of the companies, it was clear at least that the replacement of top managers was the work of insiders.

What factors predict the replacement of a firm's general director? Every increase of outside ownership and every decrease of employee ownership increases the chance that the top manager will be replaced. No wonder the top managers are so afraid of outside ownership. The general directors are replaced in more companies that are majority outsider-owned or that have no majority owner than in companies that are majority employee-owned. During 1995 top managers were replaced in significantly more companies that had large outside blockholders, and every 10 percent increase in total blockholder ownership is associated with a half-year decrease in the age of the general director. The general directors replaced since 1992 were three years younger on average than those they replaced, whereas the general directors replaced in 1995 were on average seven years younger than those they replaced. As the average age of top managers in office since before 1992 was 52, even the new general directors are certainly not untried youths.

Have the companies with new and younger general directors done more restructuring than other firms? Most indicators of restructuring simply bear no relation to the top manager's length of tenure or age. Replacement of the general director and the relative youth of the general director were significantly associated with some kinds of restructuring activities, such as increasing the amount of employee time devoted to research and development and changing managers responsible for production. There is no systematic evidence, however, that they are yet turning the companies around.

Close to half the companies changed lower-level managers responsible for production. The average company changed about 16 of every 100 production managers between 1995 and 1996. This story sounds too good to be true, and it is. In fact, a quarter of the companies changed very few managers, and a quarter had no outside directors; less than 5 percent of the companies changed more than half their production managers. The good news, then, tended to be concentrated in a few companies. An increase in blockholder ownership raised both the chance of replacing production managers and the percentage who were replaced. As blockholder ownership also increased the chance of replacing the general director, managers' fears that the sale of stock held by the state could threaten their jobs were not unrealistic.

Nikolai Medvedev, the 52-year-old new chief financial officer of a large facility in the oil industry, spoke about the speed with which an ownership change can affect a company: "At the end of last year, one of Russia's biggest banks got control of our parent company, the sixth largest oil company in the world on the basis of its reserves. They came in here to change the financial situation. The losses were astronomical. Accounts payable and accounts receivable were very, very large. The main debtor was the agricultural sector, which still tells us they prefer to pay for oil with their produce! This company simply never saw money at all. Nothing was systematized. The contracts were all agreed to over the telephone. They used an awful bank that was essentially dead. It needed one to two weeks to transfer money from one place to another. You can imagine how much the company lost as a result of inflation with such transfers. It seemed to me that the company really had no monetary relationships except with other firms in Moscow. Here people still exchanged oil for rutabagas! They were overpaying taxes because they didn't understand the laws. We're not going to give oil without payment, or free, or as a commodity credit anymore. And they were investing practically nothing in modernization, which is vital for our industry." Contrast this with the management style of a Red director in a majority employee-owned Siberian plant that's one of the hundred largest companies in Russia by market value. His strategy has been to constantly increase production since 1992 and offer as many products as possible by borrowing as much money as can be borrowed at low interest rates from commercial banks. The plant now has two hundred million dollars in debts. On the grounds there are sixty building projects that were started at various times and never finished. The factory manager had an idea to build a furniture factory, a medical clinic, and a hospital to provide jobs for the wives of the workers in the main plant. Because there was no market in Russia for the factory's products, they were exported to Asian countries. Because the transportation costs were more than eighty dollars a ton, the exports produced losses. The factory used commercial loans subsidized by the Central Bank of Russia to cover these losses. The factory manager continued to expand the enterprise. Several unprofitable factories were added, and he decided to build colleges on the premises. He opposed transferring social services to the municipality because they felt these services would die without the corporation's support. This company actually increased employment from twenty-some thousand to forty-some thousand during the last few years. This enterprise's debts to banks represent a quarter of all the money owed to banks by the entire industry the enterprise belongs to. The money needed just to make loan payments every month is staggering. In a recent interview, the manager said he believed his business strategy is correct. He explained his solution to his predicament. He filed a petition for bankruptcy but the court rejected it. In late 1995, it became impossible to go on. A quarter of the workers were laid off and all production was stopped. The manager demanded that the government intervene by controlling prices in the industry. He then asked the government to allow inflation to rise so the cheaper ruble would make his exports more attractive. And he asked the government to reduce railroad rates. This is his restructuring plan.

Restructuring Business Operations

Business operations were changing. (See Table 10, under "Organization.") The average company had cut its workforce by 23 percent since 1992. Since the average firm was working at only 55 percent of its capacity, however, it was still quite overstaffed. The average hides the fact that over a third of the companies did very little cutting, so even negative restructuring was very uneven. Sixty-eight percent of the companies changed their mix of products and added new products. Eighty-two percent of the companies added new customers, who accounted for about a fifth of sales. Fifty-nine percent made about a fourth of their purchases from new suppliers and 64 percent created a marketing department. About half the companies increased the amounts they spent on research and development by a fifth and made significant cuts in their overhead.

A closer look reveals that the average story is not the accurate story. Let's consider new products. Probably the most meaningful change in business operations a privatized company can make is to offer new products or services to respond to what consumers say they want to buy. Fifty-two percent of the companies reported that they added completely new products, which generated an average of 12 percent of their sales. But new products accounted for only a very small proportion of the sales of more than half the companies, whereas they accounted for half of the sales in less than 5 percent of companies. Thus, while it is a positive sign that companies are restructuring in this area, it is not encouraging that the most meaningful restructuring is concentrated in only about a quarter of them. This pattern is repeated in every area of business operations. When managers were asked if they restructured in some way, half to two-thirds of them said they did, but on closer examination the amount of the restructuring, measured by its impact on their sales in 1995, was found to be modest, and most of it was concentrated in a small number of firms.

Inevitably the more difficult restructuring tasks were avoided. Once the command economy gave way to privatization, many firms had to change the products they offered and find new customers, suppliers, and retail outlets. The state stopped servicing many businesses as their main buyer and seller. The difficult tasks of finding new distributors, discontinuing products that did not sell, changing technology, shifting production outside of the enterprise, and selling off unnecessary parts of the enterprise were not widely undertaken. The firms that attempted these tasks did so very tentatively; only 37 percent of the companies surveyed discontinued products, for example, and on average the products they discontinued accounted for 16 percent of sales the year before they were discontinued.

What explains the restructuring of business operations that did take place? Increases in the total percentages of outside ownership and blockholder ownership are strongly related to employee layoffs since 1992. Managers in companies with significant outsider ownership have laid off substantially more workers than other firms and report higher increases in employee productivity. Layoffs averaged almost 10 percent less in majority employee-owned firms than in majority outsider-owned firms. Outside shareholders, however, could not have caused the larger employee layoffs in 1992, 1993, or even 1994. Those were the years when privatization was just beginning. Perhaps they viewed the firms that were laying off more workers as good investments.

Outside shareholders have been able to get on the board, they have been able to join with insiders to replace general directors and production managers, and they have been able to choose firms that lay off substantial numbers of workers. Neither the presence of outside shareholders and blockholders nor the amount of stock they own, however, is generally associated with the most positive restructuring. Of the many indicators of restructuring, the only ones that are meaningfully correlated with the size of outsider or blockholder ownership are the percentages of production managers changed, employees laid off, and new distributors. In most companies, outsiders have a minority position on the board and own a minority of the stock (see Tables 5 and 6). When outsiders are the majority owners, they are likely to add new distributors for their products. But there is still no evidence of *many* far-reaching changes.

Larger firms are doing more experimenting with restructuring than smaller firms. They have changed their product mix, added new products, found new customers, used new retail outlets and transportation services, added more distributors, added marketing departments, and increased their expenditures on research and development with more frequency than smaller firms. All the same, the national impact of their activities is still minimal.

A consistent picture is emerging. Although considerable experimentation is going on everywhere, it has not yet led to widespread large-scale restructuring. Where the impact of restructuring extends beyond employee layoffs and changes in management, a few companies account for much of it.

Meaningful adjustment of business operations to the market economy is proving very difficult for most privatized companies. To reach this conclusion we gave each corporation a restructuring score based on sixty-nine specific actions to promote restructuring, which the 1996 Russian National Survey measured. (Table 10 contains a complete list.) The addition of a marketing department, for example, earned a company 1 point; otherwise it scored zero on that item. Companies that had sold enough new products the previous year to be rated among the top 50 percent in Russia scored a point; those that had introduced new products but had sold a negligible number of them scored zero. The perfect score was 69. The average score for all firms was 20, an indication that most companies were not seriously engaging in two-thirds of the restructuring activities. No company scored above 42, and only a tenth of the companies achieved a score above 30. The combined percentage of either outside or blockholder ownership made a significant difference, but the impact was very small. A 10 percent increase in outside ownership increased the restructuring score about half a point, and a 10 percent increase in total ownership by blockholders raised it only slightly more. Furthermore, the only outside owners and blockholders that are in any way correlated with restructuring are Russian commercial firms. But it is critical to remember that only 6 percent of the firms in Russia are currently owned by one blockholder alone. This finding suggests that something is standing in the way of effective restructuring.

An investigative report on the automaker AvtoVAZ in 1996 demonstrates how even the blue-chip firms are getting it wrong. AvtoVAZ is the thirty-eighth largest company in Russia, with 114,000 employees. The nearly 600,000 cars it produced in 1995 were almost 80 percent of all cars produced in the country. It has the widest range of models, which it sells through its own 140-dealer distribution system. It is located on the Volga River in the town of Tolyatti, named for Palmiro Togliatti, a founder of the Italian Communist Party and its head for many years. The AvtoVAZ factory was built by Fiat of Italy in the 1960s because the Soviet industrial system could not build a proper car. The small Fiat 124 was the model for the Zhiguli, the Soviet "people's car." At one point AvtoVAZ turned out about a million cars a year. Like the Soviet Union, Zhigulis seemed to live forever. The arrangement with Fiat did not include plans to cooperate with the Italian company on revising the car or changing the model. An auto expert at the Rinako-Plus investment company says, "The Zhiguli was the people's car. But there was no tradition of taking care of the people's comfort." The car did not change in thirty years. The company had tried earlier to make a more Western model, called the Samara, but that effort failed. Seven years after the Samara was introduced it accounted for only 15 percent of production. AvtoVAZ used to export to Germany, France, Belgium, Hungary, Turkey, and Great Britain, where the car was called the Lada. Competition in these export markets drove exports down from just over 40 percent of the cars the company made to about a quarter of the cars that rolled off the assembly lines along the Volga. As production declined, the cost of each car produced skyrocketed.

The company was privatized in 1993 with employee ownership of

35 percent. Everything about AvtoVAZ's restructuring repeats the story that our 1996 survey tells. The long-time general director, Vladimir Kadannikov, was named first deputy prime minister in early 1996 and quickly replaced by his deputy, Aleksei Nikolaev. Outside shareholders have limited influence on management. None of them are strategic investors or management experts, like the KKR team at KamAZ. AVVA, owner of a large block of shares, tried unsuccessfully to assemble the Opel Corsas in Russia. After some layoffs, the annual production per worker is 5.1 cars—an unimpressive record in comparison with that of the Czech Republic's Skoda plant, whose 17,000 workers produce 12.4 cars per worker. Some experts say the company needs to eliminate 15 percent of its workforce, but that idea makes management nervous in a town where 80 percent of the population work for AvtoVAZ and depend on the social services it provides. The firm's solution was to stop paying its employees in November 1995 while they worked on. Oleg, a young engineer with a wife and a baby, told a reporter, "It's a nightmare. We borrow off each other, ask our parents for help, but basically no one's got any money anymore." The company's finance director said that the crisis started in September 1995, when a prepayment of $20 million for ordered cars was not received.

Analysts say that the company has a bright future if it can restructure its operations. AvtoVAZ has a reputation for having a high-quality workforce and skilled engineering. It never had serious competitors and most Russians have preferred its cars. Demand for new cars will increase by 50 percent in Russia by 2000. If the market share of foreign cars continues to rise from 3 percent to 10 percent, 90 percent of the market will still be left for Russian producers. Other analysts suggest that AvtoVAZ has far more serious problems that will be complicated to solve. Debates abound as to whether the government's tariffs on foreign cars and cutting of the local sales tax on Russian cars are helping or hurting its restructuring. AvtoVAZ has great difficulty raising capital and its managers have not been able or willing to make the kind of deal KamAZ made. They have been unwilling to give any control to anyone who gives them capital and have repeatedly called for more state aid. The company issued 41 billion rubles in bonds to survive and then stopped paying interest on its loans to Sberbank, the state savings bank. Until it stopped paying its workers altogether, it had been paying them with borrowed money. It owes several hundred million dollars to creditors for loans and supplies and is indebted to the state for trillions of rubles in back taxes.

Some success stories have been reported, such as Bolshevik Biscuit

(Introduction), Baltika Beer and Lubyatov Cookie (Chapter 2), and some companies that are being restructured by domestic and foreign blockholders.

Social Services for Employees

The restructuring of Russian businesses is complicated by their tradition of providing housing, child care, and recreational, cultural, medical, and other facilities for their workers. (See Table 10, under "Social services provided to employees.") Workers depend on these services and need them, and managers have come to consider them part of the social contract between management and labor. Any restructuring of social services stirs serious conflict between the old culture of Russian enterprises and the new demand that they be competitive. It is not a small issue (see Table 10).

It has been estimated that 20 percent of total compensation paid by Russian industrial firms is accounted for by social services—twice as much as Polish firms spend. The major expenditures are not for such benefits as paid vacations and health care, which are provided to employees in many countries, but for housing, day care, and kindergartens. Employee housing accounts for about half of the social service expenses, day care for a quarter to a third.

Though privatized companies turned over responsibility for some social services to the municipalities, their social service expenditures remain high. Many continue to provide such services because the towns and cities either cannot afford to do so or levy such high taxes that the firm ends up paying for them anyway. Whatever solutions are sought, this is an issue that makes it difficult for companies to attract investors. The costs of social services reported in the Russian National Survey in 1996 were 16 to 24 percent—depending on the method of computation used—of total monthly compensation.

The manager of a clothing factory with 2,000 employees in Ivanovo says that neither the factory nor the state can afford to support employee social services. "Why, when you consider the high taxes they charge us, is the state incapable of maintaining the kindergartens, apartment houses, and sanatoriums? Before 1991, about thirty-five percent of the cost was financed by the federal and municipal budgets and the rest by the factory. Now, after privatization, the proportion is fifty-fifty. This company owns forty-three apartment buildings and four kindergartens. Only the kindergartens have been transferred to the city." Another factory manager down the road with

2,700 employees is more explicit: "The expenses for the plant's day-care centers, apartment houses, medical center, and farm take up a good part of our total sales for a month!" The manager of another nearby factory spelled out the connection between the restructuring of enterprises and the restructuring of government itself: "The Ivanovo authorities are simply ignoring the president's directive requiring them to take over the social services of industrial enterprises. They say their budget is empty and they have no money for this purpose."

Access to Capital

Most general directors of the newly privatized corporations reported that they were starved for capital to invest in new equipment, develop their goods and services, and increase efficiency; and 10 percent of the companies in the Russian National Survey Sample reported that they were receiving subsidies. In a kind of involuntary government subsidy, privatized enterprises in 1996 owed an average of 6.5 percent of their annualized sales in taxes to the central and regional governments. The average company spends just over 10 percent of the proceeds of its bank loans on new capital equipment and uses the rest for raw materials and employee compensation. But this average company is a product of statistical calculations based on a few companies that are taking out substantial bank loans for investment and the many companies that are making no capital investment at all. Three-quarters of the companies spent no part of either their last bank loan or the total bank loans they carry on their books for capital investment. Management's chief criticism of the privatization program has been that shares in their companies were sold mainly for vouchers rather than for cash. The companies got nothing from the privatization process but shareholders. Many managers derisively called their new employee and outside shareholders "pretend capitalists" because they did not lay their own money on the line. But the rapid transfer of property rights was an overriding goal, and citizens did not have the money to buy all the Russian enterprises at world market prices. The solution to this dilemma was the voucher program.

Individuals who bought shares with a few vouchers from family and friends may indeed be pretend capitalists, but the criticism does not apply to large outside investors. To secure large blocks of shares in an enterprise, those outside investors had to hand their own money over to citizens in exchange for vouchers. The money may not have gone to the companies, the price may have been low, the managers may not have been happy, but from the perspective of voucher investment funds and commercial firms, they did pay for their shares and they bear real risk.

In 1993 and 1994, when managers began to attempt to restructure their firms on their own, the Duma, which had passed the first privatization law in 1992, refused to pass a second law to authorize the sale for cash of the state-owned shares of the companies that had been held back from privatization. Some of this cash would have gone to the companies, some to the state. A very small percentage of privatized companies did later sell their remaining state-owned shares in investment tenders and cash auctions, but most of those that did so found the prices were relatively low.

The infancy of Russian capital markets complicated efforts to raise capital for investment. In a developed market economy companies can issue bonds or stocks fairly easily. The Russian stock market had not yet developed sufficiently to enable a company to make an audited and reasonably accurate financial statement available to the public quickly and a broker to conduct a sale of shares in a single day. In 1994 and 1995, many Russian banks were only a few years old. The high rate of inflation allowed many banks to make money by speculating in currency and government securities. Few had the kind of experience necessary to evaluate a company's application for a loan for a capital project. During some years, the interest rate that banks charged was significantly above the inflation rate, so that companies had very little interest in borrowing money from banks. In fact, the Russian National Survey for 1996 found that most of the companies reported that they took out only short-term loans from banks. The banks cannot be completely faulted for their attitudes. Half of the enterprises reported that they were not keeping up with their loan payments, a quarter were not keeping up with their interest payments, and almost a fifth were considering taking out more loans to retire their earlier loans. When one survey examined this problem in 1994, it found that almost a third of the loans from banks to industrial enterprises were overdue. It concluded that because overdue loans had tripled during 1994, the banks themselves were running short of capital, and their liquidity problems could cause them to fail.

To make matters worse, Russians did not have enough confidence in the banks to deposit their estimated $20 billion of savings in them, so banks lacked the capital necessary to create a major program of loans to industry. In 1994 and 1995, millions of citizens were defrauded by unlicensed investment companies, such as the infamous MMM, whose head, Sergei Mavrody, ran for the Duma in an effort— unsuccessful, as it turned out—to get immunity from prosecution. Voucher investment funds had been licensed and somewhat supervised, but other investment funds were not. A mutual fund industry that could directly attract billions of savings and fuel the market for corporate bonds and stocks had not developed in Russia by the end of 1995. In its absence, Russian citizens and corporations preferred to bank and invest abroad. The European Bank for Reconstruction and Development estimated that $40 billion in capital had been exported from Russia.

The Duma's delay until 1996 of legislation providing unequivocal protection to domestic and foreign investors and lenders and foreign investors' perception of political risk exacerbated the problems in the financial sector. Investors had little trust in the ability of the Russian courts, which had not had to deal with investment questions before, to rule objectively and enforce their judgments. Legal problems with landownership also daunted the banks.

Capital started to flow into the Russian stock market in late 1994, with the amount reaching significant amounts per month, but political events quickly put a brake on this activity. Yeltsin appointed a new deputy prime minister for privatization, but fired him when he began to talk about renationalizing some companies. Who wanted to buy stock that the government could take back? Polls began to predict a Communist victory in the parliamentary elections of December 1995, and throughout the first half of 1996 the Communists were expected to win the presidential election in June. New capital for modernization, a key ingredient of restructuring, was not available to the enterprises.

Barriers to Restructuring

Corporate governance is essential to the delivery of capital. Good governance assures the suppliers of capital of a return on their investment. How do suppliers of capital ensure that management will return some of the profits to them? How can they be sure that managers will not steal the capital they supply or divert it to other uses? How do they control the managers? Corporate governance is typically exercised through concentrated ownership. A substantial minority or majority shareholder has an incentive to collect information and monitor management, and enough voting power to put pressure on managers even to oust them through a proxy fight or a takeover.

In late 1995 the investors in the Lebedinsk Ore Processing Company, in the town of Stary Oskol, got a crash course in the barriers to stockholders who seek to add governance to ownership in an effort to effect restructuring. Lebedinsk, with a market value of almost $300 million, is the eleventh largest company in Russia. At a shareholders' meeting in November 1995 the general director, Anatoly Pomonerov, announced that the company would raise $6 to 10 million in capital by selling new shares. The money would be used to build a metal briquette plant that would cost over $200 million; $180 million would come as a loan from a consortium of German banks, and the Russian Tokobank would lend the firm another $20 million. The company created a closely held corporation called LebGOK-Invest and asked the government to allow this sister company to buy most of the new shares. The statutes of the sister company provided that the voting rights and control of all these shares belonged to Pomonerov.

The true reason for issuing new shares was not to pay for the new factory at all but to transmit control over Russia's eleventh largest company to Pomonerov personally. The new share issue would reduce the outside shareholders' control and voting rights by sixfold. Five outside shareholders, led by the Rossiisky Kredit holding company, then owned about a quarter of Lebedinsk's stock—enough to veto the new share issue. The head of Rossiisky Kredit says the new share issue would have reduced its shares and those of its clients to about 6 percent.

The committee that registered shareholders who came to the annual meeting refused admittance to the five outside shareholders, citing a ruling by the Belgorod Regional Arbitration Court. Lebedinsk's management had sued the outside shareholders, accusing them of violating antimonopoly legislation when they bought the company's shares. The court had sequestered the outside shareholders' shares so that they could not be voted. So the shareholders' meeting was held without the Rossiisky Kredit group, and management's proposal for a new issue of shares to the sister company was approved. Then, just to cover themselves, the arbitration court judges turned around and canceled the sequestering of the shares. A few weeks later the federal government's antitrust committee found that the outside shareholders had committed no violations of antitrust laws. Suits, countersuits, and appeals followed.

On March 27, 1996, with the court cases still unsettled, Dmitry Lubinin, the vice president of Rossiisky Kredit, went back to Stary

Oskol to try again. He had one word to describe that shareholders' meeting, packed mainly with 200 workers and managers from the plant: "Absurd." One worker proclaimed, "We don't need any outsiders." The others fiercely agreed. Where Lubinin proposed that Pomonerov be removed, the factory manager was reelected by acclamation. He then rushed through the agenda and the shareholders approved a new corporate charter and blocked the holding company from holding a seat on a new factory advisory panel. The Russian Metallurgy Committee says that Lebedinsk is one of the most profitable ore smelters in Russia, with $147 million in profits, mainly from exports, in 1995.

The Lebedinsk story reveals the fuzziness of the lines that separate state, corporation, management, government, and law in emerging "capitalist" Russia. It also suggests that barriers to governance are one reason that substantial outside ownership may not lead to restructuring. Russia now has a new corporate law that prohibits many of the actions alleged by Lebedinsk's outside shareholders. Earlier regulations were so unclear that shareholders could not be sure what their rights were or how the courts would view them.

The restructuring that is occurring takes many forms. Most of the activity, like the flailing about of the frog in the milk can, is ineffective, because the can is filled not with cream that will turn to butter but with water. The frog needs something solid under its feet to get out. Some enterprises have made some changes, but few have made the comprehensive changes that will ensure their survival. As we have seen, the enterprises' primary strategy has been to lay off workers, but they have laid off only a fraction of the employees they need to eliminate. Expenditures for social services have been curtailed a little. Beyond this negative restructuring, there are encouraging signs of positive restructuring, but the actual measures taken are not far-reaching, comprehensive, or radical.

Why is it that outside ownership and blockholder ownership do not seem to be having a far-reaching impact on restructuring in a large number of companies? We have observed that very large concentrated blockholders do seem to be able to take control of restructuring in some specific cases. Both the evidence available and our interviews with company managers have made it clear that increases in outside and blockholder ownership have not been associated with significant increases in comprehensive positive restructuring. Why not?

The simple presence of outside or blockholder ownership is not enough to move a firm toward strong and determined governance.

Most firms lagged in progress toward open trading of stocks, independent shareholder registers, accurate financial disclosure, democratic boards of directors, and fair issues of new stock. A deficiency in any of these areas retards a blockholder's ability to monitor a firm's operations effectively.

Only 20 percent of firms in Russia are majority-owned by outsiders, only 6 percent are majority-owned by one blockholder, and only 5 percent are majority-owned by several blockholders (see Table 11). Even majority blockholders encounter strong barriers to good governance. The bottom line of the evidence presented in Table 11 is that both the absence of concentrated blockholder ownership that is effective *and* the difficulty that existing blockholders are having in exercising their voting and governance rights may present barriers to restructuring. Most of the companies do not have independent shareholder registers or use cumulative voting, and the number of blockholders' seats on the board does not reflect the size of their ownership stakes. Many voucher investment funds that are blockholders do not have board seats. Most top managers in these companies oppose the public release of financial and ownership information.

Blockholders, for their part, have not been effective in bringing capital to the companies. Most companies that are majority-owned by blockholders made no capital investments from 1994 to 1996, and the general directors of almost half of the companies oppose new share issues. In those years majority blockholders did manage to replace the top manager at twice the rate of replacement in other firms, but the new general director was usually another insider.

In the U.S. economy, businesses are bought and sold and shareholders buy in and out of companies. People or firms that think they can improve businesses buy them and people or firms that have exhausted their competence sell them. In a country with active stock markets, shareholders who believe they cannot make much money in a company or who are dissatisfied with its management sell their stock to people who view the firm differently. In the United States, for example, an investor who wants to build a concentration of stock in a public company simply calls a broker, accumulates a blockholder stake, and begins to work with or struggle against management.

Technology, the know-how to use it, and the capital to buy it are even more complicated problems. Many of the outside shareholders who bought stock during voucher privatization do not have the deep pockets to supply capital to the firm. A 1995 study by the privatization ministry found that most Russian commercial firms that bought investment tenders at auction after voucher privatization did not fulfill their obligation to invest capital in the firms. Thus, even when managers want capital and really know how to use it efficiently, they are intensely frustrated by the slowness with which capital markets are developing. Concentrated shareholders therefore are having a hard time introducing disciplined change in management, technology, and capital investment.

In the United States, investors have almost blind faith in the functioning of the stock market. When they want to buy a stock, they have some modest confidence that that stock is available to a broker, that the broker can quickly execute the transaction on an efficient stock exchange, that the price is fair, that the ownership of the stock is registered honestly, that accurate financial information on the company will be available, and that the press, a government regulatory agency, the board, certified public accountants, and hostile investors will watch the profit-making behavior of the company closely. The United States has a system of clearly defined rules, market institutions that have a history of working, and government bodies and courts that will enforce the contracts and agreements between the parties. But some of today's general directors resemble the old Soviet manager who becomes general director of his privatized firm, puts on a new suit, gets a blow-dry haircut, and looks every inch the modern manager, but still has the history, attitudes, and skills of a Red director.

Our evidence shows that few companies are being bought and sold as a whole, and trading of stock is modest. Insiders in fact view such trading—except when management buys from employees—as betrayal. Any stock that is traded is in the largest companies, which cannot control tens of thousands of employee shareholders and whose workers can often make real profits by selling their shares. Nevertheless, outsider ownership is slowly increasing and insider ownership seems to be slowly declining. Even so, when shareholders or blockholders buy into a company, they find it difficult to monitor management, get financial information, and carry out restructuring.

So how are these firms going to get strong, determined, and concentrated shareholders who will bring the management skill, the capital, and the technology they need and make them operate efficiently? Several institutions have been established to try to jump-start restructuring. One is the Russian Privatization Center (RPC) in Moscow, which manages most technical assistance to enterprises for the Russian government. The RPC has been employing Western consultants to help managers design restructuring plans and reform their financial accounting systems. With the assistance of the United

States and other countries, several restructuring funds, such as the Fund for Large Enterprises in Russia, have been set up to make loans to enterprises. Unfortunately, the industrialized nations have moved very slowly to build such institutions, and there are too few of them and their support is too weak to enable them to stimulate the use of effective restructuring strategies.

Two key responses to this problem will be the emergence of large blockholders to concentrate ownership and the development of more open capital markets with effective protections for investors.

Restructuring Strategies

Strategic Investors. One way to overcome the barriers that deter domestic Russian investors' efforts to bring management skill, capital, and technology to privatized companies is to sell a major chunk of the firm to a single shareholder. That shareholder must be a world leader in the business with a proven track record of success and deep pockets. The shareholder takes over the firm or takes a significant amount of control and does not have to worry about constant struggles over the changes that need to be made.

Naturally, Russians are very worried about Western ownership of their country. The Communist newspaper *Pravda* (now defunct) charged that the objective of Western advisers was to develop a system of "colonialism" in Russia, and the means to keep foreign ownership in check was an issue in both parliamentary elections of December 1995 and the presidential election of 1996. Foreigners own less than 2 percent of stock in Russian corporations today, whereas they account for about 5 percent of stock ownership in the United States and Japan and 14 percent in Germany, whose industry was substantially rebuilt after World War II. Direct foreign investments in Russian corporations were less than $2 billion per year from 1992 to 1995 and less than $1 billion per year in 1994 and 1995. (Table 2 shows *cumulative* foreign direct investment.) Because of Russia's size, it is unlikely that foreign money will ever account for more than 10 percent of investment in Russian companies. Foreign strategic investors will play important roles in efforts to overcome the barriers to disciplined restructuring, but the major role is likely to be played by Russian strategic investors. The danger is that many Russian commercial firms, investment funds, privatized corporations, and banks do not have the skills to operate efficiently. They may buy other Russian firms, but can they restructure them? One alternative is for these Russian institutions to go to the world market and hire Western managers and financial experts to help them. Just over a quarter of general directors support the idea of selling their plant to a strategic investor who would bring all the know-how, capital, and technology necessary to restructure their business, and the same number report they could persuade the employees to support such a move.

How can managers and employees be sure of fair treatment in their negotiations with strategic investors? They can do what employees and managers of foreign firms do: hire competent investment bankers and lawyers to represent them in their negotiations.

Some employee-owned Russian firms have true wealth to protect. Novorostsement, for example, has the capacity to produce over 4 million tons of cement annually and exports 500,000 tons. Just a tenth of this company's stock is owned by two Russian firms, Sovintrast, a joint venture, and Alfa-Tsement, a Russian group that invests in cement plants. Top management is looking to sell up to a quarter of the stock to a strategic investor. Output has dropped by about half in the economic downturn, but as Sergei Titov, the economic director, says, "We're the only producer of cement in the North Caucasian and Kuban regions, so we won't die." But the company needs $20 million to reconstruct its quarry equipment. Preliminary examples of foreign strategic investors do exist. Rossia Chocolate sold a controlling interest to Switzerland-based Nestlé. Overnight Nestlé replaced equipment throughout the factory. The head of the technology department, Tamara Zhuravleva, said, "In the factory's twenty-five-year existence the equipment had never once been replaced." Nestlé is repairing and reconstructing the factory and installing Dutch and Italian equipment. It is building an assembly line to make its Nuts bars, with an expected annual production of 12,000 to 13,000 tons. Meanwhile, the refurbished old factory will continue to make 25,000 tons of Rossia chocolate a year. The German company HIT Beteiligungsgesellschaft, a subsidiary of Herlitz AG, invested $12.1 million in the Volga paper mill. It owns 33 percent of Volga's stock and the International Finance Corporation (IFC) owns 25 percent. IFC, an investment arm of the World Bank, reports that production has increased by 30 percent.

But Russian factory managers must make the first move, because many foreign investors are not going to battle to invest in Russia. Vlad Borisov, general director of the Severnoye Siyaniye perfume company said, "I've been looking for partners for many years, and I'm very happy to have found such a large corporation, one with liquid assets totaling forty-five billion dollars." The investor is Unilever, which transferred its production management principles and sales management policies to Russian soil. The British-Dutch giant now controls 93 percent of the perfumery's stock. Borisov had never dealt with serious finance and marketing issues before, and had to increase the number of the firm's managers tremendously. The Dutch electronics giant Phillips is now a blockholder in VELT, a Voronezh television tube manufacturer. Vyacheslav Kotelnikov, VELT's general director, said, "Through Phillips, our strategic investor, we've been able to get new equipment." As other Russian factories cut back their production by half on average, he expected his factory to quadruple its monthly output to 55,000 TV tubes in the third quarter of 1995. He did not foresee an increase in his workforce. In fact, he expected the workforce to be reduced as mechanization was introduced; but he added that Phillips intended to be sensitive to the employees and was not planning any drastic actions.

Strategic investors' power is growing in Russia. In 1996, domestic Russian commercial firms owned more than half the stock in 5 percent of all privatized corporations. Despite the average foreign ownership of less than 2 percent, foreign strategic investors own more than a majority of the stock in 1 percent of all Russian corporations.

Insider Takeovers. Employees and mid-level managers are now the dominant blockholders in Russia. Ironically, it is these insiders who have put up the biggest barriers to shareholders' rights. Most Russian trade unions and employee groups have been embarrassing failures as representatives and have not attempted to find independent outside board members with business training to represent their members' shareholdings. At the same time, managers have worked ardently and successfully to block attempts by employee shareholders to exercise their rights. Employees can be fired for selling their shares to an outsider or for attempting to institute cumulative voting to elect independent board representatives. Despite the fact that Russia now leads the world in employee shareholding, the country that so recently called itself the "workers' state" does not legally protect workers' shareholder rights.

In principle, there is no reason why Russian managers and employees could not hire financial and industry experts to advise them and take decisive steps of the sort taken by the union and nonunion employee groups and management of United, Northwest, TWA, and Delta airlines in the United States to restructure their costs by reaching compromise agreements that provided for some employee ownership, greater investor say on the board, and more corporate governance supervision of management by all shareholders. Adam Blumenthal, executive vice president of American Capital Strategies of Bethesda, Maryland, which advises the parties in such situations, says, "Given the low price paid for many of the enterprises and their value if they were properly renovated and managed, the employees do have the largest financial incentive to restructure. But they also face the highest barriers." Because workers and other managers are not well organized to mount insider takeovers, they will probably receive increasing offers of resources and organizing ability from outside blockholders, who may then join them to create a combined "employee-outsider concentrated shareholder."

Outsider Takeovers. Another possible route to restructuring is a hostile takeover by investors who see an opportunity in restructuring but cannot cooperate with current management or employee groups. Alone or in a group, investors use Russian stockbrokers, advertisements, and contacts to gather 51 percent of the stock and then replace the old board and managers, attempting to remove all the barriers to disciplined governance overnight. As average outside ownership across Russia has crept up, more and more shares have became available on the market for prospective investors. But significant barriers to takeover investors remain. A leading Moscow stockbroker has described them: only the stocks of the biggest 200 companies, together worth about $20 billion at the end of 1995, are frequently traded: less than a fifth of all stocks are in "free float," available for purchase. Obviously, a combination of high insider ownership and undeveloped market infrastructure has kept the free float low. The stocks of only 20 to 50 of the 200 largest companies are "liquid," or easily bought and sold. With the exceptions of the United States and Great Britain, this situation is typical of world stock markets.

A widely publicized hostile takeover bid illustrates the problems these barriers presented to the country's pioneer takeover investors. The Koloss food conglomerate, a unit of Bank Menatep's brokerage division, Alliance-Menatep, put ads in Moscow newspapers in July 1995 offering to buy shares of the Red October Chocolate Company at $7.50. Red October is the fifty-seventh largest corporation in the country by market value. Workers had bought their shares quite cheaply. A battle ensued. Red October's management hired another broker as its financial adviser and broadcast warnings over the factory's public address system that if employees sold their shares, Alliance-Menatep would take over the company they would lose their jobs. Alliance-Menatep announced plans to make large capital investments in the candy maker. By 1995 workers held only about a third of Red October's shares. Those workers who resisted the offer were earning dividends of up to $90 a year. Red October issued some new shares and sold them to investors, and the takeover bid failed. Yet Alliance-Menatep did manage to effect some shift in shareholder power. When the takeover began, employees, individuals, and institutional investors, including Russian investment funds and foreigners, each owned about a third. Management argued that the company was worth more than Alliance-Menatep's new offer of $9.50 a share, and Alliance-Menatep was unable to accumulate enough shares to take over the company. Red October's own position was not very strong because Moscow's biggest brokers and the Russian public had greeted an earlier attempt to sell new stock on the market with no great enthusiasm. The managers who wanted to restructure the company were shocked into the realization that they had to be nice to investors, even those who seemed to come charging through the doors. Red October then agreed to give Alliance-Menatep two seats on its board of directors and began to cooperate with the food conglomerate. Later in the summer of 1995, the Moscow city government purchased a fifth of the company. The city's purchase supplied capital for new equipment and development of the firm's urban real estate. Alliance-Menatep's experience demonstrates the difficulty of effecting a hostile takeover, even when the position of the target firm is not strong.

As the annual shareholder meetings of major Russian companies were starting in the spring of 1996, takeover struggles were heating up once again. This time, however, the clear provisions of the new corporate law emboldened shareholders. At Perm, on the Trans-Siberian Railway, Coopers & Lybrand and the European Bank for Reconstruction and Development (EBRD) were locked in a struggle with the board of directors of Perm Motors to break the company into four parts. Mikrodin, a 28 percent blockholder with minority representation on the board, was trying to run its own slate of directors and throw out the entire old board of directors. Mikrodin controlled the general director's office but not the board, and it mounted its campaign without knowing exactly how many of the 35 percent of shares supposedly in workers' hands had been sold to other outsiders, who together held another 25 percent. The balkanization of control at Perm Motors is another demonstration of barriers to blockholders' restructuring efforts. One of the quarrels between the reformers and their adversaries is over those blocks of stock: should they be sold off rapidly, thus creating the kinds of headaches for Red managers that we have seen, or nationalized, or folded into financial-industrial groups? Today most corporations in which outsiders have a minority stake are potential candidates for outsider takeovers. Twenty-one of every hundred top managers in our 1995–96 sample suspected that outsiders were trying to accumulate majority control of their firms.

Until blockholders can impose their will on management, gradual takeovers seem the most probable scenario, unless national and regional stock market institutions develop more rapidly than they have been doing and the stock of more companies becomes available and tradable. How close are most companies to such takeovers? Outsiders own more than 30 percent but less than 50 percent of the stock of a quarter of all corporations. With modest effort, many changes in control might take place.

Financial-Industrial Groups. If the emergence of large concentrated ownership stakes, the market for shares, senior managers, and capital cannot be made to work more quickly, the State Committee on Industrial Policy has said, it proposes to create closed conglomerates, in Russia called financial-industrial groups, or FIGs. Some observers believe that this move will lead to concentrated control and ownership by a few huge cartels, like the Japanese *keiretsu* or the Korean *chaebol,* perhaps with close ties to government. FIGs come in two forms, the merchant bank and the "capitalist politburo," which is based on the old networks of factories, trading companies, and suppliers in a particular industry that had ties to the Soviet "branch ministries." By some accounts, thirty financial-industrial groups are functioning or in the works. More than eight were created in 1995 alone.

The merchant bank functions as a concentrated shareholder, often very aggressively. A Russian bank accumulates deposits and then founds a subsidiary investment company. Pooling its own funds with those of other investors, domestic or foreign, the investment company typically sets out to acquire controlling stakes in companies in one industry. The merchant bank does not have to worry about stock markets, share registries, struggles with managers, or halfhearted commitment to restructuring plans. The general director of a typical bank FIG described his operation: "We are a brokerage and investment subsidiary of the bank. We got our assets from investment tenders and cash auctions that sold the state-owned shares of privatized companies. We own fifty privatized companies and have twenty people engaged in buying the stock of employees at these enterprises. We put ads on walls in town and in the media. Our objective is to get a majority stake in all of these companies. Sometimes we count management shares in this block. . . . We hold the general directors of the companies we buy to strict monthly performance standards, and we tie part of their pay to the performance of their companies. We invest in and modernize the companies. And employees make money with us."

This conglomerate is performing all the functions of a concentrated blockholder while skirting many of the barriers smaller blockholders confront. Inkombank is at the center of one conglomerate and is involved in a number of commodity exchanges, export firms, and industrial enterprises, especially in the timber and wood-processing industry. Alfa Bank controls one of the biggest investment funds and controls a group of firms mainly in the food, chemical, and cement industries. Alliance-Menatep of Bank Menatep controls the Koloss food conglomerate and is active in several other industries, including plastics, textiles, and metallurgy. It has a 78 percent interest in the oil giant Yukos, which owns Yuganskneftegaz, number 9 in the Russia 100. In 1993 Bioprotsess/NIPEK bought shares in about 100 enterprises in the chemical and petrochemical industries and civilian machine building, including about 23 percent of Uralmash, a giant equipment manufacturer with 35,000 workers. And Rossiisky Kredit is developing a group of investments in the fuel industry. It has been reported that Oneksimbank is a very powerful group with 38 percent of Norilsk Nickel (number 6 in the Russia 100), 26 percent of the jet-engine maker Perm Motors, and holdings in metals and oil. The Renaissance Capital investment banking firm sponsors the $152 million Sputnik Fund, which has a majority equity stake in five Russian companies. Renaissance is run by Stephen Jennings, Leonid Rozhetskin, and the American-born Russian investment banker Boris Jordan, who was a pioneer in the Russian stock market as head of Moscow's CS First Boston office. Maybe such banks and holding companies will themselves go public or sell stock on Western stock markets so that investors can invest in many Russian companies through them.

The main purpose of the "capitalist politburo" seems to be to protect the current management of the companies and recreate the huge associations of companies that typified Soviet industry. Anatoly Zaikin, a senior manager in the Ruskhim FIG, in the chemical sector, described his group: "We wanted to establish the old managing system, introducing a new style where economic reasons would prevail over political ones. We used to make tanks but we didn't know who would buy them. That was politics over economics."

The government has an official regulation to prevent FIGs from becoming monopolies. Companies with more than 25,000 workers or dominance in the market are barred from membership in such groups; and companies that are members of one group cannot purchase shares in companies in another group, and so cannot create an interlocking stranglehold of ownership in the emerging Russian economy. The government predicted the formation of 150 FIGs by 1997. But government officials also worried that FIGs might try to translate their economic strength into political strength. They want the strong companies to channel their capital to the weak companies, in effect to create a kind of closed capital market in which enterprise managers can deal with people they know rather than the anonymous market. The former presidential economic adviser Aleksandr Livshits, now minister of finance and deputy prime minister, has said that the main objective of the FIGs is to introduce transnational Russian companies to the world scene and allow them to become active in the economies of the former Soviet republics.

Financial-industrial groups currently have a very low average ownership of 2.6 percent of the Russian economy. They represent 7 percent of all blockholders in the country. FIGs now own over 10 percent of the stock of 10 percent of all companies, 20 percent of 5 percent of Russian companies, and over 49 percent of 1 percent of privatized Russian companies. Russian banks are playing catch-up, with holdings of over 10 percent of 5 percent of privatized Russian corporations and over 28 percent of 1 percent of the companies. The fact that the more entrepreneurial conglomerate FIGs are being organized by banks may help firms restructure, because the banks can overcome some of the barriers to concentrated shareholders.

The FIG is merely the latest manifestation of the struggle of the new economy to emerge from the old. FIGs are proliferating so rapidly that eventually they are all but certain to do battle with open company stock markets. A compromise might be found in a government regulation forcing all FIGs to go public, disclose full financial information, and essentially open themselves up to the participation of ordinary Russian citizens.

Bank Lending. Companies in most market economies do not have to change their boards of directors, their managers, and their shareholders every time they need to restructure and make a capital investment. They borrow money, pledge some of their assets as collateral, and pay back the loan from the profits on the investment. Obviously, if most of the Russian firms that are majority insider-owned came up with a radical restructuring plan that could please the most conservative banker or credit institution, most managers and workers would have no trouble borrowing money and continuing as the majority owners of their companies.

This is not the case. Banks have not been willing to risk their money with many Russian enterprises, and in some firms, insiders have not formulated convincing plans or have lacked some factor necessary to put their plans into operation. Until recently, the land occupied by the corporations was not privatized, so it could not be offered as collateral for a loan. In 1994 and 1995 domestic banks lent only about 5 percent of their available cash for long-term industrial projects. The banks prefer short-term loans or small projects—undertakings costing no more than $10 million—that promise a quick return on their investment. They are wary of the financial risks posed by the enterprises and their lack of legal recourse in an economy where nonpayment of debts is epidemic. As a result, many banks concentrate on a few customers they know well and on taking controls of companies. Inkombank's press secretary told a reporter, "Certainly the goal of our bank is not just profit; it's not just money. We want to become co-owners of major enterprises. Yes, we buy shares. And if some directors do not understand, they are doomed." The general director of a construction company in the Novosibirsk region responded, "They are monsters. They will give you money and ask for 51 percent of your shares and property. And if you become successful they will kick you out. I will never apply for a loan from a Russian bank." In effect, top management's resistance to banks as concentrated shareholders may play some role in the banks' conservatism in respect to industrial lending.

Foreign banks offer little relief. They have been drawn into the Russian government securities market, which offers high yields and none of the complications of lending money to troubled industrial firms. Fragmentary evidence suggests that the European Bank for Reconstruction and Development, the World Bank's International Finance Corporation, and a small number of German and Japanese banks are involved in major Russian corporate loans.

There are indications that Russian banks are getting ready to accumulate large pools of capital, perhaps to begin serious investments in industrial enterprises. Stolichnyi Bank Sberezheny (SBS) and Banque Indosuez have signed a three-year agreement to issue

SBS Eurobonds worth $100 million. And many Russian banks are preparing to issue American depositary receipts. Applications submitted to the SEC by Inkombank, Bank Menatep, and Vozrozhdenie are currently under review.

Mutual Funds. Of the money invested in the U.S. stock market, mutual funds supply about 14 percent, private and government pension funds supply about 26 percent, and insurance companies supply about 4 percent. Mutual funds are increasingly a means for the public to participate in the benefits of share ownership, along with the big players. Funds of this sort would offer an alternative to Russia's FIGs, which exclude small investors. Mutual funds have the advantage of including many small investors, who may have few legal protections in a transitional legal environment such as Russia's but function like big concentrated blockholders, who can compensate for poor enforcement of investor rights. Voucher investment funds own an average of about 23 percent of 5 percent of Russian companies; the holdings of pension funds and insurance companies are negligible. Few voucher funds actually put new capital into companies. Russian citizens are conservatively estimated to have $10 billion to $20 billion in cash hidden away in their homes because they have no confidence in the Russian banks, mutual funds, or stock market. The European Bank for Reconstruction and Development estimates that Russians have exported $40 billion more for investment in stocks, bonds, real estate, and money market accounts in other countries. If mutual funds in Russia could collect some of this money and invest it in blocks of stocks in companies with real governance, restructuring might be accelerated. Foreign investment amounted to less than $1 billion in 1994 and again in 1995, so only a small percentage of Russians' hidden cash would need to be drawn into the stock market to give domestic investment a far greater role in the economy than foreigners now play.

The Federal Commission on Securities and the Capital Market issued regulations in 1996 to create such mutual funds, with provisions to protect small investors by allowing class-action suits. The funds will function as unit investment trusts of both open and interval varieties. Investors in an open fund can redeem their shares for cash within about two weeks of application; investors in an interval fund can redeem their shares at least once a year. Foreigners as well as Russians can invest in these mutual funds. The commission has invited a number of unregistered investment companies to convert to mutual funds. An investment fund called Russky Dom Selenga,

with a portfolio worth about $80 million, was the first to do so. Mu-
tual funds sponsored by Pioneer First-Voucher (controlled by the
Pioneer Group of mutual funds in Boston), Asko-Kapital, and Prom-
radtekhbank are among several in the planning stage. These funds
can negotiate privately with willing managers to buy blocks of stock
in corporations, or they can simply decide where the best investments lie and buy stock in the open market. Their ability to effect
restructuring will depend on their ability to overcome the frustra-
tions that some concentrated shareholders are experiencing. As Russian and foreign pension funds and insurance companies become
more active in the Russian stock market, the economic role played
by investment funds of all types may increase.

The youth of the Russian financial markets needs to be put into
perspective. In the United States, the New Jersey Public Pension
Fund was not allowed to invest in stocks until 1960. Before that, the
fund invested in bonds and lost money on every bond it bought. In
1975 the state fund was allowed to invest a tenth of its assets in
stocks; only since then has it put a major portion of assets in stocks.
Heavy profits on those investments swelled the fund's value to $50
billion. In 1996, while governance of Russian companies and local
managers' financial skills remained in question, as did the scope
and accessibility of the emerging stock market, domestic Russian
investment funds owned more than 17 percent of 10 percent and
more than a quarter of 1 percent of all Russian privatized companies.
They may play a key role in Russia's economic future.

The Emerging Russian Stock Market

The Russian stock market has emerged from infancy and is toddling.
It is officially made up of all large and mid-sized privatized companies. The chief market regulator in Russia is Dmitry Vasiliev, a 32-
year-old cabinet minister who heads the Federal Commission on
Securities and the Capital Market, which is now establishing offices
in most of the regions of the country. On the basis of the selling prices
of stocks provided by top managers in the Russian National Survey,
the entire market of about 18,000 corporations was worth $26 billion
in the fall of 1995. This figure, however, is based on the value of
corporations in the Russian National Sample. Since our sample includes only a few of the Russia 100, the figure should be viewed as
one possible estimate of the value of the privatized corporations not
yet actively traded. The Russia 100 account for about $20 billion in

market value just by themselves. No one can really know the precise market value of privatized companies, or of the subgroup of those companies that would be likely candidates for trading in an established stock exchange in a normal economy. For the time being, the stocks of the Russia 100 are the ones that brokers and buyers consider to make up the Russian stock market. The key industry groups in the Russia 100 account for most of the value of the trading market: oil and gas, 43 percent; electric utilities, 21 percent; metals, 13 percent; telecommunications, 11 percent; paper and pulp, 3 percent; refineries, 2 percent; shipping, 2 percent; and other groups, 5 percent. But Gazprom (no. 2) alone may be worth $27 billion.

When we asked top managers to estimate the real market value of their corporations, they gave an exaggerated figure many tens of times higher than the last trading price of their stock. On the basis of the low prices for which these companies were sold during privatization and the low market prices of Russian assets in relation to world prices, a very conservative guess is that the entire stock market is perhaps worth many times the traded value. Obviously, the ultimate value of the Russian stock market depends on several factors: political risk, restructuring, and the ease of buying and selling, which in turn will depend on legal protections for investors and a positive attitude toward investment by workers and managers.

The activities of the stock market from day to day are much more narrowly focused than this potential for growth suggests. The stock market lost half its value from 1994 to early 1996, when investors began to get nervous about the future of reform amid mounting expectations of Communist electoral gains. But the stock market rebounded significantly before the presidential election in 1996. The Moscow Times Index gained 50 percent between January and June and it gained 70 percent between March and June. The CS First Boston ROS Index nearly doubled in those three months. The Russian market has been a roller-coaster market. From January 1 to August 14, 1996, the Moscow stock market gained 103.5 percent in U.S. dollar terms and was the best performing emerging market in the world. A major Moscow broker estimates that the 500 largest corporations will ultimately account for over 90 percent of the value on this market. The Russia 100—oil stocks, regional energy utilities, pulp and paper companies, and metallurgy corporations—constitute most of the Russian Trading System, which is similar to a Western stock exchange. An electronic trading system—like NASDAQ in the United States—links Moscow, St. Petersburg, Ekaterinburg, and Novosibirsk and is now being extended to about twenty other regions.

About 150 brokers use that system, and maintain it through PAUFOR, the Association of Professional Market Participants.

Most trading takes place in Moscow and St. Petersburg. There is very little trading elsewhere except on the Vladivostok Stock Exchange, in the Far East. Insiders are holding their shares, other owners are unwilling to sell, and the infrastructures that would facilitate the buying and selling of stock do not yet exist in most of Russia's regions. Even among the top 100 to 200 corporations that are accessible on the stock market, the "free float," or the stock that shareholders are willing to sell, is less than a fifth of their shares. The state, some stable outside shareholders, and insiders still own significant chunks of many of those companies, and they do not routinely trade their stocks. Daily trading in stocks was rather low, at about $10 million to $20 million in the spring of 1996, but it is picking up. Various estimates suggest that 20 to 40 percent of the daily trades are taking place on the Russian Trading System and the rest over the counter through the pink-sheet market; buyers and sellers, in other words, simply use personal contacts, telephones, or advertisements to meet. The top 20 of the Russia 100 firms accounted for most of the trading that took place in mid-1996. If the market continues to develop, the number of companies listed on the Russian Trading System, the number of companies that are actually trading on any given day, and the free float will all grow gradually. Today, however, the country has a thinly traded market and a small one.

In the second half of 1994, the buyers in the market were mostly foreign investors who believed the market would boom. In a reaction to political events, they dampened their buying through 1995. By 1996, however, they still accounted for more than half of the trading and buying.

Foreigners participate in the market in several ways. About $1 billion has entered the market through various kinds of mutual and investment funds dedicated to Russia. The Templeton Russia Fund, for example, is listed on the New York Stock Exchange. Pioneer of Boston has announced a fund. Several major Russian investment institutions, along with the European Bank for Reconstruction and Development and the International Finance Corporation of the World Bank, created Sector Capital, which plans to put $100 million into Russian stocks. A number of limited partnerships and groups have assembled other funds in the United States and elsewhere, such as the Fleming Russia Securities Fund, Russia Partners, the Firebird Fund, and Regent's White Tiger, Blue Tiger, and Red Tiger funds, listed on the Dublin Stock Exchange. Most of the major U.S.

and British investment banks and brokerages buy Russian stocks and are developing the capacity to issue reports on Russian companies, and thus to provide financial advice to potential investors. Several foreign brokerages, such as Brunswick Brokerage and ING Barings Securities, have assembled large research and trading staffs in Moscow. In 1995 the U.S. Securities and Exchange Commission (SEC) decided to allow the Bank of New York and Citibank to issue American depositary receipts (ADRs) for several Russia 100 companies.

ADRs are trading securities issued by an American bank based on foreign stocks. Mosenergo, a Moscow utility, was the first Russian firm to make ADRs available. It was soon followed by LUKoil, an oil producer, and Severskyi Trubnyi Zavod, a pipe producer in Polevskoi, near Ekaterinburg. Because of the risk involved, American authorities allow Russian ADRs to be sold only on the over-the-counter market to institutional investors, and the SEC cautions investors that Russian share registries are not carefully kept. Other Russia 100 companies are reportedly preparing to make ADRs available. ING Barings launched the Russian Depositary Certificate Program, which allows foreign investors to buy shares in a trust that owns stocks in eleven of the Russia 100 and which is eligible for investment by U.S. mutual funds. If the stock market continues to develop, we may see the inclusion of Russian stocks in emerging market funds and global mutual funds, offerings of Russian funds by more of the major mutual funds, offerings of Russian ADRs to individual investors on the major U.S. stock exchanges, and investment in the Russian market by the giant U.S., European, and Asian pension funds.

Russian domestic investors have begun to assert themselves as a force in the market. Russian brokers and banks buy shares to build a diversified portfolio for themselves, to have shares available to sell to domestic and foreign clients, and to help a strategic investor accumulate stakes. One of the leading brokerages in Moscow accumulated a controlling interest in a major pulp and wood corporation for a foreign strategic investor by slowly buying shares as they became available on the market and placing ads offering to buy shares from employees and anyone else who owned them.

As is typical in most of the world's stock markets, common citizens have remained wary. For example, a bread factory in St. Petersburg, Khlebnyi Dom, offered about 14 million shares to investors in the fall of 1995. Some citizens bought the stock, but investment houses and three of the city's large banks—Bank Petrovsky, Kredit Peterburg, and the St. Petersburg Industry and Construction Bank—bought most of the shares. Several earlier new share issues by the Red October Chocolate Company also aroused little interest among ordinary citizens.

When Russian citizens gain more confidence in the stock market, if ever they do, the next major step in the market's development will be the growth of mutual funds. In the very risky and politically uncertain young Russian market, what have brokerages and the Russian government done to justify some minimum amount of investor confidence in these stock purchases and trades? To ensure that stocks are quickly paid for when they are bought or sold, brokers and many of the country's largest banks founded the Moscow-based Depository Clearing Company in 1993. As we have seen, the Russian Federal Commission on Securities and the Capital Market has required shareholder registers to be maintained by independent registrars, but more than half the companies are not complying with this regulation. To increase investor confidence, the Russian Securities Commission worked with the Bank of New York and several major Russian banks to found the National Registry Company (NRC), which in 1995 contracted with IBM to computerize the records of up to 10 million shareholders. Corporations that want to be able to assure investors that their ownership is properly and independently registered can point to their membership in the NRC.

Many owners of stocks let their brokers hold their shares. What happens if the broker goes bankrupt or commits fraud? To respond to investors' fears on this score, many Russian and foreign banks are beginning to offer trust and custody services, so that shareholders can choose an institution other than their broker to be custodian of their shares. Western companies that offer custody services in Russia are CS First Boston, Morgan Stanley, Citibank, ING Bank, and Chase Manhattan. PAUFOR, comprising brokers and other financial institutions, pledges to adhere to strict trading rules and high standards of integrity. Finally, the government securities watchdog has declared that the way to protect the small investor is to issue licenses to market participants, and to suspend or revoke the license of anyone who violates its rules. In 1996, these stock market institutions were used mainly by foreign and large Moscow investors. Institutions to handle the custody of shares, share depositories, the Russian Trading System, and independent shareholder registries had still not expanded for beyond Moscow.

Russia's debt markets were thrown into confusion in June 1996 when it was discovered that many government bonds in circulation are stolen. Some Western investment banks faced losses as the Russian government froze the bonds until their ownership could be established. Russia will no doubt face such reverses again as it tries to build its capital markets. The maintenance of law and order and the level of investor confidence in the market will determine how many corporations view the market as an efficient way to raise capital and how many investors are encouraged to commit their money to it. The more companies that are openly traded, the more individuals, strategic investors, mutual funds, merchant banks, and traditional financial-industrial groups will use the market to acquire shares or to exit firms they no longer want to own.

Many investors have concluded that the only way to restructure a Russian corporation is to take all or most of it under their direct control. If an open and transparent stock market develops, large blockholders and other shareholders in companies with no clear majority owner might be able to cooperate on a board of directors elected through cumulative voting to choose a management team and a company strategy that might accelerate restructuring. In the future, many smaller and mid-sized corporations may end up with majority owners, or even with a single owner. But the largest companies in the country are probably not going to come under the control of a single blockholder. If these firms are to be run in the interest of shareholders, the model of a smoothly functioning public company with an independent board of directors will have to emerge. Roland Machold, director of New Jersey's $50 billion pension fund and an astute analyst of Russian investment, offered the judgment of the skeptical investor: "At the beginning of the Russian reform I visited a large company in St. Petersburg that was looking for an investor of $10 million. I asked them what they planned to use the investment for. They said that winter was coming and they would use it to buy food for their employees. That's not an investment in a corporation, it's a public function. While Americans don't want to hear it, this problem is not uncommon in our own country. Take General Motors. General Motors is not a corporation that is unilaterally committed to return profits to shareholders, it's a large defensive social and political organization that distributes some of its profits to different stakeholders. First, Russia must decide if it will have real corporations. Investors can understand high social responsibilities *in real corporations* if the corporations make them reasonable and clear. Then Russia must decide if it wants to attract a lot of capital. The stock market is small in many Western countries; for example, less than 100 companies trade on the stock market in Germany or Japan. The world stock market is worth many trillions of dollars. Russia could easily be 10 percent of the world market and bring in tens, even hundreds of billions of dollars in capital to restructure its industries. That will depend not only on having the institutions but on making them work. The difference between making life miserable for investors who look at Russia and bringing in $10 billion in the next five years and making investments in Russia uncomplicated and fair can be measured. It's worth about $190 billion more, in my opinion."

The huge gap between the 18,000 companies that could potentially trade and the small number that are actually in the trading system defines both the potential and the risks of the market. The real potential lies in the issuance of new stocks to raise capital for restructuring, in the growth of regional markets, and in the inevitable explosion in the Moscow stock market when and if stability is achieved. If Russia has a smaller stock market, then much larger blocks of concentrated ownership will probably develop as an adaptation to its realities.

5

The Future of Reform

The breakup of the Soviet Union and the immediate undertaking of privatization were crippling blows to the Soviet system. Russian privatization was rapid, extensive, and unprecedented in world history. The enterprises at the heart of an entire economic and political system were fundamentally changed. Almost 90 percent of industrial output and 80 percent of industrial enterprises passed mainly into private hands. The impact of the change in property rights on the companies themselves is a separate issue. The enterprises were torn from the state and the Party. The rapidity with which the Russian population, government bureaucracy, and enterprise management implemented the privatization program proved that economic incentives could motivate a giant shift of systems. State ownership in 60 percent of the firms covered by the 1996 Russian National Survey was zero.

The process of redistribution of ownership will continue for some time. Whether Russia will end up with broader citizen participation in its economic system as a result of voucher privatization, through the development of mutual funds and pension funds that collect the investments of individuals, or narrow concentrated ownership by a few elites is still unclear. Ownership is definitely beginning to concentrate in the hands of commercial firms, financial-industrial groups, banks, and managers. The policies the Russian government pursues and the responses of these institutions will determine the outcome. For example, future privatizations could favor broad citizen participation through mutual and pension funds or sweetheart deals for banks, as in the loan-for-shares scheme. Banks, holding companies, and financial-industrial groups could turn into publicly traded companies and become the AT&Ts and IBMs that put their investors' children through good schools. But the situation is still very fluid.

Whether the ultimate legacy of privatization is broad citizen participation in ownership will depend on the emphasis given to citizen participation in future privatization programs. Obviously ownership will become concentrated, but the form of its concentration is open to question. For reasons of political expediency, many of the country's most valuable corporations were kept out of the original program and precious blocks of shares in thousands of other companies remain unprivatized. It will be unfortunate if the initial privatization program is hailed as an exercise in citizen participation but the property of the most valuable companies—oil and gas, utilities, metals, and telecommunications—is apportioned in a way that gives ordinary citizens no opportunity for ownership. Shares owned by ordinary citizens would have to be organized in pension and mutual funds so that they could play a role as aggressive blockholders in restructuring companies. Only a limited portion of these shares could be distributed free, since these companies require serious capital investments. Some free shares, perhaps in a second voucher program, could compensate citizens for devalued pensions and savings. But other funds should emphasize cash investment by citizens.

The economic incentive that ownership and control of businesses offers will motivate the ongoing struggle for property, which will continue to be a major theme in Russian society. In many ways, the market for corporate control has just opened. However imperfectly and unpredictably, privatization has opened up a market in private property. That market is risky, it is unpleasant, it is not egalitarian; and it tempts the Russian state—whoever possesses the state power at the end of each election—to try to tame and control it in the interests of politicians. The fact is that the Russian state still owns more than 10 percent of about a third of all the already privatized corporations in the country and more than 20 percent of a quarter of them. On average, according to recent estimates, the state owns over a third interest in the top 50 corporations in the country and may own a modest interest in the next 250 large corporations, which may help determine who ultimately controls those companies. The state and existing owners or aspiring owners will struggle over what happens to this residual state interest—which does not include several thousand firms that were never privatized in areas as diverse as coal, precious metals, health, and communications services. The partial or full state role in these firms suggests a continuation of subsidies, a drain on the state budget, and ongoing attempts to combine economic and political activity.

Just the same, governance has superseded government in many corporations. The owners of privatized firms have begun to struggle over power and shareholders' rights. The protectiveness of managers is just as much a sign of this struggle as the aggressiveness of outside investors. Employees now own more of their companies' stock in Russia than in any other nation in the world, but their rights as shareholders and their power as trade union members are compromised. The state has started to play its role as civil arbiter of fair play by taking strong stands on corporate law and the regulation of the securities and capital markets. Whether the emerging corporate and securities laws and regulations develop into the stable norms of a civil society that can attract domestic and foreign investment remains to be seen.

Like new wine in old wineskins, capitalism was implemented by the Kremlin in an environment that has demonstrated more continuity with the attitudes and limitations of the Soviet past than many people had hoped. The design and the extent of privatization were influenced by these constraints. With the exception of a few notable young reformers, who themselves were socialized under the Soviet system, the national and regional officials and the enterprise managers who implemented privatization only recently replaced their Party cards with their business cards and stock certificates. It was to be expected that the mentalities and competencies of these individuals would not change radically. There is no reason to presume that many serious men and women who grew up under the Soviet system really understand the inner workings of the new corporate system in any detail. Social systems simply do not change that fast. And people certainly do not ingest new knowledge overnight. The lingering of old habits of thought becomes clear when one notes the enormous resistance to diversification of ownership in the companies, the lengths to which managers go to undermine governance, and their sheer lack of understanding of what is really entailed in the restructuring of a mature, weak, capital-starved company to make it viable in a market economy. This mentality is not their fault. It is simply a factor in this complicated and confusing transformation. Whatever fundamental changes took place under privatization, they are only the first stage of the much longer and more complicated process of reconstructing Russian society. One problem for the reformers was that in their efforts to privatize the economy, they had to focus intently on privatizing its corporations. But an economy is also people and culture. That process can never be rapid.

After a seventy-year hiatus, Russian managers and employees and investors are confronting the harsh realities of actually having to manage businesses to profitability. Once privatization was a foregone conclusion, the degree to which the larger economic environment of Russia was habitable by these new corporations became the paramount issue. This was the most notable early failure of reform. After the state began to relinquish its overall control of the economy in the period from 1991 to 1993, it failed to implement coherent and consistent programs of macroeconomic reform and political reform of its public institutions. The years from 1993 to 1995 might have gone better for large and mid-sized privatized companies had the government been able to impose a hard budget constraint on the companies and stop the subsidies in the forms of direct payments, sweetheart bank loans, tax arrears, and interenterprise debts. By the end of April 1996 the unpaid debts and outstanding payrolls of Russian state and private enterprises amounted to about 40 percent of gross domestic production, up from 25–30 percent in December 1994. Perhaps under a hard budget constraint managers would have found it not so unthinkable to change their behavior. The unwillingness and inability of the Russian government to create a stable economic environment in those years and the vague hope that perhaps the government might again assume command of the economy encouraged many top managers to drag their feet as they waited for a change of government or of policy that would return state financial aid to their firms.

Many enterprises are weaker today than they were just thirty-six months ago, and the challenge of restructuring them is correspondingly greater. The government failed to make much progress before Anatoly Chubais took over as first deputy prime minister in 1995 with the mandate to bring down inflation, restart the economy, and stabilize the ruble. Before 1996, very little progress was made toward creating a stable legal environment for domestic and foreign investment, accelerating the expansion of the small business sector, or making sense of the high and ever-changing taxes imposed on Russian companies.

Privatization was a seed that fell on hard, dry ground. After four years of reform, the nation was still struggling to jump-start national and regional stock markets and lending to enterprises by banks. Privatization had been combined with a halfhearted attempt at macroeconomic stabilization and a lack of attention to developing the institutions that provide the water and the nutrients of a civil society in a free market economy. The reason can be found in part in the fact that since 1991 every Russian government has been essentially a coalition between the forces of socialism and the forces of capitalism, each trying to moderate the other's influence. Finally, the failure to strengthen the economy as a whole only increased the toll on ordinary citizens. Many of them sought relief by supporting nationalists and Communists in elections, thus further weakening any government's ability to move decisively along the path of reform.

For its part, the government as a whole has exhibited an unfortunate lack of concern for the plight of old people, the poor, children, the sick, the unemployed, and its soldiers while it has paid close attention to the demands for subsidies, favors, and insider deals by powerful directors of big enterprises and other people with political connections. Obviously, the best social welfare will be a vibrant market economy that creates jobs and rewards individual initiative. The IMF and the World Bank have repeatedly stipulated that the government must make a social safety net a priority to aid the weakest citizens during the transition. The government has ignored this injunction, and the international community has never mobilized either aid or pressure to change this alarming situation. Any future "reform" government will confront a budget crisis of daunting proportions. It will not be able to fund social programs for the needy and at the same time pour largess on corporations and cronies. The government must start to extend aid to weak citizens directly through civilized health, welfare, unemployment, and training programs and let firms stand or fall on their own. The international community and organizations that loan Russia funds cannot continue their clear record of failure on the question of a social safety net for Russian citizens. And the Russian government needs to put its most capable ministers in charge of the social welfare ministries and give them significant political status, authority, budgets, and room to maneuver with creative ideas.

The reform team and the reform program itself were hampered by a variety of factors. First was the unfortunate fact that before 1995 the reformers never exercised unmistakable and consistent control over economic policy. The Central Bank was not under their control during most of the reform period. Though the privatization program was quickly implemented, the reform team had little influence over the larger economic world into which these infant corporations were being born. It was 1995, too late, when the reform team began to

focus on building the institutions for the restructuring of enterprises
—capital markets, technical assistance institutions, corporate laws,
management training. Even then, they ignored the potential role of
trade unions as a counterforce to supreme managerial power. Another handicap was the fact that the reform team was focusing on
reengineering the Russian economy without significant input by any
senior Russian historian, who might have helped them appreciate
the enormous drag Soviet culture and Russian history would exert
on the sprint forward and tempered their expectations.

We believe that when an undertaking of this immensity became
inevitable in Russia, a response by the leading nations of the West
and East amounting to a mini–Marshall Plan was in order. Certainly, Russia in 1991 was not like Western Europe at the end
of World War II. Russia was unwilling to give the West the kind of
allegiance the European powers gave in return for the massive aid of
the Marshall Plan, and many Russian firms could not be saved by a
simple influx of money and equipment. Nevertheless, the intensity
and focus of the Marshall Plan could have been brought to a few
worthwhile crash projects that explicitly did not emphasize direct
subsidies to enterprises but attempted to fast-track the construction
of an institutional infrastructure for a market economy. Training in
industrial management, investment banking, accounting, and law
should quickly have been provided to tens of thousands of young
Russians rather than to the tiny number that undertook these prepa-
rations.

The leading industrialized nations focused on privatization with
the intensity of a laser beam and ignored the wide-ranging institutional development Russia sorely needed and still needs. While the
U.S. Agency for International Development, the British Know How
Fund, the World Bank, the European Community, and the European
Bank for Reconstruction and Development strongly supported the
privatization program, much more should have been done more
quickly to accelerate the development of stock markets, private bank
lending to enterprises, mutual funds for citizens, investment banks,
and clear and coherent reforms in Russian law, taxation, domestic
and foreign investment, and trade unions. Programs of technical
assistance to develop these institutions should have been begun in
1992. Because the arrival of 18,000 capital-starved corporations on
the world market was so unprecedented, many billions of dollars
should have quickly been made available to a large number of privately managed enterprise restructuring funds to begin intensive
review of loans for the modernization of key Russian industries. As
it happened, this process has moved very slowly.

The only question left is whether the industrialized nations will continue to be shortsighted as Russia confronts its new crisis, the one caused by the notable lack of maturity of Russian institutions as they attempt to deal with the emerging market economy and the concomitant emphasis on private ownership. In fact, their immaturity is so marked that it threatens the entire realization of the first stage of the Russian transformation.

Was There Another Way?

The time is too short and the evidence still too scant to permit a clear perspective on the giant leap forward that Russia has attempted. One criticism of the rapid privatization program is that this project could have been better planned, done more gradually, managed more successfully. We agree with this criticism, but only in part. The Gorbachev administration bears full responsibility for setting up the game so that the only responsible choice was to force both rapid privatization and rapid elimination of state control over the Russian economy. Mikhail Gorbachev's courage and political vision, shortsighted though it was, make him one of history's great men. But he simply did not understand the extent of the economic transformation he had to manage or how to go about it. At first he lacked the power to carry it out, and when he amassed the power to do so, he squandered the opportunity. In his destructive and misguided attempt to rescue the Communist Party, he repeatedly tried to reform Russia by introducing just a sprinkling of private ownership and market reform. Gorbachev wasted the years during which Russia could have attempted a more gradual, "Chinese" approach to reform. Observers who claim that there was another way in 1991, after Gorbachev failed, are obliged to explain how the finances of the Soviet state or the Russian nation could have been managed through anything but the state's rapid exit from the economy.

What could a gradual solution to Russian reform have looked like in 1987? Gorbachev's Soviet Union could have begun with broad-based agricultural reform, turning agriculture over to private farmers and disbanding the system of state and collective farms. A banking system could have been developed to lend farmers money for seed and machinery. Instead of betting on individual initiative and figuring out a way to supply individual farmers with the resources and technical assistance they needed to develop, Gorbachev squandered billions on enterprise subsidies and inefficiency. Despite repeated decrees and laws that in theory announced such a reform, the Russian parliament was still arguing about agricultural reform in 1996. The Duma is afraid of private landownership and has been unwilling to entertain even systematic long-term leasing of land to individual farmers. In China, private farming stimulated the rural economy. Peasants went on to set up hundreds of thousands of township and village enterprises, nominally owned by the local government, that processed food, initiated manufacturing, and began to offer services to this booming economy. These enterprises provided jobs and stimulated the small business sector in the country. The local commerce and entrepreneurial initiative allowed a new private sector to grow rapidly.

In 1987 Russia could have quickly begun to encourage such a private economy. Instead, Gorbachev first allowed the creation of private businesses and then tried to apply the brakes. China allowed the creation of new private businesses, and by 1996 private business accounted for 60 percent of the Chinese economy, despite the fact that most large and mid-sized state-owned companies in China have not yet been privatized. The Chinese must move those enterprises out of state ownership and control, and now they have a more stable economic environment in which to do so. The Chinese set up special economic zones in their coastal provinces to encourage massive infusion of foreign investment and joint ventures in manufacturing. China has attracted tens of billions of foreign direct investment during the same period in which Russia has brought in $1 billion to $2 billion a year. Certainly, Russia could not call upon a vibrant financial sector like Hong Kong or the hundreds of thousands of overseas Chinese to stimulate business development, but the Gorbachev administration passed up its opportunities. There are many Russian émigrés who might have been interested in business opportunities if the environment had been more friendly. In fact, Russia did everything it could to repel foreign investment during this period.

Ironically, on one front, Russia and China are arriving at the same set of ideas. Workers and managers are pressuring provincial authorities and the central government to allow them to own stock in the township and village enterprises in provinces all over China and in the tens of thousands of state-owned companies. Employee ownership of many mid-sized Chinese companies is moving rapidly in several provinces, especially Jiangsu (Shanghai) and Shandong. Observers who argue that reliance on insider ownership was a fatal error in Russia tend also to put their faith in the more gradual route of the Chinese reform. They need only look to China once again to see that, whatever its disadvantages, insider ownership is one of the few means to quick "privatization" of a system dependent on state ownership, control, and subsidies. Eventually, however, insider ownership is destined to lead to a redistribution of ownership because employees can maintain ownership control with certainty only in the very successful enterprises. In the end, employee ownership is always earned, not given.

We agree with the analysis of Anders Åslund on the reasons why neither Gorbachev nor any other Soviet leader would have had an easy time following a path similar to the one taken by China. He notes that whereas the cultural revolution cost millions of Chinese lives and the Communist Party of Mao Zedong a devastating loss of confidence, Gorbachev confronted a conservative and committed Communist bureaucracy. He notes that Deng Xiaoping had a mandate for radical but pragmatic change, whereas Gorbachev had support only for an effort to revitalize the Communist Party. He correctly points out that China was more likely than Russia to succeed with a reform program that focused on agriculture, for "no less than 71 percent of the labor force in China worked in agriculture in 1978, compared to 14 percent in Russia in 1985." Agriculture was essentially a manual and small-scale enterprise in China; in Russia it was a big collective enterprise with associated machine tractor stations and high fixed costs. The state and collective farms would be harder to break up than the Chinese plots. The longer the Soviet system lasted, Åslund says, the more likely it was to suffer massive disruption. Gorbachev had less power to change the system than many observers believed, and he confronted a system that differed significantly from the Chinese system. Nevertheless, we believe that Gorbachev lost an important opportunity to use agricultural reform and a rapidly growing small business sector to stimulate the Soviet economy and prepare the ground for later privatization.

Some of Russia's best economists advised Gorbachev to move more forcefully toward privatization. By pushing this advice aside, he accelerated the bankruptcy of the Soviet system, and the result is an odd irony. If privatization had been implemented by Gorbachev, he might have created a commonwealth not unlike the Soviet Union under his leadership. Once he was forced to slow the movement toward reform, he hastened the end of the Soviet Union. The Russian Federation inherited a system that was at the breaking point, and its leaders felt they had no choice but to forge a new private sector immediately. The time for designs and plans was past. On the one hand, we do not understand how the Russian government could have afforded to manage and subsidize such a large state-owned sector after 1992 at the level necessary to prevent dislocations. On the other hand, we think it is unfortunate that during its first years privatization advanced rapidly while a program of macroeconomic stabilization stumbled slowly along. But the two should not be confused.

Will Russia Restructure?

Russia is an economy and a society in transition. It would be unrealistic to expect it to transform itself in a year or two. Russia must now confront the management of the system of Kremlin capitalism it has created. No one knows for sure how this new economic system will evolve. Nevertheless, some of its key challenges are unmistakable. Privatized enterprises must be restructured quickly. None of the factors that influence restructuring are worth analyzing unless Russian corporations are actually capable of being rescued. How many Russian companies are profitable? How many are profitable but need capital? How many need extensive restructuring, and how many should be allowed to go bankrupt? If many companies are very profitable, perhaps the Russian government, investors, and international observers should sit back and be patient as the more and the less profitable companies sort themselves out. If many companies are on the point of collapse or need far-reaching restructuring, removing the barriers to concentrated blockholders who want to restructure becomes an urgent necessity.

The finances of Russian companies are very complex, but for a rough analysis we can divide the corporations into four groups. The first group, the winners, are probably going to survive. These firms may be able to finance their restructuring from their own profits. The stock of these companies is going to make their employees and managers rich, unless huge errors are made. Their stock is likely to increase in value, and the companies may remain majority insider-owned. If they sell shares to outside investors and are taken over, the price will be far higher than what the workers paid. Winners either already make products that Russians want to buy or have developed export markets.

The second group, the potential winners, are profitable enterprises but they desperately need capital to buy new equipment and overhaul their operations. Their management teams, which may be satisfactory, must immediately devise radical restructuring plans and strategies for securing massive infusions of capital. If the current management teams cannot make that decision, they must quickly be replaced. These companies face a tricky decision. They have to choose the right partner, one who both has capital and can help manage the implementation of their restructuring plan. Choosing the wrong partner may spell the company's doom. In view of Russian banks' lack of experience in restructuring and the infancy of commercial lending, these potential winners are the most likely candidates for new share issues, friendly mergers, strategic investors, hostile take-overs, and acquisition by merchant banks. The insiders' stock ownership and control of the board and management will decrease significantly in this group of companies. Our estimates indicate that the average employee ownership in these companies must drop significantly in order to accommodate an investor who will bring the company the capital that the current general director says it needs.

The third group of enterprises are in an uncertain situation: they either are sliding toward bankruptcy or should be in bankruptcy reorganization now. These companies are very unprofitable and need capital to modernize and to operate. They need a thorough management change. It is doubtful that the current managers can put together a serious restructuring plan. Because of their very weak financial situation, these companies probably do not have the luxury of issuing new shares. If they act quickly, they may escape bankruptcy. Urgent action may allow them to save some stock ownership for insiders, but they probably need to be taken over completely.

The fourth group of companies, the losers, are candidates for immediate bankruptcy. They need to go bankrupt because it is impossible for them to operate successfully. Their assets and property should be sold and used to start new, smaller businesses. If these companies wind up their operations early, they may be able to salvage some assets to give to employees. Some of these companies occupy real estate that is worth more than the business. It is possible that a few of them may be able to find an investor who will bail them out and take them over, but unless the enterprises are located in downtown Moscow, it is unlikely that significant employee or management ownership can survive in these firms. Unfortunately, Russia has no efficient bankruptcy laws and the government has been unwilling to allow bankruptcies. These companies survive to provide social support and services to employees. Eventually they must be allowed to wrap up their operations in a way that provides some benefit to the employees.

On the basis of a preliminary analysis and managers' assessment of their own situations, our evaluation of the Russian National Survey of corporations in 1995 and 1996 leads to a shocking conclusion: No more than a quarter of Russian companies are clear winners, and only a small number of those firms are likely to be able to finance their modernization out of their profits. The bad news is that three-quarters of Russian corporations are in need of radical and far-reaching restructuring. At least a quarter of those firms should be bankrupt. In June 1996, after we completed our analysis, Oleg Soskovets, former first deputy prime minister, said that 35 percent of industrial enterprises were technically bankrupt. No one can know how the privatized corporations will ultimately shake out, how many of the three-quarters of those firms will end up as potential winners, in an uncertain situation, or losers. Just as it was difficult in the 1980s to predict which steel firms in the northeastern and midwestern United States would go bankrupt and which would completely and painfully restructure themselves, so it is difficult to predict what mixture of management talent, capital investment, worker ingenuity, luck, technology, consulting assistance, and market savvy will determine the outcomes for the Russian companies. They face alarming problems of access to capital and management talent.

How much capital investment is necessary to modernize all 18,000 privatized corporations? When estimates by the top managers in the Russian National Survey in 1995 are telescoped to all privatized corporations, the amount is between $150 and $300 billion, depending on which method of estimate is used. At the higher end of this estimate, the general directors are probably exaggerating the amount of capital they need because they generally think big. To them, to restructure is to buy enough equipment to increase the overall operations of their firms rather than to focus on and modernize only the potentially profitable parts of their plants. Many of these companies will go out of existence and have no need for capital if they are sold piecemeal and the proceeds used to start smaller businesses. Some senior Russian officials have put the figure as high as $200 billion, and certainly our figures do not account for the much larger capital needs of the Russian oil and metal industries or include funds for the development of infrastructure, such as highways and telecommunications. Even if the number is as small as $100 billion, it is almost twice the size of the entire 1995 Russian government budget, which was approximately $50 billion. Furthermore, these estimates include only the costs of capital investment. They do not include the costs of subsidizing wages to maintain full employment or supporting the many social services provided to employees. These figures suggest that no Russian government can subsidize its way to industrial renaissance, even if government planning and control of the economy were to prove successful, which they never have done. Can a government with seventy years of experience managing a nonmarket economy become the world's turnaround artist overnight? Not likely.

No government can afford to use its entire annual budget to modernize its industry even if it could do the job efficiently. With foreign investment in Russia amounting to no more than $1 billion to $2 billion a year since the beginning of reform, the capital that privatized corporations need represents a capital investment crisis of astounding proportions. In 1995 half of Russia's foreign investment went to the energy sector, which accounts for less than 6 percent of all employment. The European Bank for Reconstruction and Development has estimated that Russian citizens and companies have at least $40 to $50 billion in investments outside Russia—money they might repatriate if the country's investment climate were favorable. Much of the $20 billion that citizens are estimated to have stuffed in their mattresses could easily find its way into saving accounts or mutual funds. Even if foreign aid for industrial restructuring were to amount to a few billion dollars annually—highly unlikely—foreign aid could never provide the kinds of resources that a restructuring of Russia's own financial system could offer. Russia must reform its public sector so that the country can deal with these challenges.

Russia's only choice is to develop capital markets—stock markets and bond markets that efficiently put capital in the hands of corporations and banks that believe they can make money by lending it to companies. Banks must be regulated so that citizens can view them as safe havens for their funds. Mutual funds need to be developed to attract Russian and foreign capital and direct it to productive investment. Capital markets must be developed on an emergency basis to prevent the collapse of Russian industry. They must be developed in all of the country's eighty-nine regions and they must be relatively free of crime and corruption. This is a tall order.

An impediment to Russian firms' prospects for acquiring new capital is the mentality of their general directors. In the Russian National Surveys of 1995 and 1996, more than two-thirds said that they and their employees would oppose selling a majority of the shares of their enterprises to an investor who would bring the entire amount of capital necessary to modernize and restructure the firm. This mentality is suicidal. It makes no business sense. By focusing on control, Russian managers forget that if an investor buys 51 percent of their company and the insiders' stake falls from 59 percent to 20 percent, that 20 percent of stock in a restructured company will be worth more than 59 percent of a failing company. The top managers of some Russian corporations are saying they would rather let their enterprises die than get the capital they need from an investor. The longer these companies wait to find an investor, the more they will shrink and the more value in stock employees and managers will lose when and if they finally make a deal.

This consideration raises the question of the quality of top management. Unfortunately, our evidence strongly suggests that a large portion of the top managerial class is simply not up to the job. They stubbornly cling to inside ownership. They are resistant to corporate governance, they oppose outside investors, they do not understand the extent of the restructuring their enterprises actually need, and they are not willing to make such radical changes. They are on average 50 years old, so that they had over 45 years of socialization and training in a communist system as preparation for a task that would make seasoned CEOs in Ohio, Pennsylvania, and Illinois shudder. Their employees, their deputies, their investors, their lenders, and their government seem more interested in going along with most of them and thus silently cooperating in the strangulation of the enterprises. Surely there are some exceptions, but we know of no statistical evidence to suggest that changing a 50-year-old general manager for his or her 47-year-old deputy is much of an improvement.

Rather than thinking of subsidies, the Russian government should be stimulating the training and education of thousands of young Russians in the skills of restructuring, turnaround management, and bankruptcy workouts by sending them as apprentices to the regions of the major industrialized powers that have faced these crises. It should be using foreign assistance to contract with the best universities in those countries to offer eighteen-month MBA programs in the restructuring of manufacturing concerns.

As the Russian economy stabilized in 1995 and 1996, the top managers of the enterprises found that high inflation was no longer wiping out their debts or reducing their principle and interest payments. When monthly inflation is low, a loan today is a loan that really has to be paid back tomorrow. Now that they have discovered that financial games must stop and efficient management must begin, their response has been to call for higher inflation and a less stable ruble to make Russian products more competitive overseas, high tariffs on foreign products to protect Russian goods, a return to state subsidies, cheap credits for enterprises through state support of cheap money and loan guarantees for commercial banks, and continuation of the current xenophobic environment for foreign investment. They have pressured politicians to embrace these policies, and some industrial leaders have supported Communist, nationalist, and ultranationalist parties in their drive to create a strong industrial policy in Russia.

Our discussions with the managerial elite indicate that they strongly believe that the absence of restructuring is caused by the lack of state involvement in the economy and—at their xenophobic worst—by a conspiracy on the part of some of Russia's reformers and the leaders of the industrialized nations, who together seek to destroy the Russian economy. Most do not really believe that clear corporate and securities laws that protect shareholders, responsible corporate governance and its enforcement, strong and open capital markets, and openness to outside investment are the means to solve the restructuring puzzle. Many top managers respond to the gap between the capital their enterprises need for modernization and the capital available by concluding that the private sectors of both Russia and the industrialized nations have abandoned them after promising to help. Observers who reread the statements of Western leaders from 1991 to 1994 might concede that the managers have a point. But this subjective perception cannot influence the objective problem: 18,000 firms have come on the world capital market in dire need of modernization in a poorly developed legal and investment environment that both domestic and foreign investors mistrust.

The Next Reforms

The leading industrialized nations are guilty of a serious error of judgment in failing to recognize that privatization of Russia's industries was just one brick in the structure of economic reform. A system of laws and reasonable taxation must be developed to assure all participants that fair play is an enforceable objective of this system. The court system and the police and the people who staff them need to be developed and trained.

No country should extend aid to Russia except on the strict condition that Russia make rapid headway on these institutional reforms and on a modest new program to lend the resources and technical assistance necessary to implement such changes. Each new reform that is mismanaged will lessen the possibility that the trajectory of Russia's development will be upward. Russia needs emergency assistance with its health-care system. The regions require substantial technical and financial assistance to divorce the kindergartens, day-care centers, and housing complexes from the privatized enterprises. Land must be privatized immediately in order both to stimulate Russia's agricultural economy and to jump-start the real estate market in the cities and towns. Once land is privatized, it can serve as collateral for loans by companies that need capital to restructure. Some enterprises may be able to raise money for themselves through the sale of land.

Small businesses must be developed to expand both production and employment as the failing corporations contract. But predicting the future role of small business is very difficult because estimates of the size of this sector vary widely. Goskomstat says that 9 million people, just over a tenth of the workforce, were employed by 900,000 small businesses in 1996 and accounted for 11 to 12 percent of Russia's total production. Small businesses accounted for more than half the tax receipts for the city of Moscow, where tax revenues from large privatized enterprises were declining. Many of these businesses are shops and retail outlets that were privatized, but many of them are new businesses formed by entrepreneurs. The business researcher Thomas Tirone, of the Tirone Corporation in Champaign, Illinois, estimates that entrepreneurial firms make up no more than half of the Russian small business sector, and perhaps much less. The average startup firm has thirty-two persons; more than half of such firms have only fourteen persons. The typical founder of a new Russian small business is 39 years old, married with one child, and is sophisticated, intelligent, and hardworking. A third have Ph.D.'s and manage highly profitable one-product companies with an annual growth rate of 49 percent.

In a normal market economy, small businesses generally have a high rate of failure; but if a large number of the bigger Russian companies fail to restructure in the next two years, small businesses will have to grow at a rapid rate to absorb their employees and thus to serve as Russia's only safety valve. Russia is still a long way from having a small business sector flexible enough to serve as a buffer for the risky industrial restructuring the nation confronts. Enterprises with fewer than 100 employees account for 50 to 62 percent of the gross domestic product and an average of 59 percent of the workforces of Britain, Germany, Italy, France, the United States, and Japan. Russia would have nowhere to turn if its industrial restructuring stalled and its small business sector failed to boom.

Many privatized firms with fewer than 1,000 employees might be run more efficiently if they were broken up or downsized, so that they could be owned and managed by a single person or a small group of people. Businesses of this kind could account for as much as 25 to 35 percent of firms and employment. Russian industry might also develop through joint ventures. Domestic and foreign investors may be more comfortable investing in one promising department of a large privatized company than in buying stock in a big company with unclear financial and social obligations. Unfortunately, 80 percent of the joint ventures in Russia are now involved in wholesale trade, only 20 percent in industrial firms.

The Reality from Which There Is No Escape

Neither a reform nor a semireform nor a Communist government can afford to subsidize Russian industry on the scale necessary to prevent a disaster. Only a continuation of reforms can address this situation. Any government that attempts an industrial policy will be fated to pick favorite factories or industry groups and let the others die on the vine. The harsh reality is that there is no alternative to far-reaching changes in most of Russia's enterprises. They are not restructuring quickly enough. Their managers have not improved their financial condition. The companies are not being run in a way that beckons outside investors and provides adequate governance rights. Many of them are managing to exist by playing a range of conventional and unconventional finance games: reducing capacity, trimming employment, changing prices, selling inventory, obtaining subsidies, putting employees on furlough, borrowing from commercial banks at very high interest rates, and accumulating huge debts to other enterprises. If they are not restructured soon, the inevitable bankruptcies or more accelerated downsizings will send unemployment rocketing.

Hundreds, perhaps thousands of the companies that have a chance of surviving must now open their doors to new investors. No method of acquiring capital must be rejected or overlooked. The stock market and its infrastructure must be developed to make it easier for domestic and foreign investors and merchant banks to buy strategic stakes, to mount outsider and insider takeovers, and to put together blockholder investments for newly emerging mutual funds; commercial banks must be developed to make it easier for companies with some potential to get loans. The problem is not too much foreign investment but foreigners' unwillingness to enter Russian capital markets on a large scale. When foreign ownership of stock in the larger companies is less than 2 percent on average, no half measures are likely to increase it to the level of foreign investment in the Czech Republic, let alone China. A stable political climate and strong encouragement is necessary to encourage foreign investment.

Industrial leaders remain convinced that their inertia—or in some cases their grab for power—is in the interests of their factories, workforces, and communities, but they must now face a stark reality. By putting off a redistribution of ownership, correct governance, and radical restructuring, managerial leaders and boards of directors are actually exacerbating the problems they have said they hope to protect their companies against. Under one dangerous scenario, the more slowly industrial leaders accept these reforms, the more the state will be pressured to increase its subsidies and direct involvement in the economy. These actions will fuel inflation and prevent the country from abiding by the guidelines set forth by the International Monetary Fund. Further bankruptcy of the state treasury and continued policy flip-flops would restrict the development of the private sector. Russia would then be unable to save its mid-sized and big companies, be unable to afford continuing subsidies, and have no vibrant small business sector to absorb the unemployed. These are conditions that encourage military involvement in the nation's affairs or a more broad-based flirtation with Communist or ultranationalist candidates.

A constructive scenario for Russian reform envisions a patchwork of developments. The institutions of a free market economy continue to evolve rapidly. Part of the privatized corporations are saved, some die. The corporations' shareholders learn actually to share their holdings and profits. Workable corporate governance emerges. A new small business sector continues to expand to provide alternative employment to the millions who lose their jobs as some privatized firms go out of business and others continue to downsize.

In a more destructive scenario, socialism continues to crowd out capitalism. The ghosts of the past block efforts to transform the Russian economy. An iron curtain falls around the boardrooms of both the corporate giants and the mid-sized corporations. Insiders and outsiders fail to cooperate as Russian companies embark on a new cold war. The lack of an investor-friendly environment leads to economic containment as the investors of the industrialized economies shun Russia in favor of friendlier investment opportunities. Russians turn angrily inward, and an opportunity with important implications for world peace and security is lost.

Russia after the 1996 Presidential Election

On July 3, 1996, Boris Yeltsin was reelected president of Russia. The tumultuous election campaign demonstrated to the world once again that serious disagreement still exists within the Russian Federation over both the objectives and the methods of its economic and political reform. But most Russians did cast a vote for reform despite the serious evidence of social and economic distress raised during the campaign. August 19, 1996, was the fifth anniversary of the coup that brought down the Soviet Union, yet some of the forces that governed that event are still active. After their victory in the December 1995 parliamentary elections and their disappointment after the 1996 presidential elections, the Communist and nationalist parties can be expected to present a very vigorous opposition in the Duma, where they still command a very large bloc of votes, and to attempt to translate their large support in the Duma's lower house into domination of the upper house, the Federation Council. The Federation Council is made up of the governors of the eighty-nine regions, fifty-two of whom were slated to face elections in the coming months. The governors used to be appointed by the president, who thus could dominate the upper house to offset the antireformist influence of the lower house. Now that they are elected, the influence of politics on the legislative branch will increase significantly.

Evidence of the stark challenges that await the new government was not hard to find. In March 1996, the International Monetary Fund and Russia signed an agreement for a three-year $10.087 billion loan to support Russia's reform program. In the first half of 1996, inflation had fallen to an annual rate of 50 percent, and monthly inflation was under 1 percent. Reducing inflation below 1 percent a month was the overriding objective of the IMF's 1995 agreement with Russia. Gross domestic production, however, fell another 5 percent in the first half of 1996, according to preliminary figures. Enterprises with greater dependence on military production were more strongly affected. In the first quarter of 1996, the production of seven hundred Russian firms involved in defense conversion was a fifth lower than it had been the year before. Overdue wages to state employees continued to be a problem. They went up by a fifth from May to June, and strike actions proliferated around the country. Sergei Pavlenko of the Working Center for Economic Reform of the Government said that 10 percent of small and regional banks might fail. There was concern that promises of spending made during the election campaign might balloon the budget deficit. One serious problem was a decline in tax revenue, which was over a fifth below expectations. The shortfall was caused partly by enterprises' delay in making tax payments until the outcome of the presidential election was clear, partly by the decline in production, and partly by tax evasion. Some preliminary reports for the first part of 1996 indicated that the federal and regional budget deficits were approaching 12 percent of gross domestic product. The goal of the new IMF agreement was to lower inflation to a single-digit annual rate and to continue to reduce the budget deficit to 4 percent of GDP, with the hope that production would pick up in 1996. But there was evidence that foreign investment had risen to $884 million in the first quarter of 1996 alone.

The major question after the election was the direction the president and the government would take in light of these challenges. Yeltsin named Aleksandr Lebed as national security adviser and gave him responsibility for resolving the brutal war in Chechnya. Would Yeltsin make concessions to the Communists, who received over 40 percent of the popular vote, or would he name a government that favored continued political and economic reforms? Initially, there was no evidence of any concessions except the government's assurance of greater emphasis on social welfare in the next stage of reform. On the face of it, the new government does not seem to suffer from the deep splits between reformers and antireformers that have marked every previous Yeltsin government since 1991. After a power struggle, Yeltsin fired his more conservative advisers—his chief bodyguard and his chief of staff—and a senior opponent of reform in the government, First Deputy Prime Minister Oleg Soskovets. He named Anatoly Chubais as his chief of staff shortly after the election. In a far-reaching reorganization of the executive branch, the president's daughter and several other reformers joined the president's staff. A scientist and close personal adviser, she had a key role in his campaign. Chubais has said that the main focus of the presidential administration would be the gubernatorial elections, the naming of a government and collaboration with it, and judicial reform.

On August 15 the new government was named. It has a decidedly reformist tint. Viktor Chernomyrdin continues as prime minister. Thirty-four-year-old Vladimir Potanin, the president of Oneximbank, was named first deputy prime minister with overall responsibility for economic reform. Chubais and Potanin reportedly had major roles in the presidential reelection campaign. The former head of the presidential administration, Viktor Ilyushin, was named first deputy prime minister with responsibility for social welfare issues, especially Russia's bankrupt health, pension, and social service systems.

Aleksandr Livshits was named minister of finance and deputy prime minister with responsibility for tackling the tax revenue problem. Aleksei Bolshakov became senior first deputy prime minister with responsibility for the Commonwealth of Independent States (CIS). Like Chernomyrdin, who headed the giant gas company Gazprom, he is a former general director of a state-owned enterprise. Among the new government's first actions was a series of decrees that abolished all privileges and tax breaks granted since the adoption of the 1996 federal budget, including most of those that Yeltsin promised during his election campaign.

This is a hopeful start. It seems likely that Russia would have another period of reform, though the direction the reform policies will take is uncertain. Michael Ledeen of the American Enterprise Institute has pointed out that the democratic revolution sweeping the world is marked by a push for individual human rights over state power. Russia had many reasons to attempt privatization in 1992. In retrospect, the most important reason was the effort to establish the individual economic freedom that underlies political freedom and helps keep the power of the state in check. That is a task that has only just begun.

Tables: The Russian Business Economy and Companies

1. Number of private and privatized enterprises, 1991–1995

Enterprises	1991	1992	1993	1994	1995
1. All private and privatized[a]	250,000	550,018	873,509	891,462	917,937
2. Small, new and privatized	250,000	550,000	865,000	875,000	900,000
3. All privatized during year	—	46,815	42,185	23,000	10,000
4. All privatized at end of year	—	46,815	89,000	112,000	122,000
5. Small privatized during year	—	46,797	33,694	15,047	9,573
6. Small privatized at end of year	—	46,797	80,491	95,538	105,111
7. Small started during year	NA	NA	NA	NA	NA
8. All small startups at end of year	250,000	503,203	784,509	779,462	794,889
9. Mid-sized and large privatized during year[b]	—	18	8,491	7,953[c]	NA
10. All mid-sized and large privatized at end of year[b]	—	18	8,509	16,462	17,937

NA = not available.

Note: The numbers of small enterprises privatized each year may be overstated and the numbers of mid-sized and large firms privatized understated. The State Statistics Committee has defined small businesses as those with fewer than 100 employees, whereas the governmental bodies that assess privatization define small firms as those with fewer than 200 employees.

[a] Some enterprises had more than one voucher auction, so that figures on the number of enterprises sold each year at voucher auctions may overstate the total number of enterprises. The actual number of enterprises sold was 15,052.

[b] There is a contradiction in the figures for the total number of mid-sized and large enterprises that have been privatized in Table 94, "Share of nonstate industrial enterprises in different branches, June 1995," in *Russian Economic Trends* 4, no. 3 (1995): 96, and Table 3 in this book.

[c] No information is available on mid-sized and large firms privatized from July 1 to December 31, 1994, and no firms of this size are estimated for this period. For 1995, however, *Russian Economic Trends* 4, no. 4 (1995): 99 does report mid-sized and large firms privatized to September 1995, but the figure given may include some new mid-sized and large private firms.

Sources: Official Russian statistics are often inconsistent and puzzling. The data from which all other data are computed are as follows: row 2, Russian Federation, State Statistics Committee, cited in "How Russia Lags Behind in Small Firms," *Moscow Times,* April 2, 1996, p. 11; rows 3 and 4, *Russian Economic Trends,* Monthly Update, March 21, 1996, Table 12, "Privatization"; rows 9 and 10, Table 3, below.

2. What has happened in the economy as a whole, 1991–1995

	1991	1992	1993	1994	1995
1. Subsidies to enterprises as percent of GDP	NA	32.0%	9.0%	5.0%	NA
Change in production since previous year:					
2. GDP	−7.0%[a]	−14.5%	−8.7%	−12.6%	−4.0%
3. GDP at constant 1993 market prices	−12.8%	−18.5%	−12.0%	−15.0%	NA
4. Gross industrial output	−8.0%	−18.8%[b]	−16.2%[b]	−20.9%	−3.0%
5. Gross agricultural output	−4.5%	−9.4%	−4.0%	−12.0%	−8.0%
6. Exports (billions of U.S. dollars)[c]	$53.8	$41.6[d]	$44.5[d]	$53.0	$63.4
7. Imports (billions of U.S. dollars)[c]	$44.5	$37.2[d]	$34.9[d]	$41.0	$45.1
8. Change in consumer prices:					
December–December	+138.0%	+2,323.0%	+844.0%	+202.0%	+131.0%
Average over previous period	+93.0%	+1,354.0%	+895.0%	+303.0%	+189.0%
9. Change in producer prices in industry	+138.0%	+1,949.0%	+887.0%	+411.0%	+238.0%
10. Budget deficit as percent of GDP[e]	30.0%	21.8%	8.1%	10.0%	4.8%
11. Investment in economy (annual change)	−15.5%	−40.0%	−12.0%	−26.0%	−18.0%
12. Market exchange rate (ruble/U.S. dollar)[g]	59.0	222.0	933.2	2,205.0	4,562.0
13. Change in average wage at year's end	NA	+1,245.0%	+775.0%	+271.0%	+208.0%
14. Real wage index (December 1991 = 100)[h]	100.0	48.0	50.4	46.3	35.2
15. Household real income index (4th quarter 1991 = 100)	NA	47.3	56.6	66.9	60.7
16. Household real expenditure index (4th quarter 1991 = 100)	NA	54.0	60.2	65.7	63.4
17. Unemployment rate[i]	NA	4.9%	5.5%	7.1%	7.9%
18. Percent of population below poverty line[i]	NA	33.0%	28.0%	22.5%	24.7%
19. Real overdue wages (billions of rubles, April 1996 prices), year end	NA	R2,219	R6,277	R10,926	R15,043
20. Real interenterprise arrears (billions of rubles, March 1996 prices), year end	NA	NA	R73,767	R144,587	R134,544
21. Real average pension index (January 1992 = 100)[j]	NA	110.0	133.2	119.5	102.1
22. Foreign direct investment (cumulative; billions of U.S. dollars, end of period)[k]	$100.0	$1.554	$2.958	$3.629	$3.92
23. Electric energy production (billions of kilowatt hours)	1,048	1,008	957	876	862

[a] Estimated.
[b] Mid-sized and large enterprises only.
[c] Excludes transactions with CIS member states.
[d] Excludes transactions with Baltic states.

. What has happened in the economy as a whole, 1991–1995 (*continued*)

Off-budget funds balance. Includes federal and regional budgets; excludes intergovernmental
·ansfers. Includes interest payments due; excludes repayment of principal due on external debt and
·ansfers to former Soviet republics.
First half.
Average monthly.
Average wage index adjusted for CPI.
Year-end monthly average.
December value.
Direct investments made by nonresidents; excluded are contributions in kind (equipment,
now-how, trademarks, etc.). Estimates vary widely, depending on the method used to convert the
alue of foreign capital from rubles to dollars. The sources are the national balance of payment
tatistics of the transition economies, which generally reflect investments made in foreign currency
irough the banking system of the reporting country. Flows are cumulated at the exchange rates
revailing when funds were transferred.
January–June.
ources: 1, 17: World Bank.
  2, 4, 8, 9, 18 (1994, 1995): RosKomStat.
  3: World Bank, Russian Federation: Toward Medium-Term Viability (Washington, D.C.,
  1996), p. 109.
  5: 1991, Anders Åslund, How Russia Became a Market Economy (Washington, D.C.:
  Brookings Institution, 1995); 1992–95, RosKomStat.
  6, 7, 14: International Monetary Fund, Washington, D.C.
  10: 1991, Åslund, How Russia Became a Market Economy; 1992–95, World Bank.
  11: United Nations, Economic Commission for Europe, Economic Bulletin for Europe 47
  (1995): 21.
  12: Moscow Interbank Currency Exchange (MICEX).
  13: Åslund, How Russia Became a Market Economy; Russian Economic Trends, June 1996.
  15, 16: RosKomStat; Russian Economic Trends.
  19, 20, 21: Russian Economic Trends, June 1996.
  22: United Nations, Economic Commission for Europe, Economic Bulletin for Europe 47
  (1995): 100.
  23: 1991, World Bank, Russian Economic Reform: Crossing the Threshold of Structural
  Change (Washington, D.C., 1994); 1992–95, RosKomStat.

3. Voucher auctions, December 1992–June 1994

	Enterprises sold	No. of regions involved	Thousands of employees[a]	Charter capital sold (mil. rbs.)	Weighted avg. block of shares (percent)	Thousands of vouchers accepted	Weighted avg. auction rate[b]
December	18	8	43	R 513	17%	158	3.2
January	108	26	188	676	11	159	4.2
February	197	41	200	1,685	19	611	2.8
March	450	58	556	5,266	25	2,284	2.3
April	611	70	837	6,294	22	4,147	1.5
May	576	73	598	5,194	21	4,306	1.2
June	909	80	821	7,115	19	4,362	1.6
July	916	82	782	8,193	23	6,691	1.2
August	895	82	830	7,010	20	4,489	1.6
September	811	83	826	7,432	20	5,069	1.5
October	959	83	910	8,151	18	4,598	1.8
November	1,005	83	906	9,007	19	3,133	2.9
December	1,054	83	1,026	8,814	20	3,546	2.5
January	738	84	664	9,137	23	3,130	2.9
February	779	86	1,285	13,703	15	4,549	3.0
March	975	86	1,072	16,647	16	8,982	1.9
April	1,084	86	1,283	16,469	17	13,502	1.2
May	1,212	86	1,170	16,398	23	8,828	1.9
June	3,165	86	7,822	137,165	21	33,851	4.1
Total	**16,462**[c]	86	21,819	R284,869	20%	116,395	2.4

Note: There are minor discrepancies between several published sources on voucher auctions. These are the most recent figures of the GKI/RPC Performance database. See also Maxim Boycko, Andrei Shleifer, and Robert W. Vishny, *Privatizing Russia* (Cambridge: MIT Press, 1995), pp. 106–7; *Russian Economic Trends* 4, no. 1 (1995): 98; and Anders Åslund, *How Russia Became a Market Economy* (Washington, D.C.: Brookings Institution, 1995), pp. 250, 256.
[a] Figures may be overstated because of multiple voucher auctions at the same firm. These firms employed 17,362,000 workers at the time the privatization plans were written, mainly in 1992, according to *Russian Economic Trends* 4, no. 1 (1995): 97. It is possible, however, that factors other than multiple voucher auctions explain the larger employment total given here. In the end, total employment can only be estimated. *Russian Economic Trends* 4, no. 4 (1995): 93, 99, notes that the 17,937 privatized industrial firms employed 79.4% of industrial personnel.
[b] R1,000 share per voucher.
[c] Some companies had multiple voucher auctions. The actual number of enterprises sold was 15,052, according to *Russian Economic Trends* 4, no. 1 (1995): 97. However, total medium and large enterprises privatized to September 1995 are 17,937, according to *Russian Economic Trends* 4, no. 4 (1995): 99.
Source: Ira W. Lieberman, Andrew Ewing, Michal Mejstrik, Joyita Mukherjee, and Peter Fidler, eds., *Mass Privatization in Central and Eastern Europe and the Former Soviet Union: A Comparative Analysis,* Studies of Economies in Transition 16 (Washington, D.C.: World Bank, 1995), p. 82.

4. Inside and outside ownership of enterprises, 1994–1996 (percent)

	1994	1995	1996	What general directors wanted
Insiders	65%	55%	58%	69%
Management	25[a]	16	18	44
All top managers	7[a]	8	10	30
General director	2[a]	3	4.5	13
Middle and lower managers[b]	—	8	8	1
Nonmanagement employees	—	39	40	25
Outsiders, Russian	21	32	32	24
Citizens	—	9	6	—
Unrelated commercial firms	—	8	11	—
Suppliers	—	3	2	—
Customers	—	2	1	—
Other firms[c]	—	2	1.3	—
Investment funds	—	6	5	—
Holding companies	—	1	2.6	—
Banks	—	1	1.6	—
Pension funds	—	—	0.02	—
Insurance companies	—	—	—	—
Foreign corporations, banks, individuals, mutual funds	—	1	1.6	—
State	13	13	9	7

Note: Numbers do not yield the totals given because of rounding, missing cases, and irregularities in reporting by the enterprises. Some data were not available at the time the survey was conducted.
[a] Based on small samples.
[b] Estimated.
[c] Mostly state-owned firms.
Source: Russian National Survey, 1994–96.

5. Majority owners of private-sector corporations, 1995 and 1996 (percent)

Majority owners	1995	1996
Employees	59.0%	64.7%
Rank and file	26.7	30.5
Managers	2.3	4.2
Top managers	0.4	0.4
General director	0.4	0.8
No majority insider	29.4	28.8
Nonstate outsiders	17.3	19.8
State	3.1	2.6
None	20.3	12.8

Note: Numbers do not add to 100% because of rounding.
Source: Russian National Survey, 1995–96.

6. Details of inside and outside shareholders in corporations, 1995 and 1996 (percent)

This table provides a fuller picture of the way the ownership pie is divided than simple average percentiles for each group can convey. Read the table as follows: 95% of companies have more than 26% employee ownership (so that 5% of companies have less than 26%); 90% of companies have more than 33% employee ownership (so that 10% of companies have less than 33%); 50% of companies have more than 52% employee ownership (so that the other 50% have less than 52% employee ownership). This figure is called the median. All numbers have been rounded except those under 1%.

	Percentile						
	5%	10%	25%	50%	75%	90%	95%
Insiders							
1995	26%	33%	44%	52%	66%	85%	98%
1996	12	26	43	57	76	95	100
Outsiders							
1995	0	1	15	32	48	58	65
1996	0	0	13	30	48	66	83
State							
1995	0	0	0	9	20	38	49
1996	0	0	0	0	20	32	44
Among the insiders [a]							
General director							
1995	0	0	0	1	4	9	12
1996	0.04	0.2	0.7	2	6	12	17
Top managers							
1995	0	1	3	5	10	17	26
1996	0.7	1	3	6	13	23	30
All managers							
1995	2	4	7	13	20	36	43
1996	2	4	7	13	25	39	48
Rank-and-file employees							
1995	10	18	30	41	53	65	71
1996	5	11	25	39	55	73	82
Among the outsiders [b]							
Citizens							
1995	0	0	0	5	15	25	30
1996	0	0	0	2	8	20	26
Commercial firms (Russian)							
1995	0	0	0	0	13	24	35
1996	0	0	0	0.75	17	35	49
Voucher investment funds							
1995	0	0	0	0	10	20	24
1996	0	0	0	0	8	17	23
Suppliers [c]							
1995	0	0	0	0	0	13	28
1996	0	0	0	0	0	3	19

6. Details of inside and outside shareholders in corporations, 1995 and 1996 (percent) (*continued*)

	Percentile						
	5%	10%	25%	50%	75%	90%	95%
Customers[d]							
1995	0	0	0	0	0	0	16
1996	0	0	0	0	0	0	7.5
Banks or their related investment units (Russian)[e]							
1995	0	0	0	0	0	2	8
1996	0	0	0	0	0	2	10
Holding companies and FIGs[f]							
1995	0	0	0	0	0	0	0
1996	0	0	0	0	0	10	20

[a] When the distribution of all forms of management ownership is examined for the top 1% of companies, there is evidence of management domination of ownership. In 1995, the companies reported that general directors owned more than 32% of 1% of all firms, that top managers owned more than 37% of 1% of all firms, and that all managers owned more than 59% of 1% of all firms. In 1996, the companies reported that general directors owned more than 35.5% of 1% of all firms, that top managers owned more than 66% of 1% of all firms, and that all managers owned more than 76% of 1% of all firms.

[b] For foreign corporations, banks, individual citizens, and investment funds the ownership was zero in all percentiles shown. Foreign corporations owned more than 34% of 1% of all firms in 1995 and more than 51% of 1% of all firms in 1996, when foreign citizens owned more than 0.3% of 1% of all firms. Foreign citizen ownership was not measured in the 1994–95 survey.

[c] Russian supplier entities owned more than 49% of 1% of all privatized corporations in 1995 and more than 42% of 1% of all privatized corporations in 1996.

[d] Russian customer entities owned more than 44% of 1% of all privatized corporations in 1995 and more than 31% of 1% of all privatized corporations in 1996.

[e] Russian banking institutions owned more than 24% of 1% of all privatized corporations in 1995 and more than 28% of 1% of all privatized corporations in 1996.

[f] Financial-industrial groups (FIGs) owned more than 23% of 1% of all privatized companies in 1995 and more than 49% of 1% of all privatized companies in 1996. Note that the 1994–95 survey specified only holding companies, not FIGs, so these figures may not be comparable.

Source: Russian National Survey, 1995–96.

7. Ownership of common stock in the United States, Japan, and Germany, 1990 (percent)

	United States	Japan	Germany
All corporations	44.5%	72.9%	64.0%
Financial institutions	30.4	48.0	22.0
Banks	0[a]	18.9	10.0
Insurance companies	4.6	19.6	12.0
Pension funds	20.1	9.5	
Other	5.7		
Nonfinancial corporations	14.1	24.9	42.0
Individuals	50.2	22.4	17.0
Foreign investors	5.4	4.0	14.0
Government	0	0.7	5.0

Note: According to the most recent figures (1994), U.S. households own 47.7% of all stocks, bank personal trusts own 2.7%, pension plans own 25.7%, mutual funds own 13.6%, foreign interests own 5.4%, and insurance companies own 4.2%: "Percentages of Corporate Stock Owned by Various Investor Categories over Time," *Wall Street Journal,* May 28, 1996, p. R8.

Source: Peter Dittus and Stephen Prowse, "Corporate Control in Central Europe and Russia: Should Banks Own Shares?" paper presented at World Bank conference on corporate governance in Russia, Washington, D.C., 1995.

[a] U.S. banks are prevented by law from involvement in the stock market.

B. The top 100 Russian companies, by market capitalization, 1996

Rank	Company	Total no. shares outstanding	Market price as of March 7	Market capitalization (millions of dollars)	Sector
1	LUKoil Group	714,563,255	$ 4.3	$3,072.6	Oil/gas
2	Gazprom	23,673,512,900	0.075	1,775.5	Oil/gas
3	Unified Energy Systems (UES)	43,116,903,368	0.030	1,271.9	Electricity
4	Rostelekom	933,750,400	0.92	859.1	Telecommunications
5	Mosenergo	2,560,000,000	0.2375	608.0	Electricity
6	Norilsk Nickel	125,999,916	4.4	554.4	Nonferrous metals
7	LUKoil Kogalymneftegaz	14,649,934	34.9	511.3	Oil/gas
8	Surgutneftegaz	5,413,442,030	0.0875	473.7	Oil/gas
9	Yuganskneftegaz	53,366,940	6.7	357.6	Oil/gas
10	Surgut Holding	9,979,399	32	319.3	Oil/gas
11	Lebedinsk Ore Processing	118,544,530	2.50	274.9	Ferrous metals
12	Noyabrskneftegaz	78,545,000	3.5	274.9	Oil/gas
13	Moscow Public Network (MGTS)	1,277,267	200	255.5	Telecommunications
14	Bratsk Aluminum Plant	1,101,061	225	247.7	Nonferrous metals
15	Novolipetsk Metallurgical Plant	5,987,240	41	245.5	Ferrous metals
16	LUKoil Langepasneftegaz	28,479,308	8.3	236.4	Oil/gas
17	Irkutskenergo	47,668,077	4.4	209.7	Electricity
18	Tatneft	23,261,992	8	186.1	Oil/gas
19	Chernogorneft	26,771,420	5.9	158.0	Oil/gas
20	Krasnoyarsk Aluminum Plant	13,478,400	11.5	155.0	Nonferrous metals
21	Megyonneftegaz	132,209,120	1.15	152.0	Oil/gas
22	Purneftegaz	111,366,025	1.3	144.8	Oil/gas
23	Omsk Petrochemical	25,798,520	5.3	136.7	Refining/ petrochemicals
24	Magnitogorsk Metallurgical Plant	8,858,518	14	124.0	Ferrous metals
25	Tomskneft	45,032,112	2.7	121.6	Oil/gas
26	Samaraneftegaz	37,156,370	3.1	115.2	Oil/gas
27	GAZ	5,924,000	19.25	114.0	Automotive
28	Nizhnevartovskneftegaz	18,217,283	6	109.3	Oil/gas
29	Kondpetroleum	50,509,320	2.15	108.6	Oil/gas
30	Novoship	505,736,500	0.21	106.2	Shipping
31	Far East Sea Shipping Line	164,359,300	0.62	101.9	Shipping
32	St. Petersburg Public Network	15,549,160	6.3	98.0	Telecommunications

8. The top 100 Russian companies, by market capitalization, 1996 (*continued*)

Rank	Company	Total no. shares outstanding	Market price as of March 7	Market capitalization (millions of dollars)	Sector
33	Permneft	6,089,845	16	97.4	Oil/gas
34	Kondopoga Pulp & Paper	5,944,220	16	95.1	Paper
35	Cherepovets Metallurgical Plant	22,074,192	4.25	93.8	Ferrous metals
36	Komineft	56,979,451	1.5	85.5	Oil/gas
37	Syktyvkar Pulp & Paper	1,291,868	65	84.0	Paper
38	AvtoVAZ	32,124,965	2.6	83.5	Automotive
39	Bratsk Pulp & Paper	2,044,005	40	81.8	Paper
40	Azot, Kemerovo	6,799,920	12	81.6	Chemicals
41	Sakhalinmorneftegaz	81,241,175	1	81.2	Oil/gas
42	Orenburgneft	87,833,750	0.9	79.1	Oil/gas
43	Sayansk Aluminum Plant	4,917,688	16	78.7	Nonferrous metals
44	Oskol Electromed	4,000,000	19	76.0	Nonferrous metals
45	Udmurtneft	3,562,066	21	74.8	Oil/gas
46	Kirishi Petrochemical	35,180,190	2	70.4	Refining/ petrochemicals
47	Kotlass Pulp & Paper	751,002,000	0.092	69.1	Paper
48	Angarsk Petrochemical	1,637,669,429	0.042	68.8	Refining/ petrochemicals
49	Nizhny Tagil Metallurgical Plant	1,030,638,400	0.065	67.0	Ferrous metals
50	Yakutenergo	3,094,721	21	65.0	Electricity
51	Achinsk Alumina Complex	1,396,177	45	62.8	Nonferrous metals
52	Lenenergo	897,363,008	0.07	62.8	Electricity
53	Nizhny Novgorod Sviazinform	38,892,500	1.6	62.2	Telecommunication
54	KamAZ	50,035,720	1.2	60.0	Automotive
55	Krasnoyarsk Metallurgical Plant	14,631,980	4	58.5	Nonferrous metals
56	LUKoil Urayneftegaz	6,811,458	8.3	56.5	Oil/gas
57	Red October	8,355,775	6.5	54.3	Consumer goods
58	Sredneuralsky Copper Smelter	5,049,600	10	50.5	Nonferrous metals
59	Sverdlovenergo	697,384,264	0.0715	49.9	Electricity
60	Krasnoyarskenergo	754,532,940	0.065	49.0	Electricity
61	GUM	6,000,000	8	48.0	Retail
62	Babaev Confectionary	27,884,000	1.7	47.4	Consumer goods
63	Nizhny Novgorod Petrochemical	13,892,445	3.3	45.8	Refining/ petrochemicals
64	Orsk-Khalilovsk Metallurgical Plant	15,135,940	3	45.4	Ferrous metals
65	Samaraenergo	575,572,041	0.075	43.2	Electricity
66	Permenergo	7,927,410	5.1	40.4	Electricity
67	Northwestern River Shipping Line	9,623,728	4	38.5	Shipping
68	Perm Uralsviazinform	692,872	55	38.1	Telecommunication

The top 100 Russian companies, by market capitalization, 1996 (*continued*)

ank	Company	Total no. shares outstanding	Market price as of March 7	Market capitalization (millions of dollars)	Sector
69	West Siberian Metallurgical Plant	2,385,542	15	35.8	Ferrous metals
70	Kaliningrad Morneftegaz	11,889,800	3	35.7	Oil/gas
71	Ural Elektromed	5,071,400	7	35.5	Nonferrous metals
72	Moscow Refinery	7,883,320	4.5	35.5	Refining/ petrochemicals
73	Chelyabinsk Metallurgical Plant	3,161,362	11	34.8	Ferrous metals
74	Varjeganneftegaz	23,022,610	1.5	34.5	Oil/gas
75	Achinsk Refinery	20,511,760	1.67	34.3	Refining/ petrochemicals
76	Cheliabenergo	500,600,570	0.063	31.5	Electricity
77	Krasnodarneftegaz	1,111,387	27	30.0	Oil/gas
78	Northern Sea Shipping Line	957,854	31	29.7	Shipping
79	Svetogorsk	3,952,950	7.5	29.6	Others
80	Bashkirenergo	5,853,094	5.02	29.4	Electricity
81	Samara Sviazinform	2,641,340	10.75	28.4	Telecommunications
82	Primorsky Sea Shipping Line	11,061,000	2.3	25.4	Shipping
83	Tebukneft	12,537,500	2	25.1	Oil/gas
84	Irkutsk Electrosviaz	1,017,276	24	24.4	Telecommunications
85	St. Petersburg MMT	6,586,826	3.6	23.7	Telecommunications
86	LUKoil Volgograd-neftepererabotka	21,068,608	1.1	23.2	Refining/ petrochemicals
87	Novokuznetsk Aluminum Plant	3,997,170	5.75	23.0	Nonferrous metals
88	Nizhnovenergo	4,982,912	4.35	21.7	Electricity
89	Apatity Production Ass.	8,316,068	2.55	21.2	Chemicals
90	UAZ, Ulyanovsk	1,314,942	16	21.0	Automotive
91	LUKoil Permnefteorgsintez	18,882,980	1.1	20.8	Refining/ petrochemicals
92	Murmansk Shipping Line	943,000	22	20.7	Shipping
93	Sakhalin Sea Shipping Line	18,692,220	1.1	20.6	Shipping
94	Norilsk Gazprom	7,489,816	2.61	19.5	Oil/gas
95	Voronezh Aircraft Construction Co.	4,750,648	4	19.0	Aerospace
96	Krasnoyarsk GES (Hydropower)	470,000	40	18.8	Electricity
97	Arkhangelsk Pulp & Paper	780,225	23	17.9	Paper
98	Belomor-Onega Shipping Line	5,118,985	3.5	17.9	Shipping
99	LOMO	6,200,000	2.8	17.4	Others
00	Omskenergo	4,337,130	4	17.3	Electricity

Source: Brunswick Brokerage, Moscow and New York.

9. The important numbers on governance, 1994–1996

Open trading of stock, 1994–1996

Companies that reported they had open trading of shares: 96%

Average employee sales of stock, 1994: 4.3%   Companies with sales above 5%: 25%

Level at which employee stock selling exceeds this amount (10% of companies), 1994: 12%

Average employee sales of stock, 1995: 6.3%   Companies with sales above 7%: 25%

Level at which employee stock selling exceeds this amount (10% of companies), 1995: 20%

Companies in which all outside shareholders sold more than 5% of their stock, 1994: 10%

Companies that sold shares in an investment tender, 1994–96: 9%   Average sold: 17%

Companies that sold shares in a cash auction, 1994–96: 24%   Average sold: 11%

Companies that suspect someone is trying to accumulate their shares: 1995, 20%; 1996, 21%

Companies that want strict control over investor who buys their shares: 36%

Companies that do not want strict control over investor who buys their shares: 15%

Companies with no opinion: 49%

Shareholder registers, 1996*

Companies with over 1,000 Employees that did not have an independent shareholder registrar: 39%

Companies with over 500 Employees that did not have an independent shareholder registrar: 46%

Financial disclosure, 1996

General directors who oppose disclosure of financial information: 60%

General directors who oppose disclosure of ownership information: 50%

General directors who oppose giving out information on lines of business: 30%

Outsiders on boards of directors, 1995 and 1996

Companies with at least one nonstate outside representative on their board: 1995, 64%; 1996, 76%

Companies with no nonstate outside representative on their board: 1995, 36%; 1996, 24%

Average percentage of boards accounted for by nonstate outside representatives: 1995, 14%; 1996, 31%

9. The important numbers on governance, 1994–1996 (*continued*)

Typical board of directors, 1995 and 1996 (no. of members)

Total membership	7
Quorum	5
Management	4
Outside shareholders	2
State shareholder	1

Cumulative voting*

Companies that used cumulative voting: 1995, 33%; 1996, 39%

General directors' support for majority ownership by an outside investor, 1995 and 1996

General directors who would sell majority outsider ownership to an investor who brought all the capital necessary to restructure the firm: 1995, 26%; 1996, 29%
General directors who believe they could persuade employees to sell majority ownership to an outside investor who brought all the capital necessary to restructure their firm: 1995, 26%; 1996, 38.6%

Shareholder tricks*

Companies that issued new shares in 1995–96: 14%
  Companies that treated shareholders unfairly in the issuance of new shares: 7.5%
  Companies that admitted giving new shares free or at a nominal price to insiders: 6.5%
  Companies that admitted that new shares diluted outside shareholders' interest: 1%
Companies that planned to issue new shares in 1996–97: 12%
Companies that bought back their shares in 1995–96: 43%
  Companies that resold those shares to managers and employees: 29%

Corporate governance scores, 1996 (percent of companies)

Excellent	2%
Good	39
Bad	46
Horrible	13

Blockholders (shareholders who own more than 5% of a company's stock), 1996

Companies that had at least one blockholder in 1996: 74%
Percentage of company's stock owned by average blockholder: 16%

9. The important numbers on governance, 1994–1996 (*continued*)

Ownership and lack of board representation by blockholders, by type of blockholder (percent)

	Percent of all blockholders	Average stock ownership	Blockholders with no board seats
Domestic commercial firms	39%	18%	26%
Voucher investment funds	19	14	22
Individual citizens	11	11	49
Domestic banks	8	14	20
Domestic suppliers or customers	10	12	32
Domestic holding companies	7	21	19
Foreign firms, banks, citizens	5	19	48
State-owned firms	2	32	18

Voucher investment funds, 1995

Number of funds: 596
Population with investment in funds: 20.4 million (14%)
Average number of shareholders per fund: 34,255
Total assets of funds: approximately $400 million
Average holdings per shareholder: $19
Percentage of funds' portfolios in privatized corporations: 93%

* This evidence should not be considered an evaluation of compliance with the new Russian corporate law of December 1995. A compliance study is now under way.

Source: Commission on Securities and the Capital Market, Capital Market Surveillance Group, *Analysis and Monitoring of Specialized Privatization Investment Funds* (Moscow, December 1995); Russian National Survey, 1995–96.

10. The important numbers on restructuring. 1996

Management and control

Companies that replaced general director since July 1992: 33%
  New general director came from outside: 19%
  General director replaced since 1995: 12%
Average age of general directors (years): 50 (50+ in half of companies)
  Of general directors named since 1992: 47
  Of general directors in office since before 1992: 52
  Of general directors named in 1995: 45
  Of general directors in office since before 1995: 51
Board seats held by outsiders: 31% (28.6% or more in half of companies)
Companies that have one or more blockholders: 74%
Companies that changed managers responsible for production since 1995: 49%
Managers responsible for production changed since 1995: 16% (10% or more in
    half of companies)

Organization

Average layoffs: since 1992, 23%;[a] since 1993, 15%;[a] since 1994, 21%; since 1995,
    11%; planned, 2.5%
Additional layoffs that could be made if there were no social considerations: 10%
Capacity utilization in 1995–96: 55%
Companies that changed their mix of original products since 1995: 68%
  Percentage of 1995 sales represented by changes in product mix: 22% (15% or
    more in half of companies)
Companies that added completely new products or services since 1995: 52%
  Percentage of 1995 sales represented by new products: 12% (6% or more in
    half of companies)
Companies that added new customers since 1995: 82%
  Percentage of 1995 sales represented by sales to new customers: 19% (15% or
    more in half of companies)
  Percentage of most recent month's sales represented by sales to new
    customers: 17% (10% or more in half of companies)
  Percentage of sales represented by customers new since 1993: 27% (20% or
    more in half of companies)
Companies that added new suppliers since 1995: 59%
  Percentage of purchases represented by new suppliers: 24% (15% or more in
    half of companies)
Companies that used retail outlets not used in 1995: 38%
  Percentage of 1995 sales represented by new retail outlets: 10% (5% or more in
    half of companies)
Companies that added new transportation services since 1995: 4%
  Percentage of 1995 sales represented by new transportation services: 17%
    (7.5% or more in half of companies)
Companies that added new distributors since 1995: 19%
  Percentage of 1995 sales represented by new distributors: 9% (3% or more in
    half of companies)
Companies that have a marketing department: 64%
Companies that have discontinued products or services since 1995: 37%

10. The important numbers on restructuring, 1996 (*continued*)

Percentage of 1995 sales represented by discontinued products: 16% (10% or more in half of companies)

Companies that increased expenditures on research and development since 1995: 48%

Increase in employee time for R&D: 21% (11% or more in half of companies)

Companies that made significant changes in productivity since 1995: 63%

Increase in productivity per employee, after inflation: 13% (7% or more in half of companies)

Companies with significant changes in technology since 1995: 35%

Percentage of 1995 sales related to changes in technology: 29% (20% or more in half of companies)

Companies that shifted production or service activities outside the firm since 1995: 11%

Percentage of production/service costs shifted outside firm: 11% (8% or more in half of companies)

Companies that cut overhead expenses significantly since 1995: 44%

Percentage of sales to private enterprises: 56% (65% or more in half of companies)

Percentage of products subject to state price controls: 8% (5% in half of companies)

Capital

Companies that received subsidies from any government source in 1995: 10%

Companies that received subsidies from government of Russian Federation: 6%

Companies that received subsidies from their regional government: 4%

Percentage of annualized sales owed in taxes: 21%[b]

Companies that borrowed from banks since 1995: 70%

Loans due within one year as percent of sales: 9%

New capital investment as percent of all money borrowed: 10% (0% in half of companies)

New capital investment as percent of most recent loan: 12% (0% in half of companies)[c]

Wages owed to workers as percent of annualized sales: 7% (0% in half of companies)

Companies that offered shares in an investment tender since July 1994: 9%

Shares sold in investment tender: 17%

Companies that offered shares in a cash auction since July 1994: 24%

Shares sold in cash auction: 8%

Companies that issued new shares: 14%

Social services provided to employees

Cost of social services as percent of total monthly compensation (most recent month): 24% (4% or more in half of companies)[d]

Cost of social services as percent of most recent month's sales: 7%

Cost of social services as percent of gross profit in 1995: 16%

Companies that reduced expenditures for social assets (expenditures adjusted for inflation): 9%

10. The important numbers on restructuring, 1996 (*continued*)

Full-time workers in social services as percent of all employees: 4%
Companies that have eliminated some social service workers: 33%
  Decrease in social services workers: 33%
Companies that have transferred ownership of social services to municipalities: 30%
Companies that have transferred expenses for social services to municipalities: 10%
Companies that have transferred expenses for social services to employees: 5%
Companies that have eliminated some social services: 18%

Note: All numbers are simple averages unless otherwise noted.
[a] Figures for layoffs since 1992 and 1993 are from the 1994–95 survey. The 1995–96 survey collected such data only for 1994–96.
[b] The median is 1%. When the top and bottom 5% of tax-delinquent firms are excluded, the average is 6.5% and the median is 3% of annual sales.
[c] These figures are from the 1994–95 survey.
[d] When the top and bottom 5% of spending on social services are excluded, the average is 16% and the median is 7%.
Source: Russian National Survey, 1995–96.

11. Barriers to corporate governance in companies in which several blockholders own a majority of shares, 1996

* Only 20% of Russian companies are majority-owned by outsiders.
Barrier: Only a modest number of Russian firms can even be influenced by outsiders.

* Of the 20% of firms with majority outsider ownership, only 6% are majority-owned by one blockholder.
On average one blockholder owns 68% of a corporation. In 60% of the companies owned by one blockholder, the blockholder is a commercial firm or a holding company. Voucher investment funds, individual citizens, domestic suppliers and customers, and state-owned entities are blockholders in 20%, and foreign corporations are blockholders in 20%.
Barrier: There are very few Russian firms in which one blockholder can quickly introduce radical discipline.

* Of the 20% of firms with majority outsider ownership, only 5% are majority-owned by several blockholders. On average several blockholders together own 65% of a corporation.
Barrier: It is possible for blockholders to introduce radical discipline to less than one in twenty corporations in the country.

* Majority blockholder ownership typically involves four or five blockholders with an average stake of 16% per blockholder; 50% of blockholders have stakes of more than 12%.
Barrier: Each blockholder has a relatively small stake, so blockholders must coordinate their monitoring of the firm if they are to restructure it.

11. Barriers to corporate governance in companies in which several blockholders own a majority of shares, 1996 (*continued*)

* 57% of companies that are majority blockholder-owned do not use cumulative voting to elect democratic boards of directors.
Barrier: Majority ownership does not translate into control if a company does not follow the voting procedures necessary to give blockholders a proportionate number of seats on the board.

* Blockholder majority-owned companies control only 50% of their boards of directors on average, and in a quarter of these firms, the blockholders collectively control less than a majority of the board, though on average they own 65% of the stock. A voucher investment fund obtains less board representation than a commercial firm or another type of blockholder. More than a quarter of voucher investment funds that are blockholders in majority blockholder-owned firms have no board representation.
Barrier: Blockholders may have less power than their ownership stakes suggest because they are not exercising governance rights.

* 57% of majority blockholder-owned companies do not have an independent shareholder registrar.
Barrier: In the absence of active regional stock markets, individual blockholders who want to enlarge their stakes have to apply to management to identify the other shareholders.

* 90% of blockholders in multiblockholder majority-owned companies are Russian firms, individual citizens, and voucher investment funds; only 10% are foreign companies that might immediately bring technology, know-how, and capital to the firm.
Barrier: Being a blockholder is not enough; restructuring requires skills that Russian commercial firms and voucher investment funds founded since 1993 cannot be expected to have.

* A quarter of blockholder majority-owned companies made no capital investment in new equipment in the most recent 12-month period. They made no more capital investments than companies that are majority-owned by employees or outsiders or that have no majority owner.
Barrier: Blockholders who lack the ability to get the firm access to the capital it needs cannot effect restructuring.

* 43% of the general directors of blockholder majority-owned companies oppose a new issue of shares.
Barrier: Blockholders without access to capital markets cannot get the capital needed to restructure the firm.

* 35% of general directors were replaced in the most recent 12-month period in majority multiblockholder-owned firms; 28% in majority employee-owned firms; 36% in firms with no majority owner; 33% in the country at large. Most such blockholder majority-owned firms, however, simply replaced the general director with a deputy.

11. Barriers to corporate governance in companies in which several blockholders own a majority of shares, 1996 (*continued*)

Barrier: Most Russian blockholders have not radically changed the managers of the firms they own.

* 54% of general directors in majority blockholder-owned companies oppose full disclosure of financial information, 46% oppose disclosure of ownership information, and 29% oppose disclosure of information on the company's product lines.
Barrier: Individual blockholders may lack the information needed for informed judgment.

* 23% of general directors in majority blockholder-owned firms say that some outside investor is trying to accumulate their shares in an effort to take full control.
Barrier: When ownership is in flux, the stability suggested by a concentration of shareholders is replaced by strain and tension.

* Whereas 9% of all firms had investment tenders in the most recent 12-month period, the figure was 19% for blockholder majority-owned firms, and those firms offered larger packages of shares. Blockholder majority-owned firms had cash auctions at the same rate as other firms. Blockholder majority-owned firms issued new shares at twice the rate (27%) of the entire sample (14%).
Barrier: Blockholder majority ownership emerged mainly in firms that offered investment tenders and issued new shares after privatization. When privatization slowed in 1995 and 1996, opportunities to build concentrated stakes dwindled.

Notes

Our goal is to illuminate for general readers the main issues, facts, and interpretations of the privatization process in Russia. For this reason, we chose the essay form for our brief reference materials. We have prepared a more complete presentation and analysis of the arguments, an in-depth review of the statistical evidence, and a discussion of other scholarly research and publicly available information for a series of articles in academic journals. The references that follow are not meant to be exhaustive. The main sources of information for this book are interviews and surveys in a significant cross-section of the 89 regions of the Russian Federation from 1992 to 1996 and a detailed review of relevant Russian-language publications. Unless we note otherwise, quotations from interviews come from the Russian National Surveys. The book summarizes four studies; it relies mainly on the second, third, and fourth sets of surveys and interviews.

The first study involved only extensive interviews conducted from August to December 1992 at 23 enterprises in the Moscow region. Half of the enterprises had more than 1,000 employees; the average number of employees was 1,790.

The second study involved both surveys and interviews conducted from May 1993 to April 1994, after the beginning of privatization, at 142 privatized corporations in 32 regions of the Russian Federation. Half of the corporations had more than 1,200 employees; the average number was 2,776. The text refers to this survey as "the initial story in 1994."

The third study involved surveys and interviews conducted from May 1994 to August 1995 at 322 Russian privatized corporations in 44 regions. Half of the corporations had more than 961 employees; the average number was 1,967. We refer to this survey as "the 1995 study," since we visited most of the corporations in 1995.

The fourth study involves surveys and interviews conducted from September 1995 to June 1996 at 357 Russian privatized corporations in 46 regions. Half of the corporations had more than 835 employees; the average number was 1,802. We refer to this survey as "the 1996 study," since we visited most of the corporations in 1996.

The objective of these studies was to obtain a reasonably accurate picture of national trends. The 322 corporations with 612,000 employees surveyed in the third study represented approximately 1.8% of all large and mid-sized enterprises that were privatized, 4.5% of employees, and 49% of the nation's regions. The 357 corporations with 628,737 employees surveyed in 1996 represented approximately 2% of all large and mid-sized enterprises that were privatized, 4.6% of employees, and 52% of the nation's regions. Because of space constraints, we will not examine here the longitudinal evidence on Russian corporations from one study to the next, though we visited a significant number of corporations repeatedly, especially in 1995 and 1996. Because none of the data cited here are longitudinal, we are cautious about viewing slight increases or decreases in figures from the 1995 to 1996 samples as evidence of clear-cut trends. In many ways, the 1995 and 1996 samples should be viewed as two different attempts to construct representative samples of the same country. The overall similarity of the 1995 and 1996 data increases our confidence in them. We have based our conclusions on the consistency between the survey results and our close reading of qualitative interviews, an exhaustive review of Russian press reports, and corroborating data from smaller samples surveyed by other researchers. These data, like all survey data, depend on the accuracy of answers provided by respondents. It is possible that some results may be distorted by systematically inaccurate answers from the managers who responded to the formal survey. The area of financial data is one of particular concern because of the lack of standard accounting procedures in Russia and the possibility that managers are not openly discussing their financial accounts. For this reason, we have been wary of basing conclusions on financial data alone, and generally we do not discuss this material. In practice Russia still does not require public companies to report to the government on their ownership, financial condition, and corporate governance. Numbers emanating from the Russian government have always been suspect.

The names of all enterprises and managers have been altered to preserve their confidentiality; the only exceptions are firms that have been publicly identified by the media. The names of some managers mentioned in published sources have been changed.

The average number of employees in our sample fairly represents large and mid-sized Russian firms. The most recent published data indicate that such firms averaged 1,523 employees before the attempted reform (Goskomstat [State Committee of the Russian Federation on Statistics], 1987, quoted in *Mass Privatization in Central and Eastern Europe and the Former Soviet Union: A Comparative Analysis,* ed. Ira Lieberman et al. [Washington, D.C.: World Bank, 1995], Table A31, p. 78).

To supplement our four surveys, we have reviewed thousands of pages of articles published from 1992 to 1996 in the major Russian newspapers and journals and in the international financial press; and research assistants interviewed regional privatization officials about their evaluations of the problems and trends in their regions and transcribed the interviews for us.

Introduction: The Bolshevik Biscuit Company Goes Private

The Bolshevik Biscuit story is from "Danone to the Fore," *Russia Express,* March 27, 1995; Julie Tolkacheva, "Danone Buys 82% of Bolshevik Biscuit," *Moscow Times,* December 22, 1994; "Until Now Everybody Is Content," *Kommersant Weekly,* January 21, 1995, and *Forbes,* February 14, 1994. Current privatization estimates are from *Russian Economic Trends* 4, no. 4 (1995): 99, Table 93. The table provides a breakdown by industrial branch. Figures are for September 1995. The *New York* article is Robert I. Friedman, "The Money Plane," January 22, 1996, pp. 24–33. Russian banks responded in Sergei Lukianov, "Banks Bristle at Crime Link Charge," *Moscow Times,* January 17, 1996. For more detail on the economic reasoning behind the design of the Russian privatization, see Maxim Boycko, Andrei Shleifer, and Robert W. Vishny, *Privatizing Russia* (Cambridge: MIT Press, 1995). Robert Vishny, a professor of economics at the University of Chicago, advised on the design of the program. Anders Åslund has written the authoritative study of the broader economic transformation of Russia, *How Russia Became a Market Economy* (Washington, D.C.: Brookings Institution, 1995), and we have relied on it repeatedly throughout this book to give brief overviews of the economic situation during each year since reform.

For a collection of initial studies of Russian privatization, see Ira W. Lieberman and John Nellis, eds., *Russia: Creating Private Enterprises and Efficient Markets* (Washington, D.C.: World Bank, Private Sector Development Dept., 1994). For the number of privatized firms we rely on *Russian Economic Trends* (Lawrence, Kans.: Whurr, 1995), vols. 1–4 and supplements.

To indicate how well the 1995 and 1996 Russian National Survey samples represented major Russian industrial sectors, we have organized the sectors to accord with the Standard & Poor and Dow Jones Industry Group sectors for the purposes of comparison. The first figure in each group below represents the share of total employment in Russia accounted for by that industrial sector; the figures in parentheses are the shares of all employees represented by that industrial sector in the 1995 and 1996 Russian National Survey samples: basic materials, 14.0% (10.3%, 17.5%); consumer cyclical and noncyclical, 11.3% (28.5%, 29.8%); energy, 4.0% (3.9%, 0.7%); industry and technology, 52.7% (52.6%, 40.8%); utilities, 2.0% (4.7%, 11.18%); agriculture, 22.0% (0%, 0%). The source of the Goskomstat data is Giles Alfandari and Mark E. Schaffer, *On "Arrears" in Russia* (Washington, D.C.: Europe and Central Asia Country Department III, Economic Development Institute, World Bank, 1995), Table 5, p. 44. Goskomstat's figures add up to more than 100%.

Finally, in the summer of 1994 the World Bank took a random national sample of all Russian enterprises. We now compare how well the 1995 and 1996 Russian National Survey samples represent the nationwide Russian economy with reference to the number of enterprises in the various industrial sectors in a random World Bank sample. Again, Russian sectors have been grouped to accord with Standard & Poor and Dow Jones Industry Group sectors for the purposes of comparison. We have converted the number of enterprises in the World Bank study's Table 2 to percentages. The first figure in each group below represents the share of total enterprises in Russia accounted for by that industrial sector; the figures in parentheses are the shares of all firms represented by that industrial sector in the 1995 and 1996 Russian National Survey samples: basic materials, 18.3% (5.9%, 6.0%); consumer cyclical and noncyclical, 25.6% (45.7%, 48.5%); industry and technology, 49.5% (43.4%, 39.8%); energy and utilities, 5.8% (5.0%, 5.7%). Again Goskomstat's figures do not add up to 100%. The source of the World Bank data is Giles Alfandari, Qimiao Fan, and Lev Freinkman, *Government Financial Transfers to Industrial Enterprises and Restructuring* (Washington, D.C.: Europe and Central Asia Country Department III, Economic Development Institute, World Bank, 1994), Table 2, p. 35.

The Russian National Survey samples for 1995 and 1996 on which this book is based are not random samples, but they are reasonably representative of firms in the Russian Federation. Consumer firms are overrepresented, but such firms have been on the rise since reform. The use of a random sample was initially rejected because the 89 regions of the Russian Federation joined the privatization program slowly and not all enterprises in a region were privatized at one time. Since the central objective of the research was to develop a national picture of mid-sized and large privatized enterprises, regions were added to the study as they joined the privatization program. Supplied with up-to-date lists of privatized enterprises by the regional government and supplementary commercially available lists of the largest enterprises in each region, we instructed our assistants simply to go down the lists and request interviews at the largest privatized enterprises while attempting to maintain a mixture of industrial and consumer-oriented firms. We excluded enterprises in the cities of Moscow and St. Petersburg (although we included the Moscow and St. Petersburg regions) to ensure that the sample broadly represented the Russian Federation.

1. Privatization

The historical review is from the *Cambridge Encyclopedia of Russia and the Former Soviet Union*, ed. Archie Brown, Michael Kaser, and Gerald Smith (Cambridge: Cambridge University Press, 1994), pp. 92–101, 330, 389–99; and John Channon with Rob Hudson, *The Penguin Historical Atlas of Russia* (London: Penguin, 1995), pp. 5–6, 45–46, 57, 64, 80, 84, 99, 109; Alan M. Ball, *Russia's Last Capitalists: The Nepmen, 1921–1929* (Berkeley: University of California Press, 1987), pp. 1–25; Evgenii V. Anisomov, *The Reforms of Peter the Great: Progress through Coercion in Russia*, trans. John Alexander (Armonk, N.Y.: M. E. Sharpe, 1993), pp. 70–86; L. Eventov, *Inostrannye kapitaly v russkoi promyshlennosti*, quoted in "Country Feature: Russia," in Barings International Securities Services, *Perspectives, 1996* (New York, 1996), Table 9, p. 32; Nicholas V. Riazanovsky, *A History of Russia* (New York: Oxford University Press, 1993), pp. 552–54.

On corporate development at the beginning of the century, we rely on Thomas C. Owen, *Russian Corporate Capitalism from Peter the Great to Perestroika* (New York: Oxford University Press, 1995). On how the economy might develop, see Daniel Yergin and Thane Gustafson, *Russia 2010—and What It Means for the World* (New York: Vintage, 1994). Estimates of deaths during Soviet purges are from *Cambridge Encyclopedia of Russia*, pp. 110–11, 399, and Jeff Jacoby, "To the Victims of Communism," *Boston Globe*, December 7, 1995.

On the Gorbachev period, see Anders Åslund, *How Russia Became a Market Economy* (Washington, D.C.: Brookings Institution, 1995), pp. 26–43, 223–26; Jack Matlock, *Autopsy on an Empire: The American Ambassador's Account of the Collapse of the Soviet Union* (New York: Random House, 1995), esp. the chronology on pp. 746–79 and pp. 416–20, 466–68, 476–78; Boris Yeltsin, *The Struggle for Russia* (New York: Random House/Times Books, 1994); Mikhail S. Gorbachev, *Perestroika: New Thinking for Our Country and the World* (New York: HarperCollins, 1987). Åslund quotes Gorbachev on private property in *How Russia Became a Market Economy*, pp. 30–31. Matlock, *Autopsy on an Empire*, provides a detailed analysis of these events.

On the June privatization debate, see "Supreme Soviet Adopts Privatization Law," *Current Digest of the Soviet Press*, July 31, 1991, p. 11; the headline is inaccurate as the law was not passed, but a draft law was discussed. Gorbachev's decree on privatization has received little attention by historians. On the decree, see "Gorbachev-Pavlov Face-off Intensifies," ibid., September 11, 1991, p. 2. For the newspaper quote on the decree's significance, see ibid., p. 1. In another speech, Pavlov seems to accept the notion of privatization; see "Pavlov's Bid for Extra Powers is Rebuffed," ibid., July 24, 1991, p. 1, which condenses a June speech before the Supreme Soviet.

Scholars profoundly disagree on how to interpret both Gorbachev's and Yeltsin's actions from August 18 to 22, 1991. For one view, see Matlock, *Autopsy on an Empire,* pp. 578–604, and James Billington, *Russia Transformed: Breakthrough to Hope: Moscow, August 1991* (New York: Free Press, 1991); for a different view, John B. Dunlop, *The Rise of Russia and the Fall of the Soviet Empire* (Princeton: Princeton University Press, 1993), and Amy Knight, *The KGB's Successors* (Princeton: Princeton University Press, 1996), whose ideas in the chapter "The Myth of the August Coup" (pp. 12–37) are paraphrased here. For Gorbachev's view, see his book *The August Coup: The Truth and the Lessons* (New York: HarperCollins, 1991). Yeltsin explains his view in *Struggle for Russia.* For a detailed picture of how government ministries dealt with enterprises and tried to reform them, see Stephen Whitefield, *Industrial Power and the Soviet State* (Oxford: Oxford University Press, 1993).

Demographic information is from Goskomstat, the State Committee of the Russian Federation on Statistics. Only general demographic guideposts are given because Goskomstat's figures often conflict with those from other government sources. Itar-TASS reported on November 1, 1995, on new information released by the Ministry of Social Welfare on the number of people of pension age. Figures on employment in major sectors are from Goskomstat and the Center for Economic Analysis and Forecasting, quoted in *Russian Economic Trends* 4, no. 4 (1995): 93, Table 86.

On oil reserves, see "Facts on Russia," Reuter, June 16, 1996. Information on the size of Russia and the output, employment, and number of industrial enterprises in 1988 appears in Roman Frydman et al., *The Privatization Process in Russia, Ukraine, and the Baltic States* (London: Central European University Press, 1993), pp. 4, 7 (Table 2-2). The Business Information Service, now available from the Russian Privatization Center (RPC), is based on 1993 Goskomstat data that is roughly comparable to the 1988 data. The 1988 census has 7,481 enterprises with more than 500 workers vs. 6,204 in 1993 and 5,582 enterprises with 201–500 workers vs. 4,303 with 250–500 workers in 1993. Similar data are cited for the Soviet Union in Åslund, *How Russia Became a Market Economy,* p. 152, Table 5-1, although Åslund quotes Goskomstat's 1992 figures on pp. 38, 43, 46, 47. There are discrepancies among all three sources, a typical situation with Russian statistics. Information on small-scale privatization is from *Russian Economic Trends* 4, no. 2 (1995): 94, Table 93. The Goskomstat report of 170,000 small shops at the beginning of privatization is not the only official estimate of which we are aware. If 82% of small firms were privatized by April 1995, as *Russian Economic Trends* reports, then one of these figures may be inaccurate. Tables 94a and 94b show that the success of small-scale privatization varied across the 89 regions. Indeed, *Russian Economic Trends* 1, no. 3 (1995): 37 says there are 225,000 small enterprises across Russia.

Figures on employment in small businesses should be viewed as estimates because the numbers vary by source. Ours are from the State Committee on Small Business of the Russian Federation. See also Andrea Richter and Liam Halligan with Tatyana Gorbacheva, "Restructuring and the Russian Labor Market, 1994–1995" (paper presented at the Russian-European Centre for Economic Policy, St. Petersburg, September 29–30, 1995). GNP per capita and other social indicators and information on Russia's industrial structure and resource prices are taken directly from the World Bank's *Russian Federation: Toward Medium-Term Viability*, report 14472–RU (Washington, D.C., October 16, 1995), and *Russia Joining the World Economy*, report 12108–RU (October 15, 1993). Both provide excellent overviews of the Russian economy. Åslund's *How Russia Became a Market Economy*, esp. pp. 26–52, provides the insights and facts on the collapsing Soviet economy.

The source for the portrait of Gorbachev's efforts to reform the Soviet system in 1991 is *Russian Economic Trends* 4, no. 2 (1995): 131–62, supplemented by Russian government sources referred to in Åslund, *How Russia Became a Market Economy*, pp. 41–52, 275–88. The best discussion of this subject is Anders Åslund, *Gorbachev's Struggle for Economic Reform* (Ithaca: Cornell University Press, 1991). See also David Remnick, *Lenin's Tomb: The Last Days of the Soviet Empire* (New York: Random House, 1993). Yeltsin's speech on privatization is translated and quoted by Åslund in *How Russia Became a Market Economy*, p. 228, from "B. N. Yeltsin's Speech," *Sovetskaya Rossiya*, October 29, 1991. Dates and descriptions of International Monetary Fund agreements from 1992 to 1996 are based on IMF press releases 92-60, August 5, 1992; 93-25, June 30, 1993; 94-29, April 20, 1994; 95-21, April 11, 1995; and 96-13, March 26, 1996. Åslund discusses the details of the economic reform program in *How Russia Became a Market Economy*, chaps. 3, 5, 6, and 7. On the question of monopolies, see Annette N. Brown, Barry W. Ickes, and Randi Ryterman, *The Myth of Monopoly: A New View of Industrial Structure in Russia* (Washington, D.C.: World Bank Policy Research Department, Transition Economics, August 1994), which found that very few civilian manufacturing enterprises were monopolies and that enterprises with at least 35% of market share accounted for less than 4% of all employment. Though many Russian enterprises had been combined into large production associations in 1987, the 1992 privatization program privatized their units as separate enterprises.

Jeffrey Sachs has published several analyses of macroeconomic reform. See his "It Could Have Been Better: Reflections on Russian Economic Reform," *Russia Review*, May 6, 1996, pp. 1, 8–11; "Russia's Struggle with Stabilization: Conceptual Issues and Evidence," *Proceedings of the World Bank's Annual Conference on Development Economics* (Washington, D.C., 1994), pp. 57–80; with David Lipton, "Russia: Toward a Market-Based Monetary System," *Central Banking* 3 (Summer 1992): 29–53; "Strengthening Western Support for Russia," *International Economic Insights*, January–February 1993, pp. 10–13; "Russian Sachs Appeal: The G7 Has One Last Chance," *International Economy*, January–

February 1993, pp. 50–53; and three papers for Harvard Institute for International Development: "Economic Assistance to the Soviet Union at the G-7 Summit" (July 2, 1991); "Strengthening Western Support for Russia's Economic Reforms" (December 28, 1992); and "Reforms in Eastern Europe and the Former Soviet Union in Light of the East Asian Experience" (August 8, 1995).

There are many problems with estimating output declines in Russia. See World Bank, *Russian Federation: Toward Medium-Term Viability,* pp. 2–5; on state capital investments and subsidies to enterprises, see pp. 22–23, 53–59; on inflation and how prices changed, pp. 25–30 and the chart on 102; for a more complete discussion of the social safety net, pp. xiv–xv, 6–9, 22, 40–42, 48, 50, 59–78. The stories of management pilfering are from Steven Handelman, *Comrade Criminal: Russia's New Mafiya* (New Haven: Yale University Press, 1995). Yeltsin's comments on bribery were in *Delovye lyudi* [Business people] (Moscow), December 1992. Polling data on the Shatalin plan, Gaidar's reforms, and privatization are discussed in Lynn D. Nelson et al., *Property to the People: The Struggle for Radical Economic Reform in Russia* (Armonk, N.Y.: M. E. Sharpe, 1994), chap. 4.

On the employee ownership issue, see John Logue, Sergey Phekhanov, and John Simmons, eds., *Transforming Russian Enterprises: From State Ownership to Employee Ownership* (Westport, Conn.: Greenwood, 1995). Åslund, *How Russia Became a Market Economy,* pp. 25–26, describes attempts by employees, managers, and state bureaucrats to arrange the enterprises' affairs in such a way that they could be quickly privatized to them. He notes that Russian government officials were so concerned about the special advantage these arrangements gave to insiders that they banned new leasing arrangements in 1992. For a discussion of the central principles of privatization, see Maxim Boycko, Andrei Shleifer, and Robert W. Vishny, *Privatizing Russia* (Cambridge: MIT Press, 1995), pp. 1–47.

On Russian attitudes toward market economies, see Robert J. Shiller, Maxim Boycko, and Vladimor Korobov, "Popular Attitudes toward Free Markets: The Soviet Union and the United States Compared," *American Economic Review* 81 (1992): 385–400. On the economic reasoning see also Maxim Boycko, Andrei Shleifer, and Robert W. Vishny, "Privatizing Russia," *Brookings Papers on Economic Activity* 2 (1993): 139–81, and Andrei Shleifer and Robert W. Vishny, "Politicians and Firms," *Quarterly Journal of Economics* 109 (1994): 995–1025. On the optimal level of top management ownership, see Randall Morck, Andrei Shleifer, and Robert W. Vishny, "Management Ownership and Market Valuation: An Empirical Analysis," *Journal of Financial Economics* 20 (1988): 293–315.

A useful collection of privatization documents is *The Privatization Manual,* published in English by the State Committee of the Russian Federation for the Management of State Property (GKI) and the European Bank for Reconstruction and Development (EBRD) (London, 1993).

Åslund, *How Russia Became a Market Economy,* chap. 2, reviews relevant laws and legal precedents before the 1992 privatization program was enacted. The privatization law was signed on June 11, 1992, as decree 2980-1 of the Supreme Soviet of the Russian Federation. It was published in the government newspaper, *Rossiiskaya gazeta,* July 9, 1992, pp. 4–6. See GKI and EBRD, *Privatization Manual,* 2:1–19. An excellent analysis of the main privatization documents and the confusions of the text can be found in Roman Frydman, Andrzej Rapaczynski, and John Earle, *The Privatization Process in Russia, Ukraine, and the Baltic States* (London: Central European University Press, 1993). (This book is distributed by Oxford University Press.) The 1992 privatization law was the last such law passed by a Russian parliament. All elaborations of the privatization process came into legal force through regulations or presidential decrees. Yeltsin's power to issue decrees was authorized by the Supreme Soviet.

Estimates of the value of a voucher are based on exchange rates in *Russian Economic Trends* 4, no. 2 (1995): 151–52, Table A18a. The world press and public and many people in Russia evidently misunderstood the value of a voucher from 1992 to 1994. It is true that on March 5, 1993, when the ruble sank to 1,024 to the dollar, a 10,000-ruble voucher was worth less than $10 rather than the $24 it was worth in November 1992, when the program began. But it is also true that a 10,000-ruble voucher was being used to buy 10,000 rubles' worth of enterprise property at pre-July 1992 book-value prices. In one sense, it did not matter how much the ruble was worth during this inflationary period, as long as one voucher ruble could buy one ruble of property valued at a price insulated from inflation. An additional share fund, Fund Aktsionirovaniya Rabotnikov (a carry-over from the Duma's 1991 privatization program) entitled employees to buy more shares. Yeltsin's first decree on vouchers (Document G-1) was issued on July 14, 1992. His second decree (Document G-2) was issued on August 14, 1992. English translations of all relevant decrees are available in EBRD, *Privatization Manual,* vol. 2. Data on the use of the options is in Boycko et al., *Privatizing Russia,* p. 98; data on the fluctuation of the trading price of the Russian voucher from October 1992 to July 1994 are on p. 102. On the accusation that vouchers caused inflation, see Joseph Blasi, "An Analysis of Option 4" (Rutgers University, March 1993). According to *Russian Economic Trends* 4, no. 4 (1995): 100, Table 95, the popularity of option 2 fell from 1994 to 1995. In 1994, 28% of firms corporatizing chose option 1, 61% chose option 2, 3% chose option 3, and 8% had other options, whereas in 1995 37% chose option 1, 48% chose option 2, 4% chose option 3, and 11% had other options. Criticisms of privatization are quoted in *Russian Press Digest,* June 3, 9, 12, 27, 30; July 23; September 10, 14, 24; October 1, 3, 6, 1992. See also Georgy A. Abatov, "Neo-Bolsheviks of the IMF," *New York Times,* May 7, 1992; Roman Frydman and Andrzej Rapaczynski, *Privatization in Eastern Europe: Is the State Withering Away?* (New

York and London: Central European University Press, 1994); John Simmons and John Logue, "Thirteen Myths: Russian Privatization and Employee Ownership," *Izvestia,* April 1, 1992. Åslund raises the point on liberalizing prices without privatization in *How Russia Became a Market Economy,* p. 138. See also Andrei Shleifer, "The Enemies of Russian Privatization," *Wall Street Journal,* June 2, 1992. Housing privatization figures are shown in Åslund, *How Russia Became a Market Economy,* Table 7-4, and in the quarterly issues of *Russian Economic Trends.* Housing privatization continues at the rate of about 12,000 apartments per month.

2. Ownership

The opening scene was witnessed by Yelena Zakrevskaya, one of our research assistants. Boris Yeltsin's speech in August 1992 explaining the privatization program appeared in *Rossiiskie vesti,* August 25, 1992. A useful discussion of the details of the privatization program may be found in Anders Åslund, *How Russia Became a Market Economy* (Washington, D.C.: Brookings Institution, 1995), pp. 223–71; and Maxim Boycko, Andrei Shleifer, and Robert W. Vishny, *Privatizing Russia* (Cambridge: MIT Press, 1995). Information on top management ownership is from Joseph Blasi and James Gasaway, "Top Management Ownership in the U.S.," unpublished manuscript, Rutgers University School of Management and Labor Relations. Updated U.S. employee ownership estimates are based on Joseph R. Blasi and Douglas L. Kruse, *The New Owners: The Mass Emergence of Employee Ownership in Public Companies and What It Means to American Business* (New York: HarperCollins, 1994). The *New York Times* article is Alessandra Stanley, "Russian Banking Scandal Poses Threat to Future of Privatization," January 28, 1996. The *Wall Street Journal* article is Marshall I. Goldman, "The Communist Return?" February 13, 1996. See also Marshall I. Goldman, *Lost Opportunity: Why Economic Reforms in Russia Have Not Worked* (New York: Norton, 1994); David Ellerman, ed., *Management and Employee Buyouts as a Technique in Privatization* (Washington, D.C.: Economic Development Institute of the World Bank, 1993).

Boycko et al., *Privatizing Russia,* report (p. 98) that the average state-owned firm converted to a corporation had more than 1,000 employees, and that GKI and its regional offices registered more than 22,000 firms as joint-stock companies (although fewer were actually privatized). They report preliminary findings on what privatization options were chosen by the workers: "The apparent enthusiasm for corporatization confirms the generosity of worker and management benefits. The managers dominated the meetings of the workers' collectives in most firms, and made proposals that the workers rubber-stamped. In 73% of the firms, workers and managers elected Option 2, which gave them voting control. In 25%

of firms, they chose Option 1. . . . Option 3 was hardly ever chosen."
These data are drawn from Goskomstat Rossii, *Sotsial'no-ekono-micheskoe polozhenie Rossii 1993 g.* [The socioeconomic situation in Russia in 1993] (Moscow, 1994), p. 94. They are quoted also in Åslund, *How Russia Became a Market Economy,* pp. 253, 363.

The Russian National Survey of 1994–95 found that option 2 had been chosen by 53.64% of the firms, option 1 by 37.42%, and option 3 by 1.32%; 7.62% of firms had been privatized under the 1991 privatization program, by leasing, later choice of an option (usually option 2), and other means, often special decrees of the government. Several other surveys broadly confirm our findings on ownership. See Katerina Pistor, "Privatization and Corporate Governance in Russia: An Empirical Study," in *Privatization, Conversion, and Enterprise Reform in Russia,* ed. Michael McFaul and Tova Perlmutter (Boulder: Westview, 1995), pp. 69–84; Leila M. Webster with Juergen Franz, Igor Artemiev, and Harold Wackman, *Newly Privatized Russian Enterprises,* technical paper 241 (Washington, D.C.: World Bank, 1994). A study by John Earle, Saul Estrin, and Larisa L. Leshchenko, *Ownership Structures, Patterns of Control, and Enterprise Behavior in Russia* (Washington, D.C.: World Bank, 1995), finds 8.8% more total employee ownership, 12.3% less total outsider ownership, and 3.3% less total state ownership than our 1994–95 survey and more firms that are majority employee-owned than we report. One explanation is that the World Bank survey was conducted in a short period during the summer of 1994, just as our survey was beginning. Our 1994–95 survey was more likely to reflect changes in ownership that took place throughout that year as more voucher auctions, more cash auctions, more investment tenders, and more sales of shares by employees took place. A survey conducted in June 1994 by the Central European University (CEU) Privatization Project examined 148 of the 516 voucher investment funds in Russia and the investment portfolios and strategies of those funds. See Katerina Pistor, Roman Frydman, and Andrzej Rapaczynski, "Investing in Insider-Dominated Firms: A Study of Russian Voucher Privatization Funds," in *Corporate Governance in Central Europe and Russia,* ed. Roman Frydman, Cheryl Gray, and Andrzej Rapaczynski, 2 vols. (Oxford: Oxford University Press, 1996), vol. 1. The CEU study's sample was not random, but it included a quarter of all funds, and those funds represented 69% of all vouchers collected—a very impressive showing. The evidence "does not show any significant lessening of insider domination of the Russian firms," and as of June 1994, workers held majority stakes in over 60% of the companies in which voucher funds were invested, and when they did own a majority their median stake was over 80%" (p. 4). The figure of 60% for majority employee-owned firms confirms our findings in 1994–95. See also Derek Jones and Tom Weiskopf, "Employee Ownership and Control Evidence from Russia," working paper 96/1 (Hamilton College, Department of Economics, January 1996), based on 72 manufacturing firms in St. Petersburg in 1993 and 60 manufacturing firms in 1994. In 1993 the privatized firms had 63% total insider ownership and 8% managerial ownership. In 1994, insiders owned a majority stake in almost two-thirds of the firms in the second sample.

For a discussion of early privatization in Russia and elsewhere, see Saul Estrin, ed., *Privatization in Central and Eastern Europe* (New York: Longmans, 1994).

In 1995, Brunswick Brokerage assembled whatever information these companies were willing to disclose in the *Russian Equity Guide* (New York and Moscow: Burnswick Brokerage, 1995). The ownership reports are incomplete and the numbers presented are averages and should be viewed as best estimates. Our estimates from this source add up to more than 100 percent because of rounding. On *nomenklatura* continuity, see Ivan Szelenyi, Don Treiman, and Edmund Wnuk-Lipinski, eds., *Elites in Poland, Russia, and Hungary: Change or Reproduction?* (Warsaw: Polish Academy of Sciences, Institute of Political Studies, 1995) (in Polish), summarized in Jakub Karpinki, "Sociologists Compare *Nomenklatura* Members and Contemporary Elites," *Transition,* May 31, 1996, pp. 36–37.

A lawsuit was filed over allegations that a manager at the Institute of Physics in Novosibirsk set up a family front company to buy the institute's shares and then pass them to a foreign investor. See "An Academic Decided to Buy Out the Institute He Works In, Novosibirsk Court of Arbitration Receives a Claim," *Kommersant,* March 7, 1995. An indication that some rank-and-file employee groups feel they have a stake in privatization is seen in their demands for privatization of defense plants. See "Soskovets Did Not Allow Chubais to Privatize the Defense Plant," *Kommersant,* January 20, 1995. The story about the Lubyuytov cookie factory is from *Kommersant,* March 18, 1995. The Baltika Beer information is from *Russian Equity Guide* (Moscow and New York: Brunswick Brokerage, 1995), p. 28, and *Kommersant,* March 28, 1995. *Kommersant* reported on November 30, 1994, that outsiders had taken over the Sayansk Aluminum plant (no. 43 among the Russia 100); on January 27, 1995, that SemiTech had purchased a plant in Podolsk; and on February 6, 1995, that Swedes now controlled Svetgorsk (no. 79 among the Russia 100).

On cash privatization, the telecommunication auction, and loans for shares see *Russian Economic Trends* 4 (1995), no. 1, pp. 95–97; no. 2, pp. 89–94; no. 3, pp. 93–97; no. 4, pp. 97–102, esp. Table 98, p. 102, which provides bid prices for each loans-for-shares auction. (This report also updates information on federal budget revenue from privatization.) Ira W. Lieberman, *Russia: The Rush for State Shares in the "Klondyke" of Wild East Capitalism* (Washington, D.C.: World Bank, Private Sector Development Dept., March 1996), identifies the players in the loans-for-shares auctions. On recent Duma actions, see Itar-TASS reports, June 4–8, 1996: Thomas Siegel, "Prices Low in Federal Shares Auctions," summarizing a report in *Moskovskie novosti,* November 21, 1995, and Natalia Gurushina's summary of an *Interfax* report of November 17, 1995, in *Open Media Research Institute Digest. Segodnya* reported on November 9, 1995, that foreigners often buy a company's shares solely to eliminate a potential competitor from the market; see also *Omri Economic Digest,* December 17, 1995.

The Russian polling group data are from the polling organization Mnenie, cited in Åslund, *How Russia Became a Market Economy,* p. 225. The additional polling data are from the survey organization VSIOM and were provided by Marina Krasinikova. See also Elena Dzhaginova, "A Quarter of the Population of Russia Do Not Know What to Do with Their Vouchers," *Segodnya,* January 26, 1994 (quoted in Åslund, *How Russia Became a Market Economy*). On First Boston, see Richard Stevenson, "An American In Moscow," *New York Times,* September 15, 1995. On U.S. shareholders, see the table "Growing Ranks: Shareholders as a Percent of Population," *Wall Street Journal,* May 28, 1996, p. R8. The data on large firms in the Russian market are from Brunswick Brokerage. Information on small-scale privatization and housing privatization is from *Russian Economic Trends* 4 (1994), no. 1: 95–111; no. 2: 89–110; no. 3: 93–99.

On the loss of savings, see "Nation's Piggy Bank Holds Up Russian System," *Financial Times,* March 27, 1996. The Ira Lieberman quotation is from an interview conducted April 27, 1996.

For further information about who bought the small shops, see Nicholas Barberis, Maxim Boycko, Andrei Shleifer, and Natalia Tsukanova, *How Does Privatization Work? Evidence from the Russian Shops,* discussion paper 1721 (Cambridge: Harvard Institute for Economic Research, May 1995); and April Harding, *Commercial Real Estate Privatization in Russia* (Washington, D.C.: World Bank, Private Sector Development Dept., 1994).

3. Power

Sergo Ordzhonikidze was a key aide to Joseph Stalin. The article is "Open Voting: Weapon of Stockholders," *Izvestia,* September 8, 1995. The issue of open vs. closed companies is taken up by regional governments such as autonomous republics of the Russian Federation. See, for example, "The Republic President Gave an Open Joint-Stock Company Permission to Be a Closed One," *Kommersant,* February 7, 1995.

For an overview of corporate governance theory, see Andrei Shleifer and Robert W. Vishny, *A Survey on Corporate Governance,* discussion paper 1741 (Cambridge: Harvard Institute of Economic Research, October 1995).

On the design of Russia's new corporate law, see Bernard Black, Reinier Kraakman, and Jonathan Hay, *Corporate Law from Scratch* (New

York: Columbia University School of Law, December 1994). The Federal Law on Joint-Stock Companies is available in Russian and English from the International Institute for Law-Based Economy, Moscow. Yeltsin's decree on cumulative voting and limitations on insider board seats was decree 2284, December 24, 1993.

For a comparison of Russia with other countries and a discussion of other research, see Frydman, Gray, and Rapaczynski, *Corporate Governance in Central Europe and Russia*. Note that this was written *before* Russia's new corporate law was passed.

The discussion of corporate governance systems worldwide and concentrated ownership is from Rafael La Porta, Florencio López de Silanes, Andrei Shleifer, and Robert W. Vishny, "Law and Finance" (Harvard University, April 1996).

Information on government policy on shareholder registers and the new corporate law is from the 1995 press packet of the Federal Commission on Securities and the Capital Market.

On Komineft see "Big Stockholders Are Not Satisfied with Decision of General Meeting," *Kommersant*, February 1, 1995. The Sakhalin case is discussed in "A Simple Scheme of Defense Has Been Invented," *Kommersant*, March 14, 1995. On Primorsky see "Primorsky Share Issue Approved," *Moscow Times*, May 14, 1995. See also Geoff Winestock, "Shipping Industry: Worth Fighting For," *Moscow Times*, April 30, 1995. Red October is discussed in Reuter's dispatches of July 18, 19, and 25, 1995, and July 26 and 27, 1996.

On blockholders, see Andrei Shleifer and Robert W. Vishny, "Large Shareholders and Corporate Control," *Journal of Political Economy* 94, no. 2 (1986): 461–88.

On the Kuznetsk shareholder action, see *Biznes segodnya* [Business today], September 20, 1994.

The Bratsk Aluminum Plant (no. 14 in the Russia 100) has attracted considerable outside investment. Another shareholder conflict arose between a Vladivostok fishing company and an American company, Hermes Imperial Investment; it is discussed in "Morgue Is Payment for President of Open Joint-Stock Company," *Kommersant*, January 12, 1995.

The survey on worker influence in privatization is from Lynn D. Nelson et al., *Property to the People: The Struggle for Radical Economic Reform in Russia* (Armonk, N.Y.: M. E. Sharpe, 1994). On wage and pensions and strike activity, see *Russian Economic Trends* 4, nos. 1–4 (1995). On living standards, see David Stamp, "Western Living Standard Far Off in Eastern Europe," Reuter, October 11, 1995. The discussion of falling wages vs. living standards is from World Bank, *Russian Federation: Toward Medium-Term Viability*, Report 14472-RU (Washington, D.C., October 16, 1995), p. 6. See also Brian Pinto and Uma Ramakrishnan, "Wage Convergence to Western Levels: How Soon?" *Transition*, January–February 1996, pp. 6–7.

There are many problems with Russian wage figures. People under-state them to avoid taxes, official figures do not include the new private sector, and part of the large drop in real wages from December 1994 to January 1995 was due to a revision in the way Russia's price indexes are computed. For figures issued in the spring of 1996, see *Russian Economic Trends,* Monthly Update, April 22, 1996, Table 9. The average wage cost per manufacturing worker in Russia is compared with the comparable costs in other Eastern European countries on p. 5. See also *Economist,* June 1, 1996, pp. 45–46, for a chart on the decline in real wages. Re-search on household consumption and household incomes is reported in World Bank, *Russian Federation,* Report 14472-RU, pp. 6–8. See also Andrea Richter, "Keeping People Working," *Moscow Times,* August 13, 1995; Donald Filtzer, *Soviet Workers and the Collapse of Perestroika* (Cambridge: Cambridge University Press, 1994), pp. 78–88 on workers' councils and 88–94 on union struggles over privatization; Walter D. Con-nor, *Tattered Banners: Labor Conflict and Corporatism in Post-Communist Russia* (New York: HarperCollins/Westview, 1996); Simon Clarke et al., *What About the Workers? Workers and the Transition to Capitalism in Russia* (New York: New Left Books/Verso, 1993); and American Embassy in Moscow, *Foreign Labor Trends: Russia, 1994–1995* (Washington, D.C.: U.S. Department of Labor, 1995). For a detailed study of one industry based on worker surveys, see Jennifer Senick-Goldstein, "Employment Relations in Russia's Food Industry: The Social Contract Meets the Market" (Ph.D. diss., UCLA, 1996). The author finds that some enterprise-level unions are more aggressive. See also "One in Five Workers Owed Back Pay," *Moscow Times,* July 16, 1995; John Thornhill, "Trade Unions Struggle for the Trust of Workers," *Financial Times,* October 10, 1995.

The Vorovskoi Mir meeting at Vedentsovo has been reported by many sources. Much of the discussion of the Mafia relies on the best researched volume available on the subject, Steven Handelman's *Comrade Crimi-nal: The Theft of the Second Russian Revolution* (London: Michael Jo-seph, 1994). The government report on the Mafia is quoted in "Crime in Russia: The High Price of Freeing Markets," *Economist,* February 19, 1994, pp. 57–58. On recent estimates by the Academy of Sciences and the Interior Ministry see Olga Kryshtanovskaya, "Russia's Mafia Land-scape," *Izvestia,* September 21, 1995.

On corruption, see Andrei Shleifer and Robert W. Vishny, "Corrup-tion," *Quarterly Journal of Economics,* August 1993, pp. 600–616; Bill Rigby, "Eastern Europe: Mob Rules," *Corporate Cover,* December 31, 1995; "Mafia and Police Have Been Working Together," *Moscow News,* December 15, 1995; "Interior Ministry Girds for Major Anticrime Drive," *Kommersant,* August 25, 1995; Cherif Cordahi, "Egypt [Conference]: Russian Money Launderers a Threat to the West," *Guardian,* May 5, 1995; "Criminals as Insurance Salesmen," *Economist,* July 8, 1995; Mar-shall I. Goldman, "Why the Mafia Is So Dominant in Russia," *Challenge*

39 (January–February 1996): 39–47; Mikhail Gulyayev and Larisa Vos-
tryakova, "Taxes and the Mafia Burden Small Firms," *Moscow Times,*
April 2, 1996; Genene Babakian, "Poll Surveys Links to Business," *Mos-
cow Times,* July 6, 1996; "Stockbrokers Say Criminals Breaking into
Stock Market," *Moscow Times,* April 30, 1995. On Kuznetsk Steel see
Crystia Freeland, "Russia's Future Played Out in Steel Mill," *Financial
Times,* March 4, 1996.

The assertion that the Mafia controls privatization appears in Louise
Shelley, "Privatization and Crime: The Post-Soviet Experience," *Journal
of Contemporary Criminal Justice* 2 (December 1995): 244–56. The article does not support its claims with persuasive evidence. This treatment
was repeated in the popular press in J. Michael Waller, "To Russia, with
Cash," *Reader's Digest,* June 1996, p. 17. Handelman's *Comrade Criminal* was written before much of voucher privatization was complete, and
he provides little evidence of extensive Mafia ownership or control in
larger enterprises. In February and March 1996, we did an extensive
review of the Lexis/Nexis database for 1994–96 on the subjects of Russia
and Mafia or crime in a series of translated Russian and English data-
bases and a more limited search on the Dialog online database in order
to confirm independently how much evidence on the penetration of mid-
sized and large privatized enterprises by criminal elements was printed
in the press. Again, we discovered no evidence of systematic penetration,
only isolated cases. See, e.g., Anton Zhigulsky and Carey Scott (of the
London *Sunday Times*), "A Very Bumpy Ride . . . Mafia-Laden and Un-
modernized, AvtoVAZ Struggles to Survive," *Moscow Times,* March 25,
1996, about one of Russia's major car manufacturers. Serebryakov's comments are in Reuter's and Itar-TASS stories of May 21 and May 23, 1996.
The FBI and CIA comments were made in a Reuter's story of April
30, 1996, filed from Washington, D.C., by Robert Green. Gulyayev and
Vostryakova, "Taxes and the Mafia," quotes the Russian Trade Chamber,
Russia's chamber of commerce, as saying that racketeering is one of the
major problems of small businesses.

4. Restructuring

On subsidies, see World Bank, *Russian Federation,* Report 14472-RU,
p. 54, Table 2-9, which indicates that transfers to enterprises dropped
dramatically from 1992 to 1994 and that subsidies are becoming increasingly concentrated in the largest enterprises. See also Simon Commander, Qimiao Fan, and Mark Schaffer, eds., *Economic Policy and
Restructuring in Russia* (Washington, D.C.: World Bank, 1996), p. 3,
which says that 2% of firms are receiving 50% of subsidies. Subsidies
must be considered to include direct transfers, tax exemptions, and credits from the federal and local governments, often for housing stock owned
by enterprises. For a broader analysis of how criminals, managers, and

bureaucrats expropriate assets from the government, see Anders Åslund, "Reform vs. Rent-Seeking in Russia's Economic Transformation," *Transition*, January 26, 1996, pp. 12–16.

For a historical perspective on restructuring, see Evsei Liberman, "Are We Flirting with Capitalism?" in *Readings in Russian Civilization*, vol. 3, *Soviet Russia, 1917–1963*, ed. Thomas Riha (Chicago: University of Chicago Press, 1964), pp. 803–10. Liberman, a professor at Kharkov University, proposed reforms to restructure state-owned companies in the 1960s. On enterprise subsidies, see "Enterprise Support," in World Bank, *Russian Federation: Toward Medium-Term Viability*, Report 14472-RU (Washington, D.C., October 16, 1995), pp. 53–59, on which this discussion is closely based.

The KKR and KamAZ story is based on a press release in *Kommersant*, March 30, 1995, and information supplied by KKR. The brief descriptions of the economic situation in 1993–94 are heavily informed by Anders Åslund, *How Russia Became a Market Economy* (Washington, D.C.: Brookings Institution, 1995). The descriptions provided here generalize each year's developments. Åslund supplies the details on pp. 193–200. His table 6-3 shows that interest rates were negative from January 1992 to November 1993.

The fact that enterprises did not have to identify themselves as privatized when they applied for subsidies and the discussion of budget loans and loan guarantees to enterprises are based on a personal interview with the former finance minister Boris Fedorov in February 1996. Not all reformers in the government supported Chubais's stabilization program. See "Would the Real Anatoly Chubais Please Stand Up?" *Moscow Times*, June 18, 1995. The idea of dividing large enterprises into smaller ones that are independently financed is discussed in "At Shareholders' Meeting They Didn't Share the Enterprise and the Land It's Situated On," *Kommersant*, March 22, 1995. See also "Trust but Keep It under Control," *Kommersant*, March 21, 1995.

Commander et al., eds., *Economic Policy and Restructuring*, has been very useful in the preparation of this chapter, esp. Simon Commander, Sumana Dhar, and Ruslan Yemtsov, "How Russian Firms Make Their Wage and Employment Decisions," based on a survey of 400 privatized enterprises in 24 regions in mid-1994. On Zil see "The Problem Is Not in the Patriotism but in the Land," *Kommersant*, February 7, 1995.

We are indebted to Jonathan Hay for describing the way the government securities market crowded out private bank investment in enterprises. The 1995 Russian National Survey looked mainly at layoffs and actions taken to restructure social assets. The detailed evidence on restructuring is from the 1996 survey. In this chapter we examine whether enterprises did or did not do a specific type of restructuring, such as introduce new products, and attempt a detailed measurement of that restructuring, in this case the percentage of sales accounted for by new products. The available evidence on each type of restructuring indicates that most restructuring was concentrated in a small number of firms. A table summarizing that evidence is available from the authors. On Avto-VAZ see *Russia Review,* March 25, 1996, pp. 26–28.

Regarding bank loans to enterprises, see Giles Alfandari and Mark E. Schaffer, " 'Arrears' in the Russian Enterprise Sector," in Commander et al., *Economic Policy and Restructuring.*

Estimates of social services for Russian and Polish employees are from Simon Commander and Une Lee with Andrei Tolstopiatenko, "Social Benefits and the Russian Industrial Firm," in Commander et al., *Economic Policy and Restructuring.* These measurements are corroborated in the Russian National Surveys for 1995 and 1996, as reported in Table 10 and in Maxim Boycko and Andrei Shleifer, "The Russian Restructuring and Social Assets," unpublished paper, May 1994. A discussion of capital, human capital, social services, and business operations as the key restructuring problems is in Maxim Boycko, Andrei Shleifer, and Robert W. Vishny, *Privatizing Russia* (Cambridge: MIT Press, 1995).

Lebedinsk is discussed in *Ekspert,* February 26, 1996, p. 42, and "Shareholder Showdown at Massive Ore Smelter," *Moscow Times,* March 28, 1996. A related story is "Morgan Grenfell Opposes Results of Shareholder Meeting," *Kommersant,* April 5, 1995.

Whether the Russian corporate scene will develop in the direction of free and open company and capital markets or more closed hierarchies is a major question. The factors that influence such trends were first explored in detail in Oliver E. Williamson, *Markets and Hierarchies* (New York: Free Press, 1975). The ways individuals and organizations respond to decline is discussed in Albert O. Hirschman, *Exit, Voice, and Loyalty* (Cambridge: Harvard University Press, 1970). On the problems with investment tenders, see "Why Tenders Did Not Work," *Moscow Times,* International ed., June 11, 1995. The Russian Privatization Center's work is discussed in "Privatized Enterprises Need More Human Capital than Cash," *Finansovye izvestia,* March 22, 1995, and "Privatized Enterprises Are Entering the Market," *Delovoi ekspress,* March 21, 1995.

The *Pravda 5* article is "The Great Colonial Revolution in Russia," January 19–26, 1996.

The discussion of foreign capital is from *ING Barings Perspectives,* January 1996, pp. 31–33. See also Thomas C. Owen, *Russian Corporate Capitalism from Peter the Great to Perestroika* (Oxford: Oxford University Press, 1995).

On Novorostsement, see "Cement Plant Is Well Placed To Grow," *Moscow Times,* International ed., June 11, 1995. For other strategic investor examples, see "Western Sugardaddy: Secret of Their Success," *Moscow Times,* International ed., August 27, 1995.

On insider takeovers, see "United We Own," *Business Week,* March 19, 1996. Timothy Middleton, "For the Brave, an Open-End Russia Fund," *New York Times,* April 18, 1996, cites a report by Arnold & S. Bleichroeder Inc. that sixty listed stocks trade once a month and fewer than thirty trade at least once a week, and discusses the Russia Fund of Lexington Capital Management Corporation, Templeton, and Pioneer.

"The Big FIG," *Russia Review,* April 22, 1996, describes Menatep as a FIG rather than a merchant bank.

The Perm Motors information was provided by Harvey Sewikin of Eastern Star Consulting, New York City, personal communication, 1996. Mr. Sewikin manages the Firebird Portfolio Russia Fund. On FIGs, see "The Battle for Russia's Wealth," *Business Week,* April 1, 1996, which lists the key FIGs in Russia. See also Lev Frenkman, "Financial-Industrial Groups in Russia: Emergence of Large Diversified Private Companies," *Communist Economies & Economic Transformation* 7, no. 1 (1995): 51–66.

On Renaissance, see "Renaissance Man," *Russia Review,* April 8, 1996. On politburo FIGs, see "Socialism Is Being Restored in Russia's Metallurgical Industry," *Izvestia,* September 30, 1995 (available in *Current Digest of the Soviet Press,* October 25, 1995). Zaikin and Livshits are cited in "New Economic Behemoths," *Moscow Times,* International ed., August 20, 1995. Livshits's remark was made in a personal communication, May 1996. On bank lending, see "Long-Term Investment in Short Supply," *Moscow Times,* International ed., August 6, 1995.

The few reports of big investments by Russian investors are mainly announcements of intent. See, for example, "Russian Company Ready to Invest $40.5 Million in Well-Known Optical and Mechanical Plant LOMO," *Kommersant,* March 30, 1995. LOMO is no. 99 in the Russia 100. There is scattered evidence that various pools of money have been set up to allow state investment in production through assorted government agencies and friendly or related banks. "Russian Bank Reconstructs Coke Production," *Kommersant,* March 12, 1995, discusses the work of the International Industrial Bank. On Stolichnyi Bank, see *Kommersant,* May 30, 1995.

The idea that lack of investment is a sign of lack of loyalty to the Russian nation is reflected in articles about the troubled Zil automobile company: "Zil Found Patriots Who Would Help Out the Plant," *Izvestia,* January 27, 1995, and "Zil Can Turn Out to Be a Leader of Domestic Industry but in Terms of Its Bankruptcy," *Izvestia,* January 20, 1995.

On mutual funds, see "Russia Said Lagging in Capital Retrieval," *Moscow Times,* International ed., November 5, 1995, on the EBRD; "Russian Shepherd of Mutual Funds," *New York Times,* March 8, 1996; Andrew Burchill, "Is Russia Ready for Mutual Funds?" *Institutional Investor,* March 1996.

A press packet of the Commission on Securities and the Capital Market, May 1996, is the source of material on the stock market, depositary clearing, share registration, and PAUFOR. The commission publishes a newsletter and maintains a World Wide Web page. Other information on stock market operations comes from a confidential interview with a major Moscow broker in 1996.

Several stock market indexes are available for Russia. The Moscow Times Index is compiled by the Moscow Times, publisher of the English-language weekly *Russia Review,* which is available in the United States. PAUFOR maintains the Russian Trading System (RTS) Index. CS First Boston produces an index called ROS. The firm AK&M, which lists the top Russian corporations, also compiles a Russian stock index. A list of the top 200 Russian firms appears in *Ekspert,* October 24, 1995. Weekly and monthly profiles of the Russian stock market and profiles of individual companies were made available by both Brunswick Brokerage and ING Barings, with offices in Moscow, New York, and London.

On related stock market institutions mentioned, see "Survey Ranks Domestic Brokerages," *Moscow Times,* International ed., July 23, 1995; "Morgan Grenfell to Start Custodian Service," *Moscow Times,* International ed., July 9, 1995; on privatization of oil companies, "Revamp Sets Stage for Oil Competition," *Moscow Times,* International ed., August 27, 1995. On the Russian Depositary Certificate Program, see *The Russian Depositary Certificate Program: Introduction of New Companies* (New York/London/Moscow: ING Barings, 1996). On ADRs see "U.S. Approves Russian Share Issues," *Moscow Times,* International ed., September 17, 1995; "Blue Chips Plan U.S. Sales," *Moscow Times,* International ed., June 4, 1995; "Morgan Grenfell Eyes Securities Sector," *Moscow Times,* International ed., June 4, 1995; "Securities Need Private Push," *Moscow Times,* International ed., October 29, 1995.

A detailed report on share custody operations with the Swiss Hypo-Bank (Bayerische Hypotheken- und Wechselbank) is discussed in "Rossiisky Kredit and Hypo-Bank Agreement: Russian Securities Will Be Sold to Foreign Investors in Their Country," *Kommersant,* March 21, 1995. Rossiisky Kredit published an extensive list of corporations whose shareholder registers it would keep.

Information on the New Jersey State Pension Fund is based on a personal interview with its director in March 1996. On the gap between share prices in Russia and the theoretical prices in mainstream stock markets, see "Share Prices in Russia: The Reasons for Undervaluation," *Russian Economic Trends* 4, no. 2 (1995): 111–27.

On recent reports of new ADRs, see *Segodnya,* May 1, 1996. On the bond thefts, see "Russian Bond Thefts Hit Banks," *Financial Times,* June 14, 1996. For examples of detailed market data on specific market sectors, see the following industry analyses by Brunswick Brokerage, all issued in 1995: *Russian Pulp and Paper Industry; Russian Regional Telecommunications; Russian Automotive Industry; Russian Regional Power Utilities;* and *The Russian Oil Industry.* These analyses describe the structures of the respective industries and review costs, demand, competition, available financial information, and valuation issues. Russian investment recommendations will probably crash if Russia experiences further political instability. We make no recommendations whatsoever.

5. The Future of Reform

Assessments of the percentage of privatization are from *Russian Economic Trends* 4, no. 3 (1995): 96. Despite the slowing of privatization, auctions of packages of shares in companies continue in Russia's regions.

Russian Economic Trends regularly lists the biggest privatization transactions of the most recent period. Upcoming auctions of shares in privatized companies are listed regularly in the daily *Moscow Times* (in English) and at the end of most weekly editions of *Russia Review* (the new name of the *Moscow Times'* International edition) under "Upcoming Cash Auctions." Announcements of regional auctions are also carried by Interfax in an English edition available from Boulder, Colorado.

For a historical perspective, three books by Richard Pipes have proved invaluable: *Russia under the Old Regime* (New York: Macmillan, 1974), *The Russian Revolution* (New York: Random House, 1990), and *Russia under the Bolshevik Regime* (New York: Knopf, 1994). See also James Billington, *The Icon and the Axe: An Interpretive History of Russian Culture* (New York: Random House, 1966). As a general reference, see *The Cambridge Encyclopedia of Russia,* ed. Archie Brown, Michael Kaser, and Gerald Smith (Cambridge: Cambridge University Press, 1994). Space and other limitations do not allow the full historical analysis that these events certainly demand. The three most significant economic reforms that are comparable to privatization are the emancipation of the serfs in 1861, when peasants were required to redeem their land with annual payments over 49 years; the 1906 agrarian reforms of P. A. Stolypin; and Lenin's New Economic Policy (NEP), which Stalin abolished. On NEP see Alan M. Ball, *Russia's Last Capitalists: The NEPmen, 1922–1929* (Berkeley: University of California Press, 1987). Historians are bound to compare these reforms with privatization. On the emerging moneyed class in Russia, see "New Russians Aren't So New," *Russia Review,* April 8, 1996.

On the ongoing role of the state after privatization, see Roman Frydman and Andrzej Rapaczynski, *Privatization in Eastern Europe: Is the State Withering Away?* (Oxford: Oxford University Press, 1994).

On the importance of institutional reform, see Douglas C. North, *Institutions, Institutional Change, and Economic Performance* (Cambridge: Cambridge University Press, 1990).

On legal reform, see Jonathan Hay, Andrei Shleifer, and Robert W. Vishny, "Toward a Theory of Legal Reforms," *European Economic Review,* forthcoming; "When the Deal Sours, Where Do You Settle?" *Moscow Times,* International ed., June 11, 1995.

On China, see Anders Åslund, *How Russia Became a Market Economy* (Washington, D.C.: Brookings Institution, 1995), pp. 13–15. Regarding the financial performance categories of Russian privatized enterprises, general directors reported that their cash flow covered their operating costs by a lot (5.6% in 1995, 5.6% in 1996), barely (21.2% in 1995, 27.2%

in 1996), not by a lot (45.3% in 1995, 38.2% in 1996), and not by a very wide margin, with the firm in serious difficulties (27.6% in 1995, 28.9% in 1996). We are examining all available data from 1995 and 1996 to assess this issue further. Russia's Federal Commission on Bankruptcy has been hampered by weak laws and has not moved to accelerate bankruptcies. "In Russia, Even Bankruptcy Is Profitable," *Moscow Tribune,* March 7, 1995, describes how the government drove a company into bankruptcy and then allowed its management to buy it cheaply.

The insider/outsider, Russian/foreign conflict can be seen in the title of a *Kommersant Weekly* article, "The Motherland Cannot Be Sold for a Controlling Stake of Shares," March 28, 1995.

A comparative perspective is offered by Gerhard Pohl, Simeon Djankov, and Robert E. Anderson, "Restructuring of Large Industrial Firms in Central and Eastern Europe, 1992–1994," paper for World Bank, Europe and Central Asia, and Middle East and North Africa Regions, Private Sector Development and Finance Group, November 1995.

On foreign investment, see "Foreign Investment Downplayed," *Moscow Times,* International ed., July 9, 1995. Regarding management entrenchment, see Anders Åslund, "Reform vs. 'Rent-Seeking' in Russia's Economic Transformation," *Transition* 2, no. 2 (January 26, 1996): 12–17.

For a historical perspective on one-man management in Russia's enterprises, see Hiroaki Kuromiya, *Stalin's Industrial Revolution* (Cambridge: Cambridge University Press, 1988).

The data on the growth of small businesses and joint ventures are from Michael Gulyayev and Larisa Vostryakova, "Taxes and the Mafia Burden Small Firms," *Moscow Times,* April 2, 1996.

On entrepreneurial firms, see Thomas Tirone and Neli Esipova, *A Study of Russian Entrepreneurial Firms* (Champaign, Ill.: Tirone Corp., 1996). Data on the shift away from the industrial sector toward the service sector are in Phillip Hanson, "Structural Change in the Russian Economy," *Transition,* January 26, 1996, pp. 18–21. On interenterprise debts see the report on Soskovets in *Interfax,* June 11, 1996.

For a broader examination of economic issues, see Alan Smith, ed., *Challenges for Russian Economic Reform* (Washington, D.C.: Brookings Institution, 1995), and Brigitte Granville, *The Success of Russian Economic Reforms* (London: Royal Institute of International Affairs, 1995). On trends in public opinion on these issues, a series of reports is available from Richard Rose of the University of Strathcylde in Glasgow, Scotland, and Barry M. Popkin of the University of North Carolina at Chapel Hill. Periodic assessments of enterprises by their managers are now available from the *Russian Economic Barometer* and the Center for Economic Analysis and Forecasting in Moscow. Both are summarized in *Russian Economic Trends.* On law, see Bernard Black and Reinier Kraakman, "A Self-Enforcing Model of Corporate Law," *Harvard Law Review,* June 1996, pp. 1911–82.

Acknowledgments

This book would not have been possible without the dedication and hard work of our Russian research team, consisting of Daria Panina, Ekaterina Grachova, Elena Zakrevskaya, Tatyana Voronina, Aleksei Krivolapov, Iuliia Cole, and Ekaterina Dementieva, and of our administrative assistant at the Rutgers University School of Management and Labor Relations (SMLR), Joanne Mangels. The study received support from the Eurasia Foundation of Washington, D.C., and the Foundation for Enterprise Development (FED) of La Jolla, California. During 1995–96, Joseph Blasi worked on the book at the Institute for Advanced Study in Princeton as a Mellon Foundation Fellow. The support of the Andrew W. Mellon Foundation is gratefully acknowledged. The warmth and interest of the faculty of the School of Social Sciences, Clifford Geertz, Albert Hirschman, Joan Scott, and Michael Walzer, were most appreciated. George Kennan, also a professor at the Institute, offered his analysis and suggestions throughout the year.

In Moscow, the research team was hosted during 1994–96 by the Russian government's Federal Commission on Securities and the Capital Market (the Russian SEC), headed by Dmitry Vasiliev, who earlier oversaw the implementation of the voucher privatization program. The team was also hosted by the Institute for Law-Based Economy (ILBE). The ILBE's Jonathan Hay attended to the good of the research effort at many turns. Hay was responsible for drafting many of the regulations for Russian privatization. The research team began its work at the Russian government's State Committee for the Management of State Property (the privatization ministry) in 1992, when the chairman was Anatoly Chubais. At that time, the research effort received the strong support of Maxim Boycko, a top aide of Chubais, who later continued to host the team when he was general director of the Russian Privatization Center. We owe a debt of gratitude to the hundreds of managers and privatization officials in Russia's eighty-nine regions who gave of their time and their patience year after year and went out of their way to be helpful to the research team.

We are grateful for the comments and ideas of colleagues, especially Andrei Shleifer, whose insight, support, and criticism have been invaluable. Adam Blumenthal, Michael Higgins, and David Binns of the FED and David Bloom, deputy director of the Harvard Institute for International Development, also gave useful comments. Ira Lieberman, a senior manager at the World Bank who advised the Russians, offered ideas and analysis on many issues in several lengthy interviews. Jeff Sachs, director of the Harvard Institute for International Development, provided us with his studies on Russian macroeconomic reform. Robert Tucker of Princeton University commented on the historical section. Boris Fedorov, the former minister of finance of the Russian government, provided a long interview. Bernard Black of the Columbia University School of Law and Anna Tarasova of ILBE aided our understanding of corporate legal issues.

Others have provided important assistance: Andrea Rutherford and Holly Nielsen and the staff of the Resource Secretariat of the Russian Federal Commission on Securities and the Capital Market; the staff of the Russian Privatization Center, especially Marina Dobatkina, Lena Shalneva, Rolf Montag-Girmes, and Mark DiGentile Williams; Dr. Robert Beyster of the FED for his support at key moments; Brunswick Brokerage for access to their research reports on Russian companies; ING-Barings Bank for access to their research reports on Russian companies and their online searching; Dean John Burton, Betty Lou Heffernan, the staff of the Dean's Office at SMLR, and James Chelius and the Human Resources Management Department; Victor Gabor of the World Bank for his comments on statistics; Cheryl Gray of the World Bank for her comments on our corporate governance work; Erik Shultz, James Gasaway, and Ken Kujundjic, who worked as research assistants in the United States; Marcia Tucker and Elliott Shore of the Institute for Advanced Study Library and Jeff Katz, Eugene McElroy, and George Kanzler of the SMLR Library, who made an extensive library research effort possible; Eric

Johnson and Melvin Richter; April Harding, for her early but key contributions; the Open Media Research Institute and the Jamestown Foundation, for their daily press briefings; Interfax of Boulder, Colorado, for access to their press reports; and Kohlberg, Kravis, and Roberts for their discussion of the KamAZ case.

The Cornell University Press team has been heroic in working with us on this book. We thank them all, as we know each of them has been involved in some way in making the swift appearance of this book possible. We express our sincere appreciation to our editor, Frances Benson, for her patience and perseverance, and to the director of the press, John G. Ackerman, for his strong support. Our work has been enriched more than we care to admit by the close and careful editing of Barbara H. Salazar and by Holly Bailey's timely editing of an earlier draft. A special note of thanks to the outside reviewers whose criticisms immeasurably contributed to this volume.

We would be very surprised if our review and analysis of this much material has not led to some errors of both fact and judgment. We welcome comments and hope to correct any errors and offer additional perspectives in future editions that will track both the Russian National Survey and the research of others on the Russian transition. We certainly expect later studies and analysis to shed more light on many of the issues discussed here and suggest other issues that we have missed. Meanwhile, new studies and revisions will be available on the Russian Research Project's World Wide Web site.

Finally, we thank our families and friends, who suffered through our impossible schedules and the endless wait for this book to be done.

Contributors

Andrei Shleifer, Professor of Economics at Harvard University, served as the senior Western adviser to the Russian government on privatization and economic reform and headed the Harvard project that delivered strategic advice and support for the privatization program. He is co-author, with Maxim Boycko and Robert Vishny, of *Privatizing Russia* (MIT Press, 1995).

Joseph R. Blasi, Professor at the Rutgers University School of Management and Labor Relations, served as an adviser to the Russian government from 1992 to 1996 as a member of the Harvard team headed by Andrei Shleifer. He coordinates a Russian research project at Rutgers. He is co-author, with Douglas Kruse, of *The New Owners* (HarperCollins, 1992). He wrote this book while a Fellow at the Institute for Advanced Study in Princeton, New Jersey.

Maya Kroumova has been Senior Research Associate with the Russian National Survey at Rutgers University since 1992. She is completing her doctorate at the Rutgers University School of Management and Labor Relations.

Douglas Kruse is Associate Professor at the Rutgers University School of Management and Labor Relations and a research associate at the National Bureau of Economic Research in Cambridge, Massachusetts. He is co-author, with Joseph Blasi, of *The New Owners* (HarperCollins, 1992).

234

Research on Russian Reform on the Internet

The studies described in this book will be supplemented by additional research reports and articles on a regular basis at the World Wide Web Site of the Russian Research program of Rutgers University's School of Management and Labor Relations in New Brunswick, N.J. The Internet locator is: http://info.rutgers.edu/Academics/Guides/russian.html Additional studies or confirmations of the Web Site address can be obtained from: Russian Research Program, Rutgers University, School of Management and Labor Relations, New Brunswick, N.J. 08903. E-mail: jmangels@rci.rutgers.edu Fax: 908-445-2830.

Other Sources

1. The United Nations Economic Commission for Europe (UNECE) has data on foreign direct investment in the *Economic Bulletin for Europe* from Geneva, Switzerland, at: http://www.un.org or http://www.undcp.org:80/unlinks.html

2. The International Monetary Fund in Washington, D.C., has an annual report and regular press releases on the Russian Federation at: gopher://gopher.imf.org

3. The World Bank in Washington, D.C., has an annual *World Development Report,* the 1995 report on transitional economies coordinated by Dr. Alan Gelb, and other Russian reports at: http://www.worldbank.org

4. The European Bank for Reconstruction and Development in London, Great Britain, has an annual *Transition Report* on former Communist economies by Chief Economist Nicholas Stern and the *The Economics of Transition* journal at: http://www.ireland.net/market-place/eirene/eirene-95/EBRD.html

5. The Organization for Economic Cooperation and Development (OECD) in Paris, France, has the Centre for Co-operation with the Economies of Transition's *Transition Brief* at http://www.oecd.org/sge/ccet

6. The Institute for the Economy in Transition in Moscow, Russia, directed by economist Yegor Gaidar is at: http://koi.www.online.ru/sp/iet

7. The Russian Government Federal Commission on Securities and the Capital Market has information on securities regulation, shareholder rights, and capital market development at: http://www.fe.msk.ru/infomarket/fedcom

8. The Centre for the Study of Public Policy, University of Strathclyde, Glasgow, Scotland, has polling data since 1991 at: http://www.strath.ac.uk:80/Departments/cspp/

9. The Russian Longitudinal Monitoring Survey at the Carolina Population Center of the University of North Carolina at Chapel Hill, N.C., has household surveys since 1992 at: http://www.cpc.unc.edu/projects/rlms

10. The Open Media Research Institute (OMRI) in Prague, the Czech Republic, offers daily and weekly news/research briefs at: http://www.omri.cz/Index.html

11. The Jamestown Foundation in Washington, D.C., has daily and weekly news/research briefs at the following e-mail address: Host@-jamestown.org

12. The Center for Russian and East European Studies at the University of Pittsburgh is at: http://www.pitt.edu/~cjp/rsecon.html

13. The Russian Legal Server is at: http://solar.rtd.utk.edu/~nikforov/main.html

Index

Italicized page numbers refer to tables containing data from the Russian National Survey.

Kadannikov, Vladimir, 141
KamAZ, 123–25, 141, 225, 233
Kamchatka, 4
Kennan, George, 231
KGB, 21, 65
Khasbulatov, Ruslan, xv, 65, 129
Khlebnyi Dom (bread factory), 163–64
Khrushchev, Nikita, 16
kindergartens, 12, 27, 182
KKR (Kohlberg, Kravis, & Roberts), 124–25, 141, 225, 233
Koloss food conglomerate, 153, 156
Komineft (oil company), 93–94, 100, 222
Komi Republic, 93
Kommersant, 124
Koryagina, Tatyana, 46
Kraakman, Reinier, 221, 230
Krasnoyarsk, 4, 109, 112–13, 128
Kredit Petersburg, 163
Krivolapov, Aleksei, 231
kulaks, 15. *See also* peasants
Kursk, 5
Kuznetsk metal works, 108, 121, 222, 224

labor camps, 16–17, 117
Lada (car), 140
land: lack of private ownership of, xii, 42, 158; nationalization of, under Bolsheviks, 15; opposition to privatization of, xv, xvii, 21, 174; privatization of, xvii, 130, 182; sale of, under privatized enterprises, xv, 72, 73, 132, 133, 158, 177; serf ownership of, 14; unclear laws on ownership of, 145. *See also* farms; leasing
land reform, rulings on, xiii, xiv, xv, xvi, xvii
La Porta, Rafael, 222
Latvia, 19
laws: bankruptcy, 177; on cooperatives, xi, 18; corporate, xvii, 98–102, 121, 147, 154, 169, 221; on elections, xii; on enterprises (USSR, 1990), xii, 20; on enterprises and entrepreneurial activity (Russia, 1990), xiii, 19–20, 25; on enterprises owned by state (USSR, 1987), xi, 18, 108; on freedom of press, xii; on freedom of worship, xiii; on individual labor activity, xi, 18; on land reform, xiii; multiparty system authorized by, xiii, 20; on privatization, xii–xiv, 22; on securities market, xvii, 159, 169. *See also* decrees
leadership, 11–12, 38, 123, 125, 178
leasing: of agricultural land, xvii, 174; of family farms, xii, 18; of industrial firms, xv; of state enterprises by workers, xii, 18, 21, 25–26, 216; of state-owned enterprises as special deal, 37
Lebed, Aleksandr, xvii, 186
Lebedinsk Ore Processing Company, 146–47, 226
LebGOK-Invest, 146
Ledeen, Michael, 187
Legal Office of the President (of Russian Federation), 3–4

legal system(s): French vs. common law traditions, 101; investors' lack of trust in Russian, 145, 158, 161, 164–65, 170; lack of, in Soviet Union, 28, 38; need for stable Russian, 170, 172, 181, 229; poor enforcement of Russian, 102; unclear nature of Russian, 94, 96, 146–47. *See also* decrees; laws
Lenin, V. I., 5, 14–15, 18, 50, 112, 229
Lenzoloto (gold producer), 75
Lexington Capital Management Corporation, 227
Liberal Democratic Party, 129, 134
Libermann, Evsei, 16
Lieberman, Ira W., 79, 211, 220, 221, 232
life expectancy, 24
Lipetsk firm, 62
Lithuania, 19
living standards: data on, 222; in 1980s, 17; under Stalin, 16; under Yeltsin, 32, 79–80, 110
Livshits, Aleksandr, xvii, 157, 187
loans-for-shares scheme, 74–75, 80, 83, 168, 220
LOMO, 227
López de Silanes, Florencio, 222
Lubinin, Dmitry, 146–47
Lubyatov Cookie Factory, 67–69, 142, 220
LUKoil Group, 75, 163

Machold, Roland, 165–66, 228
Mafia: alleged influence of, 2–3, 11, 78, 114–21, 223–24; fears of, 36, 39, 42, 46, 54–55, 58–61, 90, 104–5; history of, in Russia, 115–16; in U.S. businesses, 57–58. *See also* corruption
management. *See* governance, corporate; managers
managers: age of, 90, 122, 135–36, 180, *203;* attempts of, to guide companies through privatization, 126–33; attempts of, to retain control, 42–43, 45, 51–53, 55, 59, 62–67, 88–90, 93–96, 98, 100, 103, 121, 146, 156–57, 169, 179–80; attitudes of, toward privatization, 77, 106; as business owners, 1–2, 36, 42, 52, 54–56, 58–67, 73, 82, 84, 167, *193, 194;* corruption among, 33–35, 37, 39, 43–44, 118, 216, 224–25; election of, by shareholders, 106; election of, by workers, 18, 36, 88, 106; and fears of outside investors, 71, 96, 103, 141, 179–80, *201, 207;* firing of, 86–87, 100, 103–4, 108, 135, 139, 148, *203, 206;* foreign, 14; lack of supervision of, 33, 40, 45, 51, 82; lobbies for, 42, 53, 59, 64–65, 89; mentality of Russian, 26–28, 71, 122–23, 125, 132, 169, 179–80; need for leadership among, 11–12, 38, 123, 125, 178; as *nomenklatura,* 33, 61, 65, 66; number of firms owned by, 66–67; numbers of, involved in privatization, 105; resistance of, to outside investors, viii, 52, 53, 62–67, 73, 93–96, 102–3, 120, 134, 135, 179–80,